12-99

123929

TITLE

MAKING SHORT FILMS

SUBTITLE

The complete guide from script to screen

NEW EDITION
OF A BESTSELLER
ENTIRELY UPDATED,
REVISED AND EXPANDED

AUTHOR

Clifford Thurlow

MAKING SHORT FILMS

The complete guide
from script to screen

SECOND EDITION

Clifford Thurlow

Oxford · New York

English edition
This edition first published in 2008 by
Berg
Editorial offices:
First Floor, Angel Court, 81 St Clements Street, Oxford OX4 1AW, UK
175 Fifth Avenue, New York, NY 10010, USA

© Clifford Thurlow 2005, 2008
First edition 2005. Second edition 2008

Berg is the imprint of Oxford International Publishers Ltd.

Library of Congress Cataloging-in-Publication Data
A catalogue record for this book is available from the Library of Congress.

British Library Cataloging-in-Publication Data
A catalogue record for this book is available from the British Library.

ISBN   978 1 84520 803 5 (Cloth)
        978 1 84520 804 2 (Paper)

Design by Chris Bromley
Printed in the United Kingdom by Biddles Ltd, King's Lynn

www.bergpublishers.com

FOR IRIS GIOIA

Contents

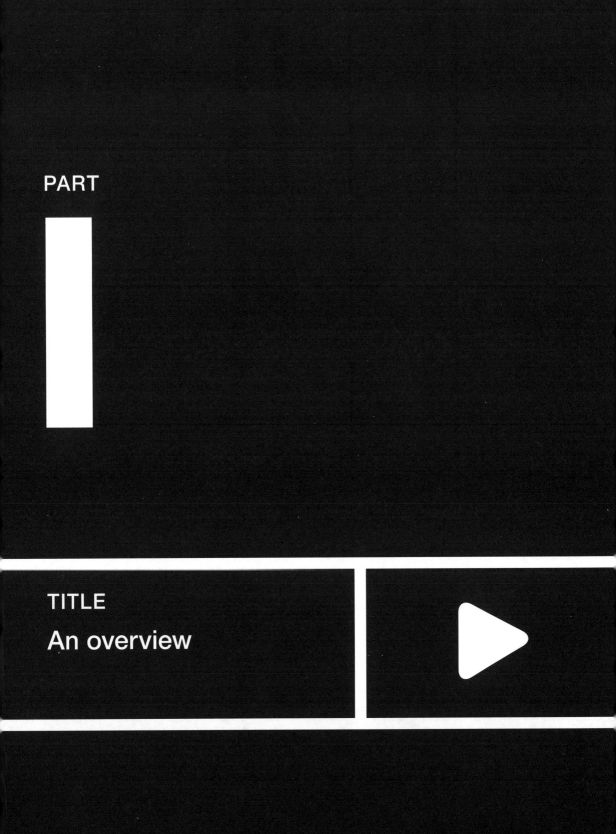

PART

I

TITLE
An overview

CHAPTER 1

Introduction to Making Short Films

In the long, hot summer of 1929, Luis Buñuel set out for Cadaqués, an isolated fishing village clinging to the last rocky outcrops of the Pyrenees and inaccessible except by sea. Under his arm, Buñuel carried the first draft of a short film and was making the journey from Aragon to the Spanish coast to see Salvador Dalí, his collaborator.

They had already made *Un Chien Andalou* and *L'Âge d'Or*, the latter "a uniquely savage blend of visual poetry and social criticism," according to writer Paul Hammond,[1] this surreal masterpiece being banned from public viewing thanks to Dalí's "subversive eroticism" and the film's "furious dissection of civilized values." Vicomte Charles de Noailles and his wife Marie-Laurie, a descendent of the Marquis de Sade, had promised funds for the new film and Buñuel was anxious to have his writing partner on board.

But that summer Dalí had other manias in mind. He needed a muse and was pursuing the Russian beauty Gala, wife of poet Paul Éluard, and a significant, if controversial, figure in the Surrealist Movement. It was said that if one of the artists—Max Ernst, Yves Tanguy, Man Ray et al.—did a particularly fine piece of work, the others would nod judiciously and whisper: "Ah, but of course, he was having an affair with Gala at the time."

Buñuel, with all the determination that was to characterize his career, followed Dalí from the shingle beach where fishermen repaired their nets, to the dining table where the local wine was said to have the bitter taste of tears, to the modest hut where his old student chum from Madrid's Residencia de Estudiantes had set up a studio. All to no avail.

In desperation, Buñuel tried to throttle Gala, to the consternation of the rest of the party: René Magritte, his dull wife Georgette, art dealer Camille Goemans, and his svelte girlfriend Yvonne Bernard. Cadaqués, despite its lack of a road, had been discovered by the Paris avant-garde and the appearance of this exotic group would be covered in the columns of the fortnightly *Sol Ixent*. Finally, his fingers prised from Gala's white throat, Buñuel packed his bag, shoved the script under his arm and sailed back around the coast, the still surface of the Mediterranean doing little to calm his fury. Salvador Dalí had worked on the scripts for two short films and Buñuel was now on his own.

He did not see Dalí again until 1937. Civil war had broken out in Spain. Fascist thugs had murdered their fellow student, the poet Federico García Lorca, and fearing that he was next on the list, Buñuel fled to New York where Dalí, always one jump ahead, was safely ensconced with Madame Éluard. He was making a handsome living painting portraits of society ladies and collaborating on movie sets with Alfred Hitchcock.

Buñuel asked him for a $50 loan. But, just as Dalí had spurned working on short film number 3, he refused his request and ended their long and fruitful friendship with a letter of such eccentric misanthropy that Buñuel's son, filmmaker Juan Luis Buñuel (*Calanda; La Femme aux Bottes Rouges*), carries the offensive missive folded in his wallet to remind him of the joys of generosity.

Filmmaking is tough. Buñuel's flight from Spain at the outbreak of the Civil War, the banning of *L'Âge d'Or* and the long years of exile in Mexico were not wasted years, however, but the very experiences that infused the wit and imagination that would make him one of the greatest filmmakers of the twentieth century, as indeed Salvador Dalí, who suffered his own array of paranoias and phobias, would become one of its great painters.

Buñuel's early films were random, scattered, indeed surreal, but he came to understand that the key to a great film is the script. If anything, the script for a short film is more important and perhaps more difficult to write than a feature, simply because the brush strokes by necessity must be fine and detailed, each moment perfect. He was learning his craft by trial and error and would have been the first to admit that he still had a long way to go. *Un Chien andalou* and *L'Âge d'Or* always head the Buñuel filmography, but he had already made, with cameraman Albert Duverger back in 1929, the forgotten 5-minute short *Menjant garotes* (Eating Sea Urchins) on 35mm. Illustrating, perhaps, the incestuous nature of filmmaking, it was Salvador Dalí's young sister Ana María who had kept *Menjant garotes* stored in a biscuit tin where it remained until her death more than half a century later.

Shot for the most part in harsh sunlight, the film follows Dalí's plump father and stepmother as they stroll through the terraces of Cadaqués before sitting down to a plate of sea urchins. Buñuel had planned his setups with care, the light filtering through the window as Dalí senior slices into his *garotes* revealing the first glimpse of a visual style that he would come to develop. But—a vital lesson to Buñuel, and all first-time filmmakers—for all the extravagance of camera angles and lighting effects, and in spite of the Hannibal Lecter grin of Señor Dalí as he slurps down the first sea urchin, the film is so slender on story it is at best rather ordinary and, at worst, plain boring.

Buñuel needed Dalí's inspired if contradictory logic and had taken the train from Aragon in the hottest month of the year to try and get it. A phrase, a gesture, a jump cut between unrelated events, a moment's silence or the introduction of music can make all the difference between success and failure, a story that grabs you, and one that's as flat as the sea in the bay of Cadaqués in summer.

Filmmaking is a team process. Often, contacts made and films shared in the early days will last through a filmmaker's career. Each film is a voyage of discovery, and adventurers who have made the journey together before will know that they are with people they can rely on. Buñuel mastered his craft making short films and that is how most filmmakers start. From Charlie Chaplin and Buster Keaton, with their first silent movies, to the current young *auteurs* Lynne Ramsey (*Ratcatcher; Morvern Callar*), Phillip Noyce (*American Pastoral;*

Dead Calm), Robert Rodriguez (*Sin City*; *El Mariachi*), and Christopher Nolan (*Memento*; *Insomnia*; *The Prestige*), they all, before tackling a feature, cut their teeth on the silver ring of shorts.

It was Luis Buñuel's passion to make films that made him a filmmaker, but there is another lesson to be learned from his flurry of activity that summer in 1929. *Menjant garotes* had been financed by his family, but getting it in the can, even if it was to remain hidden for decades, gave Buñuel the experience and, in turn, the confidence, to go out and source funds for future projects.

For anyone on the same path today, the journey has never been easier. Cameras are smaller, lighter, less expensive, and easier to use. A home PC and a few basic programs are sufficient to edit, compose music and add sound effects to a film. Films can be uploaded for distribution through YouTube and a host of streaming companies, and for anyone who wants to take the process to its ultimate conclusion, digital light processing and liquid crystal display home cinema projectors from Toshiba, Epson and others can turn the living room into a movie house. Anyone can do it.

How do you stand out in the crowd? How do you bring your movie gems into the world? Or, more important, in front of those who can make a difference to a new filmmaker's career? The aim of *Making Short Films* is to begin to answer those questions and to inspire filmmakers through the stages of writing, producing, financing, casting, directing, editing, and exhibiting short films. The book includes an analysis of the scripts of five very different shorts: a modern surrealist film, a country house haunting, a high-tech horror, a comedy with Nick Moran as a fighter pilot, and a *noir* thriller adapted from a short story.

In Buñuel's era, revolutionary politics or a flash of thigh was enough to make a film controversial. In an age when almost nothing is controversial, films will need other qualities. *L'Âge d'Or* would remain banned for many years, but has since been shown on television, can be viewed at the surrealist galleries at the Tate Modern, London, and can even be found on YouTube. When it was first screened in Britain, in Cambridge, in 1950, the sole complaint was from the Royal Society for the Protection of Animals. Bare breasts and a nun being thrown from a window caused no offence, but one of the characters is seen booting a small dog up the backside. Social mores had changed, but not the English.

STOP

CHAPTER 2

A Brief History of Short Films

AN INVENTION WITHOUT A FUTURE

1 The Lumière Brothers

2 The Lumière Brothers' projection of a steam train

It was a cold December night three days after Christmas in 1895 when guests filed curiously into the dimly lit basement at the Grand Café on the Boulevard des Capucines in Paris. It was the age of marvels, of new inventions, and what the people had come to see that night was a magic show performed by Auguste and Louis Lumière.[1]

The Lumière Brothers had set up a box of tricks called Le Cinematographe and, after a brief introduction, the lights were extinguished and the audience waited expectantly in the darkness. The machine in its wooden case with brass fittings was cranked into life and people saw, projected on the wall, a low-angle close-up of a train looming down the tracks in a swirling cloud of steam. There was no sound, but so realistic was this magic trick that as the train drew closer, people threw themselves under the tables and chairs screaming with fear.

The lights were lit again. The members of the audience quickly regained their composure—such are the effects of magic—and watched the rest of the show. The Lumière Brothers screened ten short films lasting twenty minutes, and that December night in 1895 those people were, without knowing it, witnesses to a moment in history. The cinema had begun.

Auguste and Louis Lumière had been on the trail of the moving image for most of their adult lives. They had attended a technical school in Lyon and had grown up surrounded by the paraphernalia in their father's photographic studio. During the last years of the nineteenth century, photographers and inventors across Europe and the United States had been trying to film and reproduce motion, but it was Le Cinematographe, a handheld, relatively lightweight device functioning as an all-in-one camera, projector, and printer, that was the first to screen what can accurately be called short films to an audience.

The Lumière Brothers had taken their camera out into the street and shot what they called "actualities"—scenes of everyday life, the steaming train being the best known. Being techies, they didn't immediately grasp the potential for creating entertainment. Louis Lumière famously said: "The cinema is an invention without a future"—a remark that was to transform from irony to paradox through the years of his pioneering work as a filmmaker. Even before aircraft were seen in the skies, the Lumière Brothers had captured the first aerial shots and, in the coming years, they would go on to shoot almost 1,500 short films and create the first short film catalog.

Louis Lumière lived long enough to regret his slip of the tongue. Far from having no future, the movies instantly appealed to the public imagination. Fine art and literature habitually serve an educated elite. The theater requires actors on stage to be paid day in and day out. But a cinema program can be shown eight or ten times a day and, with such economies, every factory worker and housemaid at the turn of the twentieth century could afford a ticket. Finally, we had an art form/entertainment/business—call it what you will—that had mass appeal and, moreover, could reach the entire world. James Cameron's *Titanic* took $1.8 billion at the box office and has been seen by hundreds of millions of people.

There is, as is often said, something magical about the movies, something that appeals to our primitive nature. As we sit in the darkened auditorium waiting for the show to begin, we are taking part in the same cultural ritual as our ancestors when they squatted around the campfire staring at the flames and listening to the elders. Through time and across cultures, man has been recounting legends that endorse and celebrate our humanity, our innate belief in equanimity, our sensitivity to the needs of others, and what George Orwell called "common human decency." You find the parable of the Good Samaritan in Luke 10:25–37, but with variances on the theme, every religion and society tells same story.

IN SEARCH OF THE MOVING IMAGE

Man has always been intrigued by the moving image and since the dawn of time people have watched the sun and moon describe reflections on the landscape. We are captivated by the way in which birds and animals appear as shadows on the wall when we shape our fingers before a light. We are mesmerized by visual trickery, optical illusions, mirages, and the mystery of the camera obscura.

The first credible moving pictures were projected by a magic lantern. A simple version can be created by drawing a silhouette on a sheet of paper and rolling it into a tube. The tube is cut strategically with flaps and placed on a circular base that revolves on a pivot. The heat from a lighted candle drives the tube in circles and the figure—a galloping horse, for example—will appear to be racing along as its shadow crosses the walls. In the seventeenth century, Athanasius Kircher,[2] the Italian inventor credited with coining the term "magic lantern," created a lens through which images from transparencies could be projected on a screen using a candle as the source of light: an early design for the slide projector. Examples of seventeenth-century magic lanterns can be found in museums, although their use goes back much further. In Britain in Victorian times, the magic lantern became a sophisticated piece of apparatus used to aid lectures, as well as for entertainment in lantern theaters.

A flick book (a progression of drawings, each slightly different) will provide the appearance of movement if you flick quickly through the pages. This illusion of motion was described as "the persistence of vision" and was first studied by the British physician Peter Roget in the 1820s, although the public didn't get its first taste, or rather glimpse, of the movies until 1832 with the invention of the Fantascope. The machine was the work of a Belgian, Joseph Plateau, whose device simulated the same motion as a flick book. A string of separate pictures showing the changes, moment by moment, of an activity such as juggling balls, or a dancing bear, were sketched around the edge of a slotted disc. When the disc was rotated before a mirror, the viewer was treated to the perception of the balls moving though the air, or the bear stamping its feet in a dance.

Plateau's Fantascope was quickly superseded in 1834 by the Daedalum, created in Britain by William Horner. He placed strips of photographs or drawings in sequence in a rotating drum. When the drum was set spinning, the viewer could see a moving image through regularly spaced slots. The device was improved and renamed the Zoetrope in 1867 by an American, William Lincoln.[3]

The quest to capture the moving image was growing intense. Back in France, Charles Emile Reynaud took the Zoetrope a stage further in 1877 with what he called the Praxinoscope, a drum interspersed with mirrors, rather than slots, and the first machine with the capacity to project a series of images onto a screen. Several years before the Lumière Brothers rolled up at the Grand Café with Le Cinematographe, Reynaud had shown a 15-minute "movie" at the Théâtre Optique in Paris.

Two years after Reynaud's success, another invention with a fanciful name came from British photographer Eadweard Muybridge,[4] whose Zoopraxiscope created a more persuasive illusion of motion by projecting images, from photographs printed on a rotating glass disc, onto a screen in rapid succession. He called his machine a motion picture projector.

Muybridge's photographs were widely published at the time and had been used by his rival Charles Reynaud for his Praxinoscope, cut into strips like film. Muybridge found a wealthy patron in the United States after demonstrating his photographic "loco-motion" studies; for example, at the race track in Sacramento, California, he set up a row of a dozen cameras to record the movement of a galloping horse, the sequence showing that all four of the horse's feet were, at certain moments, off the ground at the same time.

SHOOTING FILM

Up until this time, innovators had merely been able to create the illusion of motion. We return to France for the illusion to become reality. In the 1880s, the Parisian physiologist Etienne-Jules Marey[5] was studying animals in motion and developed what he called a "photographic gun," a camera that that could, in rapid succession, take twelve photographs per second and record these multiple images of movement on the same camera plate. He called the development "chronophotography," although the more evocative "photo-gun" caught on and the term "shooting film" almost certainly derives from Marey's developments.

Rather than Auguste and Louis Lumière, it is Etienne-Jules Marey who is normally described as the "inventor of cinema"—and for good reason. After recording his multiple exposures on glass plates, his revolutionary step, which took us closer to the modern movie camera, was to expose his photographs on strips of sensitized paper that passed mechanically through a camera of his own design. Further experimentation was conducted by Marey's fellow countryman Louis Aime Augustin Le Prince, who developed rolls of sensitized paper covered with photographic emulsion for a camera that he devised and patented. A fragment from his 1888 film *Traffic Crossing Leeds Bridge* is available on Google.

`www.video.google.com/videoplay`

Le Prince said at the time that he filmed Leeds Bridge because it provided action. A valuable movie lesson had been learned.

While Le Prince was filming in Leeds, UK, in the United States that same year George Eastman was preparing to launch his celebrated black box Kodak with celluloid film on a roll. His camera was for photographing stills, but movie innovators took special note a year later when Eastman put perforations in the celluloid.

Thomas Alva Edison's[6] electric light bulb first flickered to life in 1879 and now provided the stable, continuous source of light essential for shooting movies. It was at Edison's laboratories in West Orange, New Jersey, over the following years, that some of the most important developments in film technology took place thanks to the appearance of William Kennedy-Laurie Dickson. A French-born Scot related to the House of the Royal Stuarts, Dickson's mother, Elizabeth, was a talented musician immortalized in the ballad "Annie Laurie," and his father, James Waite Dickson, was an artist and astronomer who drew a line back through his family tree to the painter William Hogarth. As a young man (with these weighty antecedents) Bill Dickson had packed his trunks and set sail for New York with the intention of making a name for himself.

At Edison's laboratories, Dickson outlined his theories for coordinating film with sound, and was given a job. His experiments were largely unsuccessful, but as he became familiar with movie cameras, he devised (in 1890) what he called the Kinetograph, a motor-driven machine with a synchronized shutter and sprocket system that advanced film across the lens under the controlled speed of an electric motor. Like Eastman's Kodak, the addition of sprocket holes was designed to keep the celluloid rigid and allow the film to be paused momentarily before the shutter to create a photographic frame.

That was the design, but the 19mm film turned out to be neither stable nor constant. Dickson calculated that in order to maintain stability it would require film practically twice that width and, in the long run, progress the technology. It set off one of the great debates in movie history. Edison, his co-designer and funder, was at first reluctant to go to the expense of building a new machine, but Dickson finally won the day and received his patent for 35mm double-sided sprocket film on January 7, 1894: the standard that remains to this day.

Having developed the Kinetograph, Dickson began to experiment with his Kinetoscope, a projector based on William Lincoln's Zoetrope technology. The device he constructed was a cabinet as tall as a man, standing on its end like a grandfather clock, and which allowed a single viewer to watch a continuous loop of film on a small screen. A decade before motorcars rolled down the conveyor belt at the Ford factory in Detroit, Edison had recognized that only mass production would make the inventions coming out of his workshops commercially viable. If people were paying to see vaudeville, he concluded, they would pay to watch movies. After convincing Dickson, they added a coin-operated mechanism to the Kinetoscope, then took their vision to Andrew and George Holland,[7] Canadian businessmen who had dabbled in publishing, shipping, typewriters and, most important, the Edison Phonograph.

The Holland Brothers bought five machines and in April 1894 opened the first Kinetoscope Parlor in the heart of New York's Broadway theater district. Some 500 people came to pay 25 cents and watch films such as Blacksmith Working and Highland Dancing. Within a month, the brothers opened a second parlor at the Masonic Temple in Chicago with a further ten machines and some exciting new titles: Trapeze, Barber Shop, Cock Fight and Wrestling. The "peep show" craze caught on immediately and spread like a prairie fire, with new parlors opening in major cities across the United States. By setting up a delivery system, the framework for cinema distribution was taking shape.

As with the birth of stills photography, as soon as filmmakers had the expertise to screen the moving image, the bawdy crowd were shooting soft-core pornography. In the belle époque, when the sight of a woman's ankle set a man's pulse racing, What The Butler Saw must have broken box office records.

The Kinetograph became known in Britain as a "What The Butler Saw" machine and the contraptions filled arcades at seaside resorts showing a minute's worth of a woman undressing or a woman posing as an artist's model. Where the British enjoyed the saucy nature of the peep show, in France films of a more refined eroticism were already being shot in 1896 by Eugène Pirou and Albert Kirchner under their company name Léar. The oldest surviving film is titled Le Coucher de la Marie and shows Louise Willy performing a striptease. Kirchner is also remembered as the first cineaste to produce a film about the life of Christ: Le Passion du Christ.

With the growing demand for peep-show product, in 1893 the first film production studio was constructed in the grounds of Edison's New Jersey laboratories. Edison and Dickson filmed vaudeville and magic shows, boxing matches, Broadway plays, and acts from Buffalo Bill's Wild West Show. Most of the clips were short (about one minute) but the private, voyeuristic nature of the Kinetograph was mesmerizing and people remained glued to the screens even when the activities they were watching were mundane and repetitive.

Dickson parted company with Edison in 1895. He formed the American Mutoscope Company[8] and began developing his hand-cranked peep-show machine at a time when the boom was about ready to bust. That same year, while Dickson and Edison were undergoing their acrimonious parting of the ways, Auguste and Louis Lumière were constructing Le Cinematographe, their portable, all-in-one camera and projector, and with it stole a march on the Americans by screening the first films to an audience. The Lumière Brothers used Dickson's 35mm film and shot at a speed of 16 frames per second, which remained the standard until the talkies twenty years later, when 24 frames per second became the norm.

The word "cinema" derives from Le Cinematographe. The age of the Kinetoscope was at an end.

A TRIP TO THE MOON

The first cinema built for the sole purpose of screening films opened in Paris in 1897. The first in the United States was the 200-seat Electric Theater launched by Thomas L. Talley in Los Angeles five years behind the French, although a steady supply of one-reelers lasting 10–12 minutes were being exhibited as part of vaudeville shows, at fairgrounds, at carnivals, and in church halls. Films in the dying days of the Gay Nineties on both sides of the Atlantic were in the main *actualities,* documentary-like scenes from everyday life, although the first comedies were being shot and were instantly popular.

The breakthrough—to what we think of as movies today—was made largely by the French pioneer Georges Méliès.[9] Where the Lumière Brothers had been content to record a train pulling into a station and workers flooding from factory gates, their compatriot was a stage magician versed in the art of bringing rabbits from a hat and silk scarves from the palm of his hand. Méliès realized that it was the manipulation of film that made it interesting and, with his theatrical ability to deceive the eye by skilful intercutting, he can safely be described as the father of film editors.

Méliès—as producer, writer, director and actor—experimented with the medium by making more than 100 shorts before completing, in 1902, *Le Voyage Dans la Lune* (A Trip to the Moon), a 14-minute one-reeler considered to be the first true movie.

3 *Le Voyage dans la Lune*

With a rocket voyaging into space, circling planets, and alien life forms that wouldn't look out of place in a George Lucas film, Méliès had planted the magic seeds that would grow into the palms that edge the boulevards of Cannes and Hollywood and turned moving pictures into the great art form of the twentieth century.

When the former Kinetoscope operator Edwin Porter[10] was given the job of directing a narrative documentary called *The Life of the American Fireman* on Edison's New Jersey lot in 1903, he made a study of Méliès's work and came to realize that it was the Frenchman's astute editing that made his films compelling. In his 6-minute short, rather than merely filming firemen at work, Porter had them restage various activities, used close-ups to show emotion and, whether in homage to or imitation of Georges Méliès, took the viewer into the heart of the drama by crosscutting between the interior and exterior of a burning house.

What Porter brought back to the lot was so original, at least in the United States, that it took Thomas Edison months of rewatching *The Life of the American Fireman* before he fully appreciated what the director had achieved; as many of the most inventive *auteurs* and artists discover, anything too novel, too ahead of its times, will be met by confusion, even anger. Hollywood moguls aren't looking for the unique and innovative: they want to see a fresh spin on the previous year's blockbuster.

Edison, though, was a shrewd entrepreneur, as well as a filmmaker, and later that same year, 1903, put Porter back in the director's chair to shoot a fictionalized account of a true story. Just as young American directors in the 1960s analyzed the work of the iconoclastic *Nouvelle Vague* (New Wave) aesthetics of François Truffaut, Claude Chabrol, Jean-Luc Godard, Éric Rohmer and Jacques Rivette, Edwin Porter steeped himself in the work of

4 Edwin Porter's *The Great Train Robbery*

▶▶ P.20

filmmakers working across Europe before beginning to film his milestone movie *The Great Train Robbery*.

The 10-minute short was taken from a popular stage play loosely based on the real-life heist by Butch Cassidy's Hole in the Wall gang in 1900. Butch (George Leroy Parker) and the boys halted a Union Pacific Railroad train in a sparsely populated stretch of wilderness outside Table Rock, Wyoming. They threw the fireman off the moving train, forced the conductor to uncouple the passenger cars and dynamited the safe in the mail wagon before escaping with $5,000 in cash.

Porter dressed locations in New Jersey to look like the Wild West and, in what was the first true Western, created the stock elements of the genre: the robbery, the shoot-out, the chase on horseback, the gathering of the posse. Using newspaper transcripts and the structure from the stage play, Porter, in fourteen scenes, created a vibrant narrative; but what made *The Great Train Robbery* so important was Porter's extension of film language. First, it was one of the first films not to be shot in chronological order. Porter showed parallel action between simultaneous events—intercutting, for example, between the bandits and the telegraph operator—and moved between scenes without using fades or dissolves. Another first was this: having shown the fireman as he is about to be thrown off the train, Porter cuts back to see the figure (a dummy) rolling into the dust. A final Porter innovation was an added scene that could be placed either at the beginning or the end of the film (depending on the exhibitor), which showed a bandit shooting his six-gun directly at the audience.

Edison was aware that he had a hot property on his hands. In the film catalog of January 1904, *The Great Train Robbery* got the following billing:

This sensational and highly tragic subject will certainly make a decided "hit" whenever shown. In every respect we consider it absolutely the superior of any moving picture ever made. It has been posed and acted in faithful duplication of the genuine "Hold Ups" made famous by various outlaw bands in the far West, and only recently the East has been shocked by several crimes of the frontier order, which fact will increase the popular interest in this great Headline Attraction.

A STAR IS BORN

Edwin Porter achieved a great deal with his 10-minute film: he established the Western as an American genre, he co-wrote (with Scott Marble) and directed the first film to make a significant financial return, he showed the unlimited scope for fiction, and he proved that, far from being just another vaudeville act, film had the potential to grow into an industry.

Another "first" for Porter was launching the career of Gilbert M. Anderson,[11] a key figure in movie history belatedly honored with a lifetime achievement Oscar in 1957. Anderson, a traveling salesman and failed stage actor, got his movie break in Porter's intriguingly titled *Messenger Boy Mistake* in 1902. The following year, in *The Great Train Robbery*, Anderson was cast in three roles: a bandit, a shot passenger, and a "tenderfoot dancer"—the guy who hops about with bullets from the baddie's six-guns spitting about his feet: another cowboy cliché introduced by Porter.

5 Edwin Porter's mobile wardrobe

After *The Great Train Robbery*, Anderson continued acting in short films and finally hit the big time playing Bronco Billy in *The Bandit Makes Good*. Over the course of the next several years, he appeared in almost 400 Bronco Billy one-reelers and became one of the first recognizable stars. While still acting and directing, Anderson teamed up with George K. Spoor to form the Essanay company, the name taken from the first letters of their surnames. They opened studios in California and produced a series of films featuring Ben Turpin, the New Orleans-born vaudeville and circus performer with trademark cross-eyes and an act so similar to that of the well-spoken young Englishman Charlie Chaplin that it remains debatable as to who gave birth to the Little Tramp.

Charlie Chaplin left the Keystone Studio in 1908 and at Essanay was given the freedom to develop his amiable if hapless hobo across a slate of ambitious movies where character development and plot were beginning to prevail over mere slapstick to capture the hearts—and loyalty—of the audience. Chaplin and his contemporaries created a language as central to filmmaking as the rules for drama set down by the Greeks. Filming techniques developed in the silent era evolved at a frantic pace, as did the supremacy of the omnipotent studios. In Europe, the First World War brought progress to a standstill, but in the United States the industry flourished with the growth of Hollywood. When Charlie Chaplin left Essanay in 1916, he was one of the biggest stars of all time and American movies were reaching audiences across the world.

It had taken just ten years from the release of Porter's *The Great Train Robbery* for film's capacity to influence the public to be understood and co-opted by forces more potent than the moguls. President Woodrow Wilson was reelected as the "peace candidate" in 1916 and forged a nation of immigrants into a homogenous whole through a propaganda machine fueled by war newsreels and Hollywood movies with titles such as *The Kaiser: The Beast of Berlin* and *Wolves of Kultur. To Hell With The Kaiser* was so popular that Massachusetts riot police had to be summoned to deal with an angry mob denied admission at a full house.

In 1917, America went to war.[12]

A night at the cinema had long been a passion. Now it had become a patriotic duty. Movies were affectionately known as *flickers*; the term "short film" didn't exist. All films were short films. With the coming of the two-reeler, the prototype feature, the short continued to play a fundamental role at the studios as a training ground for writers, directors, cameramen, and the flood of wannabe actors and actresses arriving in Hollywood looking for their shot at the big time. As star-led features began to dominate theater programs, short films were sold to cinema chains as part of a "block booking," the package including the feature, a cartoon, a newsreel, and a serial that ended with a cliff-hanger that ensured the audience would be filling the auditorium the following week.

It could be said that the American Dream was born in the cinema. People worked hard for modest wages, often in conditions where strikebreakers and criminal involvement in big business was the norm. For the price of a ticket you could live the dream, at least for a couple of hours. The movies were an escape and what people wanted from their films was glamour, adventure, a glimpse at other worlds and, at the same time, confirmation of their own values. What the studios typically provided was just that: morality tales that reinforced a Puritan ethic, clearly defined leads, subplots that added wisdom or humor, usually played by popular character actors and, for the most part, a fairy tale ending that sent the people home with a spring in their step and the energy to get up and go back to their jobs next day.

A night at the *flicks* was an occasion. It was special. Perfect for first dates. For families. People relaxed. They smoked cigarettes. They wore their best clothes and uniformed doormen dripping in gold braid greeted their arrival as they hurried up the polished steps for this weekly ritual. Theaters were plush, with imposing entrances like temples, thick cushioned carpets, comfortable seats, and the alluring whiff of popcorn and hotdogs. Before the advent of sound in the 1920s, in the pit below the screen there would be a piano or an organ, and in some cities with competing theaters, a full orchestra would file in just as the lights went down. Music that enhanced the mood and action on screen was crucial—in general that remains the case—and complete scores normally arrived with the big cans of film stock. The talkies quickly eclipsed silent movies as well as the careers of some of the most famous silent movie stars; many had come from Europe and a lack of good American English didn't sound right to the native ear. The American gift for risk-taking, for forging ahead, even through war and the Depression, resulted in the combined film product from across the world representing only a fraction of the films being produced in America. The cinema wasn't an American invention, but they had made it their own.

THE NEW WAVE

Before the term "short film" gained wide currency, shorts in the US were known as the "short subject" and included cartoons, travelogues, news clips and comedies featuring stars such as Buster Keaton, Laurel and Hardy, the Three Stooges, and the ever popular Charlie Chaplin.[6] After the 1930s, fewer shorts were made for theatrical release; they were generally produced by picture companies that either owned their own theater chains, such as Loews Theaters, or that obliged theaters to take their shorts by selling them in the same package as their big-name features. When the practice of "block booking" was judged illegal by the US Supreme Court, the theater chains were required to sell off their movie studios and this commonsense division between production and exhibition remains in place.

6 *Chaplin and the Kid*

Back at the turn of the century, Georges Méliès had experimented with color by hand-painting film negatives, but audiences seemed indifferent to color and its introduction was a slow process that only gathered speed when producers saw the need to compete with television, a principally black-and-white medium right up until the 1960s. Shorts continued to be made as an educational tool (the corporate video/DVD continues the practice), but with the rise of the double feature, the commercial short film was virtually dead, and the cartoon short was on its way to the same celluloid grave.

While new writers and directors in Hollywood now cut their teeth making B-movies, among independent filmmakers in Europe the short continued to be a showcase for experimental films and new talent. France had produced more than its share of film pioneers and, as the light in the art world is said to move from one part of the globe to another, the short film light was switched

7 *À Propos de Nice*
promenade on the Boulevard

on in Paris with the emergence of *la nouvelle vague* (the new wave),[13] the term coined to describe a loosely knit assortment of young filmmakers who, in the 1950s, rejected classical movie structure to develop new narrative forms and a radical visual style.

As students at film school today are likely to be trawling through the subtleties of Todd Solondz (*Happiness*), Paul Haggis (*Crash*)*,* and the Korean masters Park Chan-wook (*Oldboy*) and Takashi Miike (*Audition*), so the French new wave were inspired by Jean Renoir, Jean Vigo, Orson Welles, and Alfred Hitchcock—directors with a style written like a signature into their work. They deconstructed every reel of film that passed through Paris, and outlined their theories in—among other publications—*Cahiers du cinéma,* the influential film magazine co-founded by André Bazin, the legendary critic considered the most prominent film-writer since the end of the Second World War.

Cahiers du cinéma continues its tradition in excellent movie criticism and can be read online in English (free).
www.cahiersducinema.com

8 Francois Truffaut
◼ ▶▶ P.20

Enouraged by Bazin, *Cahiers du cinéma* writer François Truffaut directed his first film in 1955: the 8-minute short *Un Visite.* Jacques Rivette was behind the camera and, the following year, Rivette made his debut short, *Le Coup du Berger*, written by Claude Chabrol with a cast that included fellow film critics Truffaut, Jean-Luc Godard, Chabrol, and Rivette himself. It was this group of filmmakers, with Éric Rohmer, who set out to redefine film as art and created the mood that would lead us to independent cinema.

New wave films were sensual, melancholic, capturing the Zeitgeist and reflecting the turbulent social and political changes that characterized the 1950s and 1960s. The Paris riots in May 1968 could have been scripted by writers of the new wave. Through critiques and editorials, they conceived the principle that the director, like the author of a book, was the *auteur* of the film and introduced the credit "A Film By"—a format adopted by directors everywhere. More significantly, *nouvelle vague* filmmakers challenged the commercial Hollywood notion of movies as being *just* entertainment—or business, or propaganda—and perceived film as an art form. As *the* art form.

9 Ashvin Kumar directing
◼ ▶▶ P.20

Although these writer/directors inevitably moved on to make features, they had provided new dignity and a sense of place to the short film. In a short there is an opportunity to reshuffle the cards of film language and take on themes commercial producers avoid on both commercial grounds and the fear of the new. There is a certain comfort in the dull warmth of Plato's cave, our backs to the sun, watching shadows on the wall. Show us a glimpse of life beyond the walls of our own narrow world and the mind will not immediately compute what it is seeing. Thomas Edison had faced this moment of doubt the first time he viewed *The Life of the American Fireman.* Anything strikingly original is likely to be rejected by the status quo, yet it is the brave artist prepared to swim against the tide who in the long run often finds the greatest success, or at least critical success.

The growth of impressionistic, poetic, surreal, transgressional, boundary-breaking, avant-garde films gave rise to the festival circuit, as well as the introduction of the independent art house cinema where audiences could expect to see films that were difficult, complex, controversial, or just plain foreign. The hegemony of the American studios with their undemanding diet of thrillers, actioners, romcoms, war, Westerns, and gangster films had been broken and, in the wake of the French new wave, young American *auteurs* such as Martin Scorsese, Francis Ford Coppola, Spike Lee, Jim Jarmusch, Robert Rodriguez and Quentin Tarantino rose up in a rolling tsunami that washed away preconceived conventions and introduced a new American aesthetic. Big-budget actioners still storm the box office but indie films made by indie filmmakers have carved out a sizeable niche in the market.

YOUTUBE

According to a report by the Pew Research Center, ten years ago one in fifty Americans got their news from the Internet.[14] Today, that figure is one in three. Some 25 million Americans downloaded videos to their computers in 2005; projections for the future are off the charts. Streaming short films over the web—drama, animation, documentaries, video diaries, hidden camera comedies, and mishaps—has grown prodigiously since the coming of net broadcasters such as YouTube, Google Video, iFilm and Putfile.

Before Robert Rodriguez made his classic low-budget *El Mariachi*, he shot the 8-minute *Bedhead*. The first title on Martin Scorsese's filmography is the short film *Vesuvius VI*. A hundred years ago William Dickson and Thomas Edison were making 1-minute films for the Kinetograph machine. Today people are shooting and sharing 1-minute films on their mobile phones. A hundred years ago the Lumière Brothers screened a train steaming down the tracks. Today Internet broadcasters are screening the same kind of actualities on the net. Major television channels are finding more slots for the short, the number of festivals dedicated to short film is on the increase, and the oldest of film genres is alive and kicking.

10 Oscar nominee Ashvin Kumar

 P.20

PAUSE

THE RISE OF YOUTUBE

YouTube was launched in February 2005 as a personal video-sharing service and has grown into an archive with many hundreds of thousands of short films. Anyone, anywhere in the world, can take part in showing and commenting on a vast range of shorts—and they are doing just that, watching a staggering 70 million films on the site daily.

Many of these films lack narrative drive, and some are of dubious taste, but what makes Internet distribution so appealing is that the viewers are directly involved in the process of choosing, playing, and sharing files. It isn't PR—or star—led interviews that make a film popular, but the unmediated impartiality of viewers' downloads.

The *vérité* effect of YouTube is often mesmerizing: the blank, locked-off camera work, the uninterrupted shot, the unedited deep-focus contributing to the sort of lo-fi video aesthetic born from the ideals of the French new wave and *Danish Dogme (Dogma)* film movement. People tune in to watch snapshot films about their interests, eyewitness accounts of current events, and to find the quirky, the bizarre, and the original. The popularity and artistic freedom of YouTube has attracted mainstream directors to its ranks. Through YouTube, as the company points out on its home page, people capturing special moments on film are being empowered to become the broadcasters of tomorrow. What's more, it's free.
`www.YouTube.com`

PAUSE

11 *Un Chien andalou*

12 *À Propos de Nice—* exotic dancers

13 *Duck and Cover*

14 *Little Terrorist*

STOP

10 SHORT FILMS YOU MUST SEE

1. Ballet Méchanique (1924): Dadaist film by Fernand Léger and Dudley Murphy, with cinematography by Man Ray, showing abstract shapes moving hypnotically to the music of George Antheil.

2. Un Chien andalou (1929): Luis Buñuel and Salvador Dalí collaborated on this surreal masterpiece where a woman's eyeball is sliced with a razor, priests and dead donkeys are strapped to a piano, and live ants pour from the palm of a woman's hand.

3. À Propos de Nice (1930): Jean Vigo's legendary travelogue takes us along the Riviera revealing the rich and poor living their separate lives together.

4. The Mascot (1934): Wladyslaw Starewicz's macabre *bal masque* features Satan and a multitude of gruesome creatures made from household items. Sometimes titled *The Devil's Ball*.

5. Duck and Cover (1951): Uncredited, wickedly parodied civil defense training film showing children how to protect themselves from nuclear attack by diving under school desks.

6. The Red Balloon (1956): Albert Lamorrise's award-winning film is a childhood story about innocence found and lost, and lessons learned.

7. La Jetée (1962): Chris Marker's puzzling study of time, memory, and imagination, a premise that inspired Terry Gilliam's *12 Monkeys*.

8. The Hold Up (1972): Abel Ferrara's short film about three men who plan to hold up a gas station after being laid off work shows the early promise of *Driller Killer* and *Bad Lieutenant*.

9. Tale of Tales (1979): This awe-inspiring film by the Russian Yuriy Norshteyn was selected by an international jury as the best animated film of all time at the 1984 Los Angeles Olympiad of Animation.

10. Little Terrorist (2004): Ashvin Kumar's Oscar-nominated film tells the story of Jamal, a 10-year-old Muslim cricketer who by accident crosses the landmine-strewn border between Pakistan and India. Returned in safety by a Hindu Brahmin, the film brilliantly captures the absurdity of divisions and borders everywhere.

4 Poster from Edwin Porter's 1903 masterpiece *The Great Train Robbery*

8 Francois Truffaut

9 Ashvin Kumar directing

10 Oscar nominee Ashvin Kumar

14 Scene from Ashvin Kumar's *Little Terrorist.* © Alipor Films

CHAPTER 3

Careers

So—you want to be in the movies?

Making a short film could be the first step. A short that gets noticed may fund the next short, festival awards, a feature, fame, and a first-class ticket to Hollywood. That is the goal of many who set out on this path but, like baby turtles scurrying out to sea, the odds are tough: only one in a thousand returns to its place of birth to breed as a fully grown turtle. You have to be determined and conscientious, you have to go the extra mile, you need bundles of talent; you have to know movies like a GP knows how to treat his patients—classics as well as new trends and innovations, film language, and film news. And like the surviving turtles, you need to be lucky.

The media, and filmmaking in particular, is the most popular and sought-after career path in the world today. Students dream of being film directors and newsreaders. But these jobs are at the tip of an iceberg consisting of all the other crafts in the many behind-the-scenes departments. If you do want a career in film, you have to be realistic about what it is you personally can do. Do you have the mind-set, flair and creative energy to be a director? Or are you methodical, good with numbers and organization? More a producer? Would you be happy spending several hours a day fretting over the turning points, conflicts, reversals, and beats of a 10-minute screenplay? That's the writer's job—and many successful screenwriters dream of being directors. Are you more comfortable with the kit than the cast? Because there are fulfilling careers to be had in the camera department, the editing suites and sound studios, set design, costume, and makeup.

Many producers begin their career as the lowly runner and, on a short film, the runner gets to know exactly what is done in each department and how those departments interact. On a well-planned film, nothing is left to chance. The dress the leading lady wears will be chosen by the wardrobe mistress in consultation with the art director's sketches for the sets and will need to be costed by the line producer and approved by the director—while, incidentally, the director is busy drawing storyboards (with an artist or with his own pen), creating a shot list with the director of photography, and discussing locations with the location manager, if he's lucky enough to have one.

Where do you fit in this intricate puzzle? By getting involved in filmmaking at any level and learning as much as you can about the different career paths, you are more likely to find where your talent lies and where you should focus your energy and training in order to reach your goal. What distinguishes film crews from professionals in most other occupations is their total commitment to the cause. Making a film, even a short film, is like a battle, an addiction, a race—against time, the weather, the bank balance. People don't take a day off because they might have a cold coming, or someone's scheduled to repair the roof. They take flu remedies and let the roof leak. Like the good doctor, film is a vocation, a calling—and if you are called, you are called for life.

As you will have read in chapter 2, *A Brief History of Short Films*, none of the film pioneers had formal training. The Lumière Brothers, William Dickson and Georges Méliès developed their own equipment, devised stories suitable for the new medium, and improved their skill base by making films. Life in the digital era is much easier. Most universities and colleges in the US and across Europe offer film and media courses with knowledgeable tutors and loads of gear to play with. Watching movies and discussing the merits of different directors may seem like a soft option. But the soft option, conversely, requires greater tenacity, commitment, and involvement in the process.

If a group of friends or students are making a film and you get the chance to take part, then do so: do anything. The next generation of filmmakers will be those who work as runners whenever the opportunity arises, the people who offer to carry the gear, stand in the rain holding light stands, help clean up a location and return home, flip a DVD in the laptop and study the last short they worked on. Some 50,000 people in the UK are regularly employed in film and television production. In the United States the number is about ten times that figure and, across the world, those numbers will grow. Runners graduate to being third assistant directors, assistant editors, focus pullers, clapper loaders. With the constantly changing technology, directors, DOPs, and even producers and writers need to be multiskilled in order to be able to communicate fully with the other departments. The process is accumulative. The more you know, the more you can do, the more you have to offer—and the more you extend your network of contacts. If you are certain that film is your calling but are unsure of your career options, there is a list of job profiles at uknetguide.

www.uknetguide.co.uk

To get a general grasp of how movies work, consult Film Education, which is a registered charity funded, since 1985, by the film industry and the British Film Institute (BFI). The wide range of teaching material is designed for students to develop their analytical and critical skills and is linked to the National Curriculum in the UK. Film Education organizes training courses, conferences, workshops, seminars, and events including the National Schools Film Week in October each year.

www.filmeducation.org

INTERNSHIPS

A warning: internships are a good way to get your foot in the door, but there are unscrupulous companies that take on students and young filmmakers to do work that has nothing to do with film production—filing, answering phones, sorting newspaper clippings, delivering packages, and collecting coffee. People will take on these jobs for no pay because they hope it will look good on their CV and lead to paid employment. Perhaps it will. But do be aware of exactly what you are expected to do as an intern and what you may learn. If you do take on a job and there is a possibility to get out on location with the crew, work doubly hard until you get the chance.

Students graduating from film and media courses will be made aware of their options by tutors and contemporaries—the grapevine is alive and well in the film industry. For those people with an inclination to pick up a camera and go out and shoot guerrilla-style, a wide variety of courses and workshops can be found in just about every major city—go to the library, telephone the film officer in the local government offices, and hit the Internet. Courses may be one-day events: writing a horror movie, directing actors, or film festival survival; or night classes spread over several weeks where you may learn the basics in shooting, directing, and editing a short film. At the very least, what these courses do is allow new filmmakers to be in a film environment and get their hands on the equipment.

As of January 2007, the BFI directory lists 5,938 media and multimedia courses in the UK. Film, television, video, radio, and web authoring courses are included. In Australia, the number of courses has doubled in five years, and in the United States there are too many to count. There are far too many to consider listing more than a few and those I have chosen here are those that I know from personal experience.

www.bfi.org.uk

National Film and Television School
A leading international center for professional training in the film, television, and media industries. The school offers full-time MA, diploma and project development programs, a wide range of short courses for industry professionals, training in post-production effects and computer-based animation.

www.nftsfilm-tv.ac.uk

Raindance
The pioneer of independent filmmaking in the UK, Raindance courses have inspired filmmakers including Christopher Nolan (*Memento*), Julian Fellowes (*Gosford Park*) and Guy Ritchie (*Lock, Stock and Two Smoking Barrels*). "Raindance tutors are all working industry professionals who will teach you how films are really made."

www.raindance.co.uk

Arista Development
Europe's largest private film development agency has a range of activities: developing fiction film projects, and providing training courses for producers, screenwriters, and developers. Arista acts as a film development consultant internationally and promotes good practice in film development.

www.aristadevelopment.com

New Producers Alliance

To the established Nine-Point Producer Training program, the NPA has added a similar program for directors. The courses are part-time over twelve months and result in an industry-recognized qualification. There are various workshops in scriptwriting, surviving Cannes, etc.

www.npa.org.uk

City Eye

Based in Southampton, UK, City Eye runs one-to-one tuition schemes, workshops in video production, editing, introduction to screenwriting and short free film courses for writers and poets.

www.city-eye.co.uk

Initialize Film

This London-based company is dedicated to what they call Personalized Film Training. They have created an interconnected web of courses for training, mentoring, and marketing designed for writers, directors, and producers. Tutors at Initialize assist students in developing projects from script stage through development to funding.

www.initialize-films.co.uk

University of New South Wales School of Media, Film, and Theatre

The University of New South Wales in Australia offers undergraduate honors and postgraduate programs in media and communications, film studies, dance education, media, culture and technology, and theater and performance studies. The institution maintains close contacts with the film and theater world in Australia and helps graduates find their way into the profession of their choice.

www.media.arts.unsw.edu.au

New York Film Academy

With their philosophy of "learning by doing," the academy, since its inception in 1992, has been offering short-term filmmaking and film production workshops with an array of options for courses and programs ranging from one week to one or two years—not only in filmmaking, but screenwriting, 3D animation, acting, editing, and new digital technologies. NYFA now has colleges in London, Florence, Milan, Barcelona, Bilbao, Paris, and Porto.

www.nyfa.com

PAUSE

THE TRUE FILMMAKER'S GUIDE

What true filmmakers have in common can be summed up in four words: passion, focus, commitment, and resiliency.

Talent, perhaps, too. But you'll never really know if you have talent without the other four. Despite the common view that talent is either in you or not, I've seen the work of a lot of filmmakers mature in ways I never would have imagined through their passion, focus, commitment, and resiliency.

True filmmakers are obsessively creative people who constantly find ways to feed their creativity, even if it has nothing to do with filmmaking. All make their films without regard for their commercial potential, nor their own career aspirations, nor how the film will, in any other way, "pay off"—even though many of those thoughts take center stage when their films are complete and in major festivals.

True filmmakers make their film by hook or by crook, some having all the money and resources practically handed to them, while others take years and use every trick in the book to push their film to completion.

Having a life as a filmmaker is not dependent on having a career as a filmmaker. Few will have a career as a filmmaker, but nearly all of us can build a life as a filmmaker. And if a career is your goal, it will not come to you unless you have committed to a life as a filmmaker. That is, if you are not passionate, focused, committed, and resilient.

Jacques Thelemaque, *Withoutabox*[1]

www.withoutabox.com

STOP

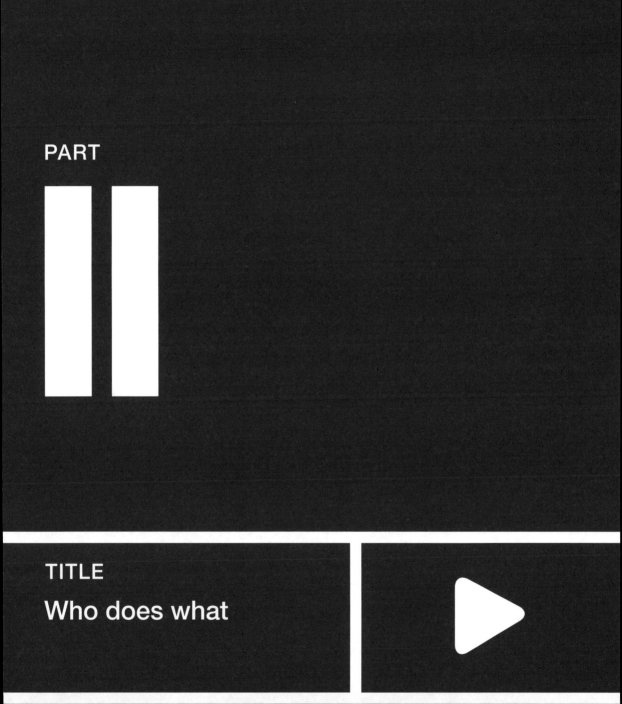

PART

II

TITLE

Who does what

▶

CHAPTER 4

The Script

How do you write a short film?

There is a certain irony in the question, inasmuch as the secret of writing a short film is the same as writing anything: first, it ain't easy, and second, the secret is that there is no secret. It's plain hard work. Scriptwriting is rewriting. Whatever goes down on paper, however well it looks (and with the abundance of scriptwriting programs and story-creating paradigms, it's probably going to look super), that first gush of words is unlikely to produce anything of great value. What that gush will do is give you something to work with. It is the cloth from which the tailor fashions a suit; the suit fittings are the rewrites, the new drafts.

It is often said that you should write about what you know about. I would amend that to say it's better still to write about what moves you: your passions, dreams, and desires. You have to get into the midst of the story before even you, the writer, know what it is you are trying to say. Character drives plot, but the underlying theme, the message, is what holds the narrative together.

CHARACTERS

Once you give birth to your characters, they are responsible for their own actions, and the effects caused by those actions. Put a volatile character in a compromising situation and he will swing out with both fists; neither he nor you will be able to prevent it. Put temptation in the way of a thief and just watch his eyes light up as he sees the main chance. Are we, the reader or viewer, interested in these people? Do we want to follow their story? Do the characters start at point A and shift subtly, cleverly, gradually and convincingly through dilemma, reversals and crisis to point B? Will the brute learn self-control; the thief not to take what isn't given? Do they have obstacles to overcome? Most important: is there conflict? All stories progress through conflict—action and reaction.

Boy asks girl: "Will you go to the movies with me?" Girl says: "Yes." No conflict, no story. Boy asks girl: "Will you go to the movies with me?" Girl says: "No. I can't stand men with beards."

Now we have a story: *The Boy with the Beard*. Will the Boy shave off his beard for the Girl? Will he shave it off in order to get her to see the movie with him, then grow it again once they're an item? And if he does regrow his beard, will she break off the relationship?

THEME

Now we have conflict, the grist of every TV soap, but what underpins the story is the theme: the writer's viewpoint, the attitudes and issues the writer wants to explore. A theme can normally be expressed by a well-known saying, in this case: You can't tell a book by looking at the cover. In *The Wizard of Oz*, Dorothy discovers that there's no place like home. *Rocky* learns that if at first you don't succeed, you try, try, and try again.

The Boy with the Beard is about superficiality, the comical aspects integral to the plot adding light relief and underpinning the theme. When the Boy sees that the Girl is merely frivolous, he will stop pursuing her. The Girl, oblivious to her own nature, and rather than looking introspectively, will look outside herself and seek ways of punishing the Boy. The initial point of conflict is the beard. The first turning point is when the Boy shaves off his beard to get a date. The plot requires another turning point, the second hook, to swing the story into a new direction.

In this case, we will add the Rival, the key element to most love stories and the third spar in the eternal triangle. Our Rival is a clean-shaven, shallow character with an equal fondness for taking girls to the movies. When the Girl goes out with the Rival, she finds him self-centered and conceited, his conversation dull. She still hates beards, but she will now look inside herself and realize that she has been superficial to worry over such trivialities. She has started to look inside the book, not just at the cover and, as if she were looking in the mirror, she will glimpse in the reflection the danger of losing the man she really loves.

It is the emotional journey that holds readers and grabs an audience. To begin with, the Boy was pursuing the Girl. Now, the turnaround is complete. She will start pursuing him, extending the theme and highlighting this aspect of human nature: the tendency to reject what we have and miss it the moment it's gone.

With the story dynamic in flux and the characters now familiar, the scenes should turn with greater urgency, racing us to a conclusion that should achieve two goals:

1. To be both what the audience expects…
2. … yet not exactly in the way they expect it.

The audience wants to be surprised, not disappointed by the obvious.

CONSTRUCTION

Each scene should have its own beginning, middle, and end, a minor conflict leading to resolution and on to the next scene, the characters growing from each development. The effect is like placing tiles on a mosaic path, each contributing to the story's journey and driving us forward to a satisfying conclusion. If the story has been well told, the characters will have gone through changes. We will have observed their small imperfections, foibles, and flaws, the acts of kindness and humanity that add up to the sum total of what they are: a representation of ourselves.

The metaphor of the sculptor releasing the figure from the block of marble is familiar and can be extended to the part played by the writer, the unique mannerisms, word patterns, strengths, and weaknesses of his characters[1] laid bare as each new challenge chips away the outer layers to reveal the individual beneath. Our own dreams and deepest desires often remain a mystery to us; we are a collage of inconsistencies. But the writer must know his characters and their motivations; they must remain consistent *even as they change* in order for them to become interesting to the audience.

The Girl of our story will have fallen in love with the Boy for what he is, not how he appears, and will accept his facial hair. The Boy, conscious of her love and aware of the compromises she has made, will stop being so obstinate about his beard, perhaps shave it off for their wedding day, when the priest—this now being a Greek Orthodox story—has the longest beard known to mankind. The Rival, too, will have changed. He lost the Girl, but has learned that you can't tell a book by looking at the cover. He'll probably grow a beard as well.

The Boy With The Beard is a morality play that evolved *while I was writing it*. It began as a romantic comedy, but the weighty undertones could, with careful writing and rewriting, draw us into new depths: perhaps the Boy is a recent immigrant and wears the beard for religious reasons? Perhaps the Girl was once assaulted by a bearded man carrying a knife and the memory still haunts her?

If we take the cross-cultural theme, I would now name my characters: let's give the Boy the heroic-sounding name of Alexander, and name the Girl Wendy—something fresh and easy on the tongue. The Rival we'll call Dirk, for reasons that will become clear. Writers keep books with titles like "Naming Your Baby" on their shelves and pay as much attention to christening their characters as parents give to naming their newborn infants. In Spain, people remember Don Quixote more than Cervantes, his creator. Great names of fiction live forever in our minds: Scarlett O'Hara, Sam Spade, Luke Skywalker, Lolita, Robin Hood, Nurse Ratched, Scrooge, Bond—James Bond. In *Pat Garrett and Billy the Kid*, the chameleon-like Bob Dylan is named Alias.

The film *In The Heat of the Night* turns on the scene when gum-chewing police chief Rod Steiger asks Sidney Poitier his name.

"So, boy, what do they call you up there in the north?"

"They call me Mr. Tibbs."

The response earns Poitier respect and he states his name with such power that the producers used the line to title the sequel. Good line; bad script. In the original, Poitier is picked up on a murder rap for no other reason other than he's black. His knowledge, detective skills, and humanity move the plot along and secure his release, but as a gritty look at Southern racism, the film is not about Poitier, but Steiger, as he comes to terms with his bigotry, his lack of humanity and, for good measure, his personal loneliness.

They Call Me Mr. Tibbs is about *what it's about*, without subplots or theme; it lacks authenticity, the quality the writer should be striving for. If a scene doesn't work, only by looking for the veracity of the scene, for the

15 *In the Heat of the Night*
▶▶ P.40

authenticity of the characters' needs, desires, and actions, will we unearth its weaknesses.

When a scene is stuck in as a device to move the plot along—*"Hi, John, fancy seeing you here. Are you going to Anne's party at the country club on Saturday?"*—the filmgoer knows that he's being made a fool of; it's a subtle thing like an instrument out of tune in an orchestra, but you can sense it in the auditorium when, instead of watching the screen, people are glancing around or—the ultimate nightmare—talking. You still see the above "Hi, John" scene, or the girlfriend opening a drawer "by chance" and finding a gun hidden among the handkerchiefs, but this is lazy writing and it's growing harder to get away with it.

In this chapter and throughout the text, examples have been taken from features, not short films, simply because there are so few universally recognized short films to quote from. The structure of short films, and all stories, is essentially the same, and writers of short films are presented with special difficulties: the challenge of space and time, or the lack of it. Once they overcome those challenges, they will be ready to write a feature.

Going back to Wendy: if we want to run with the idea that she was assaulted, we could remap the story as gothic horror, a now clean-shaven Alexander becoming an avenging hero who pursues the bearded attacker to a haunted house on a windy cliff top where the rivals fight to the death. And who is the bearded attacker? Dirk, of course, in another guise, so named for the knife he carries.

When I was looking for a story to make the above example, a number of films rushed into my mind. But I needed something less complex: a fable, more than a feature. I was sitting with my morning coffee flicking through the local paper, avoiding the computer hum in the office next door. Writing is hard; it's always hard—any diversion to avoid it will do. I turned finally to the newspaper's back page and there was an attractive woman and a young man with a full beard pictured at their wedding; in their optimistic expressions was *The Boy With The Beard*, waiting to be found.

STORYTELLING

According to American writer and scholar Joseph Campbell, the stories are already there, inside us, bursting to come out.

Whether we listen with aloof amusement to the dreamlike mumbo jumbo of some red-eyed witch doctor of the Congo, or read with cultivated rapture thin translations from the sonnets of the mystic Lao-tsu; now and again crack the hard nutshell of an argument of Aquinas, or catch suddenly the shining meaning of a bizarre Eskimo fairy tale: it will be always the one, shape-shifting yet marvelously constant story that we find, together with a challengingly persistent suggestion of more remaining to be experienced than will ever be known or told.[2]

The above paragraph comes from *The Hero With A Thousand Faces*, Campbell's analysis of world folk tales, which shows how common threads and themes in storytelling bridge the frontiers of culture, religion, and time. It was Campbell's study that inspired Christopher Vogler's *The Writer's Journey*, an insider's look at how writers can utilize mythic structures to create powerful narratives that are dramatic, entertaining, and psychologically authentic. Since its first publication in 1998, *The Writer's Journey* has become the Hollywood "bible" on the screenwriting craft.

The stories are there aplenty, in the depths of our own subconscious, and I quote Campbell to counter the postmodern belief that everything under the sun has already been seen and every story has already been told. In writing classes and spats among movie addicts someone will invariably remark that there is only a handful of different stories—the exact number always varies—and writers throughout time just keep retelling them: *The Boy With The Beard* is *Romeo and Juliet*; the man with the fatal flaw—*Achilles*; the precious gift taken away—*Orpheus*; virtue finally recognized—*Cinderella*; a deal with the Devil—*Faust*; the spider trapping the fly—Circe; change or transformation—*Metamorphosis*; the quest—*Don Quixote*.

To the list we can add the coming-of-age plot (*Gregory's Girl*; *On the Waterfront*); rivals (*Chicago; Amadeus;* Nolan's *The Prestige*, mentioned above); escape (*The Great Escape*; *The Shawshank Redemption*); revenge (*Hamlet*; *Gladiator*); the con (*House of Games*; *The Sting*); manipulation (*Svengali*). These stories have been reshaped over and over again, but it is the reshaping and combination of plots that makes them fresh and original. Cross *Romeo and Juliet* with *Cinderella* and we end up with the Richard Gere/Julia Roberts film *Pretty Woman*; change *Cinderella* for *Orpheus* and we have Nabokov's *Lolita*. The genius of George Lucas is that he borrowed from them all to create *Star Wars*, a mythical adventure in the tradition of *Gilgamesh*, the pre-Biblical epic still on the bookshelves today.

The themes running through Clint Eastwood's Oscar-winning *Million Dollar Baby* are little different from Sylvester Stallone's *Rocky*. But the deadbeat loser Rocky transforms to the girl fighter Maggie Fitzgerald (Hillary Swank), and the story in this incarnation is more about Frankie Dunn (Eastwood), her trainer. The most important lesson Dunn teaches his fighters is "always protect yourself." But we discover that Dunn, on bad terms with his daughter, is himself emotionally vulnerable. Maggie Fitzgerald is a poor waitress, already past thirty, trying to make something of her life through boxing. At first reluctant to allow a female boxer in his gym, old Frankie finally takes on the girl, teaches her everything he knows, and puts the emotional heart back in his own life. Maggie realizes her dream, becoming a great boxer, and the conclusion does just what it's supposed to do: it takes us to the big fight and pummels the wind out of us with a knockout punch of a surprise ending not to be given away here.

Million Dollar Baby is an old story made fresh in its modification. In the time of the Greeks people were saying there's nothing new under the sun. The fact is that in art, each new creation is a reworking of the old, and it is that reworking that gives a story new life. We are still discovering species of bird, insect, and fish unknown to mankind. Every generation has its own hopes and fears, its own tales to tell: melting ice caps, vanishing rain forests, GM crops, terrorism. What makes our story special, what draws in the reader or viewer, then, is not the underlying mechanics of plot, but the characters. Great characters move the audience and, as plot unfolds through conflict, great villains make great stories.

Once born, before a word of narrative goes down on paper, writers should sketch out complete biographies of their characters, their ages, idiosyncrasies, disappointments, hopes and dreams; not caricatures or stereotypes, but flesh and blood originals with all the qualities, doubts and nervous tics that make us all one-offs. Characters need a past; a network of relationships. They will show the audience just a fraction of this in the drama—the tip of the iceberg—and then usually at a time of crisis. But from this study, you should be able to extract the essence of your characters and summarize them in a few sentences.

Callie Khouri does it marvelously in her screenplay *Thelma and Louise*, describing Thelma's husband (the perfectly named carpet salesman, Darryl) in three swift brushstrokes:

16 *Thelma and Louise*

▶▶ P.40

Darryl comes trotting down the stairs. Polyester was made for this man and he's dripping in men's jewelry. He manages a Carpeteria.

Darryl is checking himself out in the hall mirror and it's obvious he likes what he sees.

He exudes overconfidence for reasons that never become apparent. He likes to think of himself as a real ladykiller. He is making imperceptible adjustments to his over-moussed hair. Thelma watches approvingly.[3]

What Callie Khouri did was take the traditional buddy movie and put two girls in the lead roles. In the story, while Louise is fighting the demons from the past, Thelma is finding herself, both in their own way "coming of age." When they have fully matured into new beings, they know they can never go back to what they were; they are ready for the ultimate metamorphosis: the drive over the cliff edge into the Grand Canyon.

Each story will have running through it what is called the Active Question: Will they get married? Will she stop using drugs and run in the Olympics? Will he get revenge? Will they escape—the robbers with the bank haul, Thelma and Louise from the tyranny of men? If the characters we create have a tale worth telling, they will *want* something: to get the girl, exact revenge, achieve justice, steal the goose that laid the golden egg, gain a sign of self-worth, or find the road to El Dorado. A story becomes interesting when the writer sets up obstacles that prevent the heroes getting what they want (Thelma and Louise first lose their money, essential for their flight). The story hooks us as they overcome those obstacles and/or villains and thereby grow and change in the process.

In order to grip the audience, the characters must be seen to go through a range of emotions: fear, self-doubt, sorrow, elation. The screenwriter achieves this through conflict (*you will never marry that man; I will never go out with a boy with a beard; you'll never be good enough to run in the Olympics*). As the conflict unwinds, the audience will be seeing themselves in the hero or heroine and will be sharing those emotions. Conflict is to drama what sound is to music. It is the heart of drama, the soul of drama, the secret of suspense, the key to emotional engagement, that thing that keeps filmgoers on the edge of their seats. If you laugh out loud while reading a book or feel a tear jerk into your eye while you are watching a movie, the writer has done his job.

Thelma and Louise is often quoted on film courses and Callie Khouri's script should be on the reading list of every writer who wants to turn his pen to film, shorts, or a feature—not only for its pace and dialogue, but for the symbolism neatly woven into the plot. *Thelma and Louise* is about male dominance; Darryl's comic machismo, the attempted rape, and the truck driver's lecherous behavior subliminally underpinning that theme. Male domination is an abstract concept, but Callie Khouri has written scenes as symbols of that concept to make the abstract real and easier to understand.

On the list of memorable names above is Nurse Ratched (Louise Fletcher) from *One Flew Over the Cuckoo's Nest*. The perfect use of symbolism is explored in this movie through the use of the water fountain that McMurphy (Jack Nicholson) has failed to budge on the various occasions when he tries to lift it. McMurphy is a free spirit gradually crushed by the institution. In the final scene, Big Chief (William Sampson) seizes the fountain and crashes it through the bars—to escape from the despotic asylum.

As a subplot, Big Chief's strand of the story tells us more about McMurphy, Nurse Ratched, and oppression, underlining the theme. Subplots contribute color, comedy, and nuance; they serve to confirm the main plot, reveal the contradictions of the principal characters and place obstacles in the hero's path. Characters who serve this function need as much fleshing out as the main characters and, ideally, will go through changes during the course of events from one state to another: in the case of Big Chief, from tyranny to freedom.

One Flew Over the Cuckoo's Nest holds our attention because of the power of the characters drawn in Ken Kesey's novel. We as people are interested in the joys and sufferings, the ups and downs of our neighbors and friends; as Marcel Proust once said, at heart everyone is a gossip. Disney cartoons and science fiction monsters are anthropomorphic, and it will take rare skill for a writer to keep us involved in a plot where the hero goes into battle against some anonymous adversary such as nature, disease, the tobacco companies, or big business. The enemy needs a human face—Christopher Eccleston in Danny Boyle's virus nightmare *28 Days Later*; Michael Douglas as Gordon Gekko in *Wall Street*. In *El Laberinto del Fauno* (*Pan's Labyrinth* in English), writer/director Guillermo del Toro combines the harsh reality of Franco's Spain with the imaginary, fairy-tale world seen through the mind of a young girl played by Ivana Baquero. But it is the human face of fascism brutally revealed by Sergi Lopez that allows us to comprehend the human cost of the dictatorship.

In life, the whistle-blower usually loses his battle against the corporate giants. It is the role of the writer to put the world back in balance and show us the little guy fighting back; except in downbeat *noir* and ironic tales, people come away from films more satisfied with positive endings. As Oscar Wilde reminds us: "The good ended happily, the bad unhappily—that is fiction." Whether it's James Bond entering Ernst Blofeld's fortress, Rocky Balboa in the boxing ring, or Charlie Sheen challenging Michael Douglas in *Wall Street's* final reel, the hero and the antagonist must have this conclusive, face to face confrontation to send the audiences home contented. The little guy rising to the challenge and overcoming evil appeals to our deepest humanity. We are the little guy.

THE WRITER'S CRAFT

One thing that first-time writers and filmmakers need to prevail over is that everyone has grown up on the same diet of countless movies and endless hours of television. We know how it's done because we've seen it done, over and over again. It looks easy. Film courses and textbooks, including this one, light the road before us. The struggle then, as Luis Buñuel understood, is to break the mold of our education and environment, think in fresh ways, and use new technology to find our own originality.

Writing has laws of perspective, of light and shade, just as painting does, or music. If you are born knowing them, fine. If not, learn them. Then rearrange the rules to suit yourself.[4]

What Truman Capote is saying in the above is that storytelling has rules, but like the moon and stars to the navigator at sea, we must still pilot our own course through the darkness.

Imagine a journey by land from London to Athens. We may take the ferry to Bilbao in Spain, cross the Pyrenees and hug the Mediterranean coast. Alternatively, we can take the Eurotunnel to France, slip through Germany and Austria, then follow the Adriatic. The two journeys will be touched by different languages, foods, customs, and landscapes; different people with different skills and knowledge will cross our path along the way. But the destination is the same and the journey will be the hero's own personal and unique experience, the material face of the more profound internal journey.

While the script for a short film will require conflict, emotional engagement, and resolution, as discussed above, there is the added difficulty of wrapping it all up in (preferably) under ten minutes. Surreal or experimental short films may be useful for filmmakers to show a new narrative or visual style. In drama, the best short films have a simple plotline and, in my experience, can generally be noted for containing these three elements:

- One main character.
- One story or conflict.
- One result or resolution.

On the list of "Ten Short Films You Must See" (see Chapter 2: *A Brief History of Short Films*) is Ashvin Kumar's 2004 Oscar-nominated short *Little Terrorist*. This perfectly illustrates the point made above: one main character; one story; one result.

Ten-year old-Jamal is playing cricket with his friends on the Muslim side of the India–Pakistan border. When the ball is hit into the minefield dividing the two countries, Jamal slips under the barbed wire and picks his way among the mines to rescue the ball (in this poor community a cricket ball would have greater value than in our consumer-driven society). Jamal is seen by guards and escapes their gunfire by fleeing into India. Hunted by the police, he is taken in by a Hindu Brahmin who disguises Jamal by shaving his head and leaving a single curl of hair at the crown—a Hindu custom. The audience sees that life in the Hindu village is the same as life in the Muslim village beyond the barbed wire and that "common human decency" is the same the world over.

The Brahmin knows his way across the minefield and returns the boy that night. They stop at a tree with cricket stumps painted on the trunk: as a boy, before India–Pakistan partition, the old Brahmin played cricket in this very place. Jamal runs safely home to his village, only to be given a good spanking by his mother for cutting off his hair. Result: boys will be boys, mothers will be mothers, and Jamal has seen a glimpse of life beyond the minefield. The plot of *Little Terrorist* is simple, but Kumar's nonpartisan exploration of universal themes and his eye for detail makes the story compelling to watch and satisfying in resolution.
`www.little-terrorist.com`

TIPS

All stories, long or short, for film or the written word, benefit from structure. In *The Writer's Journey*, cited above, Christopher Vogler outlines the twelve-stage journey the hero normally takes in those stories we find ultimately satisfying. A short film will lack time for all the intricate stages and archetypes, but a sense of structure is still crucial.

The eight-point guide below remains true to Vogler's principle, but is more practicable for a short film. I have applied the framework to both the short story and short film script in Chapter 21, *Greta May—The Adaptation*, and a careful reading reveals the eight steps that hold the story in place. The eight-point guide is not a formula, but a road map, and the best stories will take the framework and bend it into a new shape. Note also that the eight points do not have to be in sequence; with flashbacks and flashforwards, they may appear in any order (except, perhaps, the resolution), for example *Pulp Fiction* and Alejandro González Iñárritu's dazzling multilinear, multilingual and multifaceted *Babel*, a film every new writer and director should watch many times.

17 *Babel*

P.40

PAUSE

EIGHT-POINT GUIDE TO MAKING SHORT FILMS

1. Introduce main character(s); set the scene.

2. Give the character a problem, obstacle, obsession, or addiction.

3. Let the character work out a plan to overcome the problem.

4. Before setting out to solve the problem, there may be a moment of doubt that will require the hero to seek advice from a mentor such as a teacher or best friend. This is an opportunity to let the audience know more about the problem and weigh it up in their own minds. What would they do?

5. With new resolve (and often a magical gift from the mentor: the watches Q gives James Bond; Dorothy's ruby slippers), the hero sets out to overcome the problem, obstacle, obsession, or addiction.

6. Overcoming the problem or challenge (getting the girl; escaping tyranny; saving the world) will be met by extreme opposition from the rival, who will usually have greater but different strengths and will in some ways bear similarities to the hero: the nemesis is the hero's dark side.

7. The hero will appear to fail in his quest. He will give up or glimpse defeat, even death, and will require superhuman effort to overcome this daunting final task.

8. The hero wins the final battle with an opponent or enemy or with himself, and returns to his natural state wiser, or stronger, or cured, but not necessarily happier. The journey has made him a different person. He has glimpsed death and can never go back to the simplicity of what he once was.

To the eight-point guide above, I would add the following recommendations when tackling a script.

PAUSE

TEN TIPS

- Don't trust in inspiration, unless you want to be a poet. The first idea you get is often borrowed from every movie you've seen and every book you've read.
- If you do work on that inspired project—rewrite, rewrite, rewrite. These are the most important three things you will ever learn about scriptwriting, and I repeat: rewrite, rewrite, rewrite.
- See your writing from the other side of the screen, from the audience point of view; if there is no audience, there is no message.
- Do not adjust your writing to the market by attempting to stay abreast, or even ahead, of changing trends; such work is a form of cultural static lacking veracity and, often, even relevance.
- Be true to your own vision. Write about what you know about? Absolutely. But then write what you believe in.
- Four steps to writing a short film scenario: find the ending, then the beginning, then the first turning point—the event that gets the story going, then the second turning point—the scene that swings the story around and sets up the ending.
- Enter your story a short time before the crisis that ignites the drama.
- Scenes are like parties: arrive late and leave early.
- Persevere.
- Listen to criticism. But don't always take it.

I repeat the first line of this chapter: How do you write a good short film? It requires the same intense work as writing a feature or novel; it's just shorter. Finally, a quote from Jean Cocteau:

Listen carefully to first criticisms of your work. Note just what it is about your work the critics don't like—then cultivate it. That's the part of your work that's individual and worth keeping.[5]

Poet, dramatist, novelist, film director, the kind of guy you could really grow to hate, Cocteau began his career with *The Blood of a Poet*, a short film.

STOP

15 Sidney Poitier and Rod Steiger reaching boiling point in the racially charged *In the Heat of the Night*. © BFI

16 Ready for the long ride; Geena Davis and Susan Sarandon in *Thelma and Louise*. Photo Roland Neveu. © BFI

17 *Babel* film poster. © BFI

CHAPTER 5

The Producer

When a novelist completes his manuscript, the job is done (apart from the rewrites and brawls with the editor). With a screenplay, the journey is about to begin.

With short films, the writer, director, and producer will often be one and the same. Filmmakers, though, will mostly find that life is too short to keep so many balls in the air all at once and, when they find what they are best at, they stick to it.

The foundation of every film, as the previous chapter makes clear, is the script, but it is the producer who will nurture the writer through the new drafts, fork out for the cappuccinos, then present the final version to the director, casting agent, actors, and funders. He will draw up contracts, speak to lawyers, settle feuds, and stroke the high-strung sensitivities of his family of creatives.

In the 2002 *Simone*, Winona Ryder is furious with Al Pacino because her trailer, while the biggest on the lot, isn't actually the highest. At first Pacino tries to let the air out of the tires on the offending vehicle, but when his patience runs out, he does the only self-respecting thing left to him and fires her. In this parody on the movie business, Miss Ryder, in a refreshing self-parody, is replaced with a computer-generated star character. Such technology isn't yet with us, but the scene illustrates perfectly the relationship between the producer and his team, his role as best friend, adviser, marriage counselor, guru, psychiatrist and, ultimately, the boss. From the moment a film goes into production, whether it's a Hollywood feature or a first short, the meter is running and the producer has to keep his eyes on the clock.

FINANCE

It is often assumed outside the industry that the producer has a fat wallet from which he pulls fistfuls of dollars like Michael Lerner as the odious Jack Lipnick in *Barton Fink*. Not in real life. Tim Bevan and Eric Fellner at Working Title are responsible for a string of hits—*Four Weddings and a Funeral*, *Notting Hill*, *Bridget Jones's Diary*, *Love...Actually*, *Wimbledon*—but are backed by American studios. The producer uses other people's money and only when he hands that money back with a slice of the profits will he raise funds for the next project.

There is another common misconception to bear in mind: even a no-budget film is going to cost somebody something somewhere along the line—the camera and equipment, postage, labels, pre-production planning, post-production film developing or transfer … and that's apart from the bus fares and bacon sandwiches during production. The producer with the pared-down micro-budget short may not have investors to worry about, but will need to show flair with his debut in order to attract some cash next time around.

It's not essential for the producer to have a sister working in Barclays in Soho or a college buddy at the Chase Manhattan; what he does need is a nose for a story and the passion to convince backers and funders (more on that later) to finance his project over the many competing and perhaps equally good packages that flood across their desks. You will notice that in the mind of the producer, the script has become the product and the product, with its added elements, becomes a package.

DIFFERENT HATS

The producer, then, is a salesman, a PR shape-shifter; he can sell plans for a bridge when there isn't a river; he is a UN peacekeeper between warring factions—the writer, director, leading lady—a shepherd who should guide his creatives and, as such, is a creative himself. You don't have to be able to score music to appreciate Mozart or Ry Cooder's seductive blues. Likewise you don't need to know what the *f*-stops do on a camera, or how an editor adds fades on an Avid Composer. What the producer understands is human nature. He knows how to get the best out of his people and gives the best in return.

Producers are characterized as tough guys, the cigar-chomping tightwad, and while this might be true of a Hollywood Jack Lipnick, the parody is the exception and, in my own encounters with industry heavyweights, I have experienced only kindness and that species of vibrant, boundless energy it takes to be interested in everything and everyone they come across: the energy it requires to make movies.

PAUSE

▌▌

SIX QUESTIONS TO ASK WHEN YOU READ A SCRIPT

1. Who is the hero?
2. What is the active question: will he, will she, will they…?
3. Who or what opposes the hero?
4. From whose point of view is the story being told?
5. Theme: What's it about?
6. What is the visual style of the film?

One time, when I was writing a book about Salvador Dalí, I met Hal Landers, the man behind such classics as *What Ever Happened To Baby Jane?* I mentioned that I was a writer—writers can't help themselves—and Hal asked to read the manuscript. It was something I would not normally have done, showing someone unfinished work, but I was swept along by Hal's enthusiasm. The following morning, he insisted on calling a publisher he knew. That same day, the publisher was calling me and by the end of the week I was reading a contract. There was nothing in this for Hal Landers—except the dedication in the book—but he had used his contacts to pull the deal together, extended his own network and made life seem truly magical.

Hal Landers once bumped into Queen Juliana of Holland in a store in Paris. "Hey," he said, "aren't you the Queen of Holland? I'm from New Jersey; I've never met a queen before. Why don't you let me buy you a cup of coffee?" The queen was so overwhelmed by the approach that she agreed, and they remained friends from that day on.

What these anecdotes illustrate is that the qualities Hal Landers brought to his daily life are the very qualities required by a producer: enthusiasm, energy, generosity, a good eye for product (the Dalí book is now in its fifth edition), an agile mind, the verve to think laterally, and the personality to do the unusual. Like invite a queen for coffee.

ALEXANDER SALKIND

One time when I was in Paris, I was invited to the premiere of *The Rainbow Thief*, a whimsical fantasy written by Berta Dominguez D, directed by Alexandro Jodorowsky and pairing Peter O'Toole with Omar Sharif for the first time since *Lawrence of Arabia*. I met the producer, Alexander Salkind, and at his prompting I told him that I was trying to interest broadcasters in a documentary project. He didn't make any phone calls on my behalf, but led me to the bar and told me how he got started in the film business.

He had arrived in France from Russia, penniless, and was taking a train from Paris to Lyon where he thought he might have more luck finding work. In the carriage, he met a man who owned three shoe shops. Alex told him a story he wanted to turn into a short film. By the time they arrived at their destination, the shoe shop owner was so intrigued that he decided to sell one of his shops and fund the movie. Financially, it was a disaster. Salkind was depressed, but it was his first film and his collaborator, the shoe shop guy, considered the experience so valuable that he sold a second shop to finance the next film. That, too, was a flop, but he had started out on a course from which he saw no way back: he sold the last of his shops to fund one more film and lost everything.

Alex Salkind had to go elsewhere for finance, but he now had a showreel and was on his way. As for the shoe shop proprietor, he'd left the footwear business behind him forever. He'd caught the film bug, worked as Salkind's assistant and had a long career as a cinematographer. Salkind had learned the three essential lessons:

1. How to inspire potential finance.
2. How to manage a budget.
3. How to tell a good story.

With these skills he went on to make an enormous variety of movies, from Kafka's impenetrable *The Trial* (1962) to *The Three Musketeers* (1973) to the *Superman* movies where, due to deft negotiations and deceptive scheduling, his name is lent to what lawyers call the Salkind Clause: that an actor must be told *how many movies he's making*. When he filmed Christopher Reeve in the first *Superman* in 1977, the outtakes contained much of the footage used in *Superman II*.

Salkind by then was a powerful figure, "a Russian producer who moves somewhat mysteriously in international circles,"[1] according to writer John Walker, but he had learned, when he was penniless, the value of a penny and never took his eye off the ticking meter. The producer will always be pushing the production manager and first assistant director (first AD) to keep to schedule: that's his job. But the enthusiasm and passion he brings to the project must animate them to give their best. He will develop the bilingual skill of telling his director two things at once: The rushes are great. Get on with it. He will know when his leading lady needs stroking or firing. Producing is a multiskilled pursuit and communication skills form the basis of all the others.

The bigger the budget, the more of other people's money he's spending and the good producer will always be aware of that responsibility. He makes a modest living from the fee written into the budget. He makes the big money for those fat cigars from the points—the percentage of profits negotiated with finance or the studios. The success of a film will leverage up those points for future projects. Failure will make it that much more difficult to finance the next one and sobering statistics from the Film Council show that the majority of first-time filmmakers never make a second feature.

To turn the written word into film needs everyone from the stars whose names go up in lights to the runner on a work experience scheme. The process of mixing and shaping the many disparate elements is like taking base metal and turning it into gold. The producer is the alchemist. Behind the scenes he will be working harder than anyone. It's his reputation that's on the line.

WRITERS

A variety of prefixes shore up the title "producer": "assistant," "associate," "executive," "line," and the modest "co-." However, what we are dealing with here is *the* producer, the man or woman who finds the raw material: the book, play, short story, original script, a script adapted from another medium, an idea on the back of a pack of Marlboro, or inspired by a photograph on somebody's shelf—and what he sees is the film flash before his eyes.

This talent is more acquired than innate and for the producer to get started, the short film provides the same demands of storytelling and filmmaking found in a feature or TV drama. The constraints of budget and the need to answer to backers or broadcasters will encourage the producer to seek out a story that works for a wide audience, and that's not a bad thing. However, if you do have the urge to make something culturally or socially valid, or a personal crusade, or a showcase for your six-year-old twins, or something zany and completely off the wall such as Martin Pickles's *G.M.*, a short homage to Georges Méliès (discussed in Chapter 20), the short film has all the challenges of a feature without the risks—critically as well as financially.

The first job is to find the script or find the story and put a writer to work on it.

Where do you find a writer?

Throw a stone out of the window and you'll probably hit one. Finding a good writer—finding a great writer—takes time, practice, patience, and luck.

If you announce that you're looking for material, proposals will start dropping through the mailbox along with whining letters that diligently explain the story—always the kiss of death; if a script needs explaining, it isn't ready. Andrea Calderwood once remarked that when she left BBC Scotland for Pathé, the same scripts followed her down the M6 to the capital. She took on two assistants; they read 700 scripts between them and rejected the lot. That isn't to say, of course, that the 701st isn't going to be *the one!*

It's an odd contradiction, but even with all those rookie writers out there, producers from the narrow streets of Soho to the gleaming glass offices looming over Santa Monica Boulevard are pulling their hair out, weeping over the scarcity of good scripts. There was a time when every man leaning on every bar imagined that he had a book in him. Now it's a screenplay. In fact, mention the movie business and he'll whip it out of his shoulder bag, dog-eared and coffee-ringed, and ask strangers, casually met, if they would like to take a look. If you meet Andrea Calderwood in a bar, she'll probably tell you she's a dentist.

While there are thousands of people writing scripts, producers continue to complain that there isn't anything worth filming, and with the complaint being ubiquitous, there must be something to it. Producers are therefore rejecting the scripts sliding over the transom and are making calls to publishing houses in search of the neglected novel, the remaindered gem, the out-of-copyright book. Others are venturing out of London's West End to see fringe plays, and also to hole-in-the-wall experimental theaters in New York's wind-blown canyons off Broadway. If it's worth publishing or staging, it must be worth taking a look at.

But here lies the dilemma. The novel is about ideas, about the internal life of the characters. Proust, in *Remembrances of Things Past*, wanders off for a dozen pages to describe the smell of *madeleines.* Try getting your writer to put that in his screenplay. Or try getting him to take it out if he's attempted to slip it in. The stage play is about words, plays on words, the taste of words. There is a mass of material that can be adapted, but as anyone who has ever done any adapting soon learns, you have to read the original, take out the kernel and sling the rest to the pigeons. An adaptation is just as hard to write as an original screenplay: perhaps harder.

A friend of mine recently quit making corporate videos to adapt a biography, the hardest of genres. Within days he was phoning to chat about migraine and insomnia, his attraction to cliff tops and razor blades. Suddenly he was fighting with his girlfriend (her fault) and arrived late for appointments; he was drinking too much or, alternatively, claiming he no longer drank at all (first sign of the alcoholic). Finally, he turned up at a meeting wearing odd shoes. He talked about the "verbal" power of silent movies then handed me a Post-it with this on it:

The true way leads along a tightrope, which is not stretched aloft but just above the ground. It seems designed more to trip than to be walked along.[2]

He'd found Franz Kafka, or Franz Kafka had found him, and this is where the producer becomes the psychiatrist, the healer, the script editor. My writer friend was filled with self-doubt; not that he had done a bad job with the screenplay—he just needed someone to tell him he'd done a good job, a great job … just a few tweaks here and there, get the first turning point forward a few pages, put some action into that soggy middle … maybe cut out that section on page 73 where the cop explains the whys and wherefores to his sergeant.

Producer Maureen Murray (*The Sea Change*) puts smiley faces beside the bits she likes in a script and her writers are more able to cope with the cold straight lines that slice like razors through the bits she doesn't. She makes suggestions, but expects the writer to find solutions: the two skills are different and must complement each other like yin and yang in a perfect, if reversed, fit. A producer is not a writer who has too much in the in tray to write, but must be able to distinguish good writing when it's on the page and bad writing that needs erasing. Rewrites are a form of torture: "the main condition of the artistic experience,"[3] according to Samuel Beckett, but no screenplay surfaces through the slush piles without them. A film may not live up to the script's potential, but there has never been a great film made from a bad script.

Producers are not always looking for the best script that they can find. They may be looking for a script that appeals to them for their own reasons. J. Arthur Rank[4] was a Methodist lay preacher who showed films to children at Sunday school. In 1932, when he discovered more people went to the cinema than to church, the wealthy young mill owner entered the movie business with the intention of making and distributing films that had a positive social content. In the competitive movie market, the Rank Organization had to make films with one eye on the audience but Rank, in looking at scripts and dealing with producers, never lost sight of his original aims.

Rank was concerned with the moral and ethical state of society in his time, as an examination of this theme can provide useful and entertaining material at any time. No one who saw *Syriana* and *Good Night, and Good Luck,* two films in 2005, would have missed the filmmakers' allusions to, and reflections on, the Iraq War. The actor/producer George Clooney was the prime mover behind them both and his political stance got him in a whole lot of trouble with the American right wing press: If you're not with us, you're against us. But Clooney was big enough to swim against that particular tide and come fall 2006, Americans were swimming the same way, voting the Republicans out of power in both Houses of Congress. Clooney's films did that? No, of course not. But they were a valuable part of the drip, drip, drip of opposition that finally encouraged the American people to take a fresh look at the entire Iraq crisis.

From the early days of Chaplin's Little Tramp movies, film has evolved as a primary source of social and philosophical debate. Film—with greater facility and playing to a larger audience than literature—can convey complex ideas through the intentions, actions, and relationships of the characters; those actions, and the results of those actions, involve the audience on an emotive level.

18 *Good Night and Good Luck*
▶▶ P.53

Day in and day out we hear stories of rape, robbery, muggings, violence at school and on public transport on the news. We watch a movie about Joe Wright, a man doing two jobs in order to help his sister Maria pay for an operation to right a crooked leg. We meet Bill Black, his neighbor. Black's a small-time dope dealer in trouble with the mob. When he robs Joe Wright at the very moment when enough money has been saved for the operation, our heart goes out to Joe and Maria. We are glued to our seats until Bill Black get his comeuppance, and we'd kind of like to see Maria walk straight again. Audiences watching the soap story of Joe and Maria Wright will be moved far more deeply than by listening to a priest in church telling the parable of the Good Samaritan, as J. Arthur Rank realized when he first showed films at Sunday school.

TELLING A STORY WELL

19 *Taxi Driver*

▶▶ P.53

Some writers are good at dialogue, others at structure, others can see the big picture and take on adaptations. There are writers such as Paul Schrader—*Taxi Driver*; *Cat People*—who go alone into the desert for a week, work twenty hours a day and return with a finished scenario. Maybe it needs fixing, but there's another kind of writer unique to the film industry called the script doctor, and that's what he does—not original work but, like a picture restorer, he fills in the fine details. The role of the producer is to match the writer with the story; in Hollywood, of course, they'll use a combination of expertise and leave the Writer's Guild to resolve the credits.

There is yet another kind of writer the producer must watch out for and he's the one who does a single draft and is reluctant to do more because he knows the script will be overhauled when a director comes on board. He's right, of course: it will be. But a director won't come on board if the script isn't fully developed in the first place. These writers, normally very competent, make a reasonable living writing first drafts and can't understand why it's rare for their scripts to turn into films. They are often wonderful raconteurs and can slip marquee names, with their business cards, into every conversation. These are the writers to avoid. Their stories are verbal, not on the page, and it is easy to be fooled by a colorful personality unless the producer has knowledge of script mechanics and the insight to enjoy their company and leave it at that.

If the producer has learned the art of managing money, he should max out his credit cards and spend some time on a desert island finding out how stories work. Read Æschylus, the lives of the great Olympians, Oedipus, and on to Shakespeare and Chaucer. Dip into the wise worlds of Lao-tsu and Confucius; look at some Jacobean drama, and don't forget the exquisitely constructed short stories of Hemingway and James Joyce. See Sam Beckett's absurdist plays (demand them on your island) and study the greats: Dickens, Thomas Hardy, E. M. Forster, Daphne du Maurier, F. Scott Fitzgerald, Flaubert, William Golding … and on to Tolkein, Nick Hornby, J. K. Rowling … Gore Vidal, José Saramago and Michel Houellebecq.

You can learn a lot about making films by watching films, but you learn storytelling from the written word. Buñuel hitched his wagon to Dalí's genius to get started, but he was a voracious reader and became a masterly writer

20 *Belle de Jour*

with the breathtaking *Belle de Jour* and Academy Award-winning *The Discreet Charm of the Bourgeoisie*, to name just two of his many films. To get there, like Buñuel, it makes sense to start with shorts. Once you get those right, you'll have a showreel for Andrea Calderwood to brighten her quest for the perfect script.

THE DISCIPLINE OF SHORT FILMS

Unlike the United States and in Europe, many short films made in the UK have a sameness about them, no doubt because the majority are produced by young filmmakers eager to enter the industry and whose background and education is similar. They have the mixed good fortune not to have lived through the hard times of Alexander Salkind, who fled Russia, or Hal Landers, who grew up in the mean streets of New Jersey during the Depression, though, naturally, it is those experiences that shaped them and gave them an edge, and the nerve it takes to approach strangers on a train and royals out shopping.

According to Dawn Sharpless, creative director at Dazzle Films, one of the UK's top outfits for sales, distribution, and the exhibition of short films, shorts in the UK are falling behind because insufficient time is spent on their development. Short films are often seen as merely a stepping-stone to features and filmmakers are in such a hurry to take that step that they are not putting the time into creating powerful short scripts. The short film discipline is a genre in its own right, and only when that is fully recognized and appreciated will short films improve. "Occasionally something makes you sit back in your seat and you realize that here's a filmmaker with a story to tell," Dawn adds.[5] "But the sad thing is that for every fifty shorts I see, you sit back only once with real excitement."

What's the problem?

"Inadequate planning. I think the whole secret is in pre-production," she says. "New filmmakers need to be more daring. Stories should take us to places we have never been to before—and that takes courage."

Her observation is substantiated by Elliot Grove, who heads the Raindance Film Festival. Some 2,000 shorts are submitted to him each year from forty or so countries and 200 make it into the annual festival, the largest showcase of shorts in the UK. He has noticed that every year there is a flood of good shorts from a different country. Last year it was Poland; a few years ago, South Africa. "It's always somewhere new, but it has been a few years since I have seen anything in the UK that really knocks your socks off."

Elliot Grove has noticed that most British short films are dialogue-driven, while those in the United States and Europe tend to be more visual. "It's an odd dichotomy, because those British films that are visual usually go around the world winning prizes."

In the United States and Canada, young filmmakers have grown up on a diet of MTV, while in the UK, a lot of the scripts and films that Grove sees have been inspired by TV soaps, with their incessant banter and lack of action. With shorts, filmmakers should be exploring ideas and learning their craft, says Grove. They should study as many short films as they can, especially at festivals, where they will come into contact with other filmmakers meeting the same challenges and where they can ask each other how they got this effect or that shot. Film is a collaborative process, and Elliot Grove has been constantly and pleasantly surprised at how willing filmmakers are when it comes to sharing information.

Grove compares the difference between writing a short film and a feature as creating a haiku poem and a sonnet. "It requires different techniques, different skills, a different sensibility. With a good short film you have a calling card. And every time we have shown filmmakers with great storytelling skills, they have moved on to making successful features."

Raindance first showed Christopher Nolan's shorts before he made *Following* and *Memento*, and showed Shane Meadows before he made *TwentyFourSeven*.

USING SHORT STORIES

If, in the search for a feature, producers look at novels and plays, for a short film, one surprisingly untapped source of material is the short story, sadly neglected by mainstream publishers and mainly found in the hermetic world of the literary magazine.

There are thousands of small press journals with a constant flow of new stories, usually by writers experimenting with style and who view publication as an end in itself. Few journals can afford to pay contributors, but the competition to get into print is still fierce and the quality of writing often very high. Short story writers know that every word counts and, as a form, the short story has similarities to the short film that do not apply to the novel and play. Both make use of suggestion, atmosphere, nuance, the subtly implied gesture. Both are a riddle, every word having to carry its own weight, justify its existence. The short story weaves fine lines more than broad strokes. Explanation is death. A published story will have been honed and refined, every gesture thought through to such a degree that if the woman in the story runs her tongue over her lips, there is such a good reason for it that you'd better make sure your script contains the same instruction and your director heeds it.

Where do you find these literary and small press magazines? On the web; in the library; on the shelves in independent bookshops. Find one and you find them all. Research is money in the bank, the first weapon in the producer's armory. And if you do discover a writer with a fine short story, he will already be well versed in rewriting and prepared for it when you option a short script. And who know, perhaps he has a feature script lurking in the bowels of his laptop?

Short stories are subtle, often enigmatic, with carefully drawn characters, and when filmmakers alight on them they tend to think in terms of features, not shorts. There are many examples of successful adaptations, among the best known coming from three Philip K. Dick stories: Ridley Scott's *Bladerunner*, from the imaginatively titled *Do Androids Dream of Electric Sheep?* (later published as a short novel), Steven Spielberg's *Minority Report*, and John Woo's 2003 adaptation of *Paycheck*, a story about a machine that can read the future and just as relevant in film terms half a century after it was first published in 1953. Dawn Sharpless was unable to come up with any examples of short stories that have been turned into memorable short films, but yearns for the day when that hole in the genre is filled.

As mentioned above, many short story writers see publication as their main goal; now that is as likely to mean on the web as on paper. There are many short story sites. I have found FanStory and ABCtales particularly good.

`www.FanStory.com`
`www.abctales.com`

SMALL FISH

Instead of doing their research and finding material, producers will, in frustration, often turn to directors and accept their scripts, not because they're better (often it's the contrary) but at least they know the director is committed and they haven't got to go through the birth pains of yet another draft. The result, though, as Dawn Sharpless has observed, are too many forgettable films—shorts and features—written by non-writers and backed by producers too uncertain of themselves to find a writer and put in the hours bonding and working together. Writers tend to be introverted. Directors are charming, outgoing, and more fun to work with. But producers should be wary and heed William Goldman's haunting counsel: there are three essentials that come before you sign up a director. The Script. The Script. And the Script.

When Goldman's *Butch Cassidy and the Sundance Kid* came out, New York's three leading papers devoted many pages to reviews. Two of the critics were in raptures over the Redford–Newman coupling and forgot to mention the writer. The third hated the picture and blamed the script. Goldman had spent five years sitting in his New York apartment writing it.

Critics are not going to go easy on writers. The producer must. He should cultivate the wisdom of ancient China, where an emperor once sent an emissary to Lao-tsu asking for advice on how to rule the kingdom. You should rule the kingdom, replied the sage, as you would cook a small fish.

Producers are emperors. Writers are small fish. Don't grill him, don't batter; bone him and leave him gutted. Writers are delicate: fine porcelain, thin ice on winter morning ponds, a love affair. Imagine the plumber coming three days late to repair the toilet. He shoves a new tube into the ball cock, fingerprints the tiles with lubricating oil, and you feel a wave of gratitude when he accepts $300 cash and agrees to screw the government out of the taxes. Your writer drops in with three typos and an oxymoron fleshing out a secondary character and you want to kill him. Those stains on the bathroom walls have to be douched away and where better to spray some ammonia than at the self-doubting wordsmith. Writers cry easily. Don't use words such as "pretentious," "slow," "lacking," "boring," "depressing" or "another day," as in: "We'll talk about it another day."

He'll worry himself sick waiting for that day. Let slip the word "pretentious" and you're leaving yourself open to the pretensions of defining the term. Tell a writer that his script is slow and he'll shuffle down to Starbucks for a double espresso with whipped everything, including the skin on his back. Tell him that his work's depressing and he'll get depressed, swallow a fistful of codeine and consider Hemingway's last dance with a shotgun.

The major production companies work with established writers and, more than ever, are sourcing material from novels, biographies, plays and—a disturbing trend—old movies (*The Wicker Man*, *The Four Feathers*, *Psycho*, and *Vanilla Sky* from Alejandro Amenábar's *Abre los Ojos*; all, in my opinion, inferior to the originals). The new producer is more likely to be working with an inexperienced writer who, like the producer, is learning his craft. The writer will work for weeks and months before presenting what he believes is a masterpiece and it will require tact and patience for him to see that what he has typed is probably little more than a glorified treatment.

PAUSE	TAKING ADVICE
▐▐	There's a great saying: When nine Russians tell you you're drunk, lie down. I always think of that. If people say, "That's a ghastly idea"—and I'm certainly capable of ghastly ideas—then it might be worth listening. You have to listen, and it's desperately important to find people whose opinions you can respect and value. Anthony Minghella[6]

When Lee Hall's script for *Billy Elliot* first went to the BBC it was about the miners' strike in Thatcher's Britain. Billy's desire to dance was a subplot. Hall's standpoint was socialist, more than aspirational. Three years of development changed a story about class solidarity to class betrayal, from Old Labour to New Labour, and created a film for our times. Hall's first draft, like all first drafts, was not a film but a road map leading to a film; a guide, not the place it became. When you read first drafts you are looking for a spark, originality, an individual voice, not gold dust but the iron ore that can be mined and shaped into a bridge to span the gulf from development to production. A producer should identify all that is good in a script. If only ten percent is good, salvage it, compliment it. Get rid of the other ninety percent and start again.

Billy Elliot spent three years in development. *Good Will Hunting* needed seven. Richard Attenborough was white-haired and twenty years older before *Ghandi* was ready to go. Scripts are hard to write, as difficult or more difficult than novels. They need many drafts and time; lots of time. Producers must face that. They choose a companion as much as a project. Their writer becomes their brother, their sister, their child. According to Cyril Connolly, writers are just that: infants crying in their cots for attention. A writer needs faith, patience, and passion. A producer needs all of that and a box of Kleenex to wipe away the tears.

There is no science for putting producers and writers together, although an experiment to do just that has been created by two London-based organizations, the New Producers Alliance and Screenwriters' Workshop, with their script initiative *Match*. Screenwriters armed with treatments are paired with first-time producers, recognized script editors are attached as godfathers and, with their input, projects are developed for their journey into the industry. Since the year the scheme started, in 2001, Marcus Lloyd's script *Cuckoo* has won the prestigious £10,000 Oscar Moore Foundation Screenwriting Prize, and other projects have been optioned by major production companies.

When a producer finds his writer, he sticks with him. *The Claim* (2000) was produced by Andrew Eaton with Frank Cottrell Boyce writing and, by the time Michael Winterbottom began directing in Canada, they were already working on *24-Hour Party People*, the next project.

At a Script Factory screening of *The Claim* in London, Cottrell Boyce spoke about the long process he'd gone through to take the themes from Thomas Hardy's *The Mayor of Casterbridge* and transpose them to the 1849 gold rush in the American West. He told the audience that the first drafts (that's plural) of his script were done *just to see what the themes were*. The next drafts have to be a good read so that the *Suits* with the checkbooks can see the story in their minds. The script that goes out to actors is slightly different again. *But every draft is different to the shooting script*. Those earlier drafts contain an explanation of themselves that you don't need when you're ready to shoot. It's a leaner and fitter thing. "I love this stage. It's really great when you feel something coming to life. It's like cutting diamonds."

Frank Cottrell Boyce did not choose to write *The Claim*. Andrew Eaton chose it and stuck Hardy's novel on his desk. Of course, writers want to write their own stories. But it is the job of producers to know what they can market. With a short film, the producer has an added burden: telling a good story in ten minutes is hard and finding slots for films that are longer is harder still, as we shall discuss later when it comes to distribution.

Once the producer has survived the writing process and has a script in his hand, he moves to the next square on the board, where he must find a director and build his team.

STOP

18 George Clooney and fellow travelers take on commie hunter Senator Joseph McCarthy in *Good Night and Good Luck*. © BFI

19 *"Are you looking at me?"* Robert de Niro in *Taxi Driver*. © BFI

CHAPTER 6

The Director

The writer has labored over his ten descriptive and lively, but tightly written, pages, and the producer hands these precious objects to the director. It is hardly surprising that writers want to direct their own work but this impulse is, in a historic sense, a relatively new trend and many subscribe to Hitchcock's faith in what he called "The Trinity: Writer. Director. Producer." By keeping the roles of writer and director separate, the producer has greater control.

In the case of Hitchcock, while he was directing one film, he would have breakfast every morning with the writer he'd set to work on a new project. He didn't read the pages or interfere with the ongoing narrative, but like the operator of a Punch and Judy show, his hand was manipulating the twists and turns from behind the scenes.

The director, whatever his modus operandi, will invariably work on the script and his name often finds its way on to the writing credits, something Hitchcock grandly renounced. The director also gets the debatable designate *A Film By…* just above or just below the title, depending on his status and the power of his agent when it comes to negotiating the contracts. The deifying of the director in this way occurs because he is the creator of the finished work, the artist who takes the raw material of the script and combines the elements of *mise-en-scène*, a phrase borrowed from the theater and meaning "to put on stage."

In film terms, John Gibbs, in his excellent study *Mise-en-Scène*, suggests a useful definition might be that of the contents of the frame and the way those contents are organized, both halves of the formulation being significant:

What are the contents of the frame? They include lighting, costume, decor, properties, and the actors themselves. The organization of the contents of the frame encompasses the relationship of the actors to the camera, and thus the audience's view. So in talking about *mise-en-scène*, one is also talking about framing, camera movement, the particular lens employed, and other photographic decisions. *Mise-en-scène* therefore encompasses both what the audience can see, and the way in which they are invited to see it. It refers to many of the major elements of communication in the cinema, and the combinations through which they operate expressively.[1]

In the novel, the word alone must convey mood and meaning. In film, every frame is packed with information—a shadow, a ticking clock, the breeze fingering the curtains: every detail is significant. Stephen Fry, while directing *Bright Young Things* (2003), from the Evelyn Waugh novel *Vile Bodies*, was shown several cigarette cases from the 1930s by the props department to choose from. That cigarette case might only be seen for a fraction of a second—it may be edited out of the final cut—but it is the attention to detail that creates audience identification with characters and involvement in their lives.

The director must have an eye for every small detail. He decides who does what, when and why; this multiplicity of detail described by actor Gary Oldman after the first time on the floor as "death by a thousand questions."[2]

The fusion of these disparate parts is the puzzle the director (with the editor's help) assembles and it is his vision that we see on screen. Of all the jobs in film, the director requires the least training and the least experience with technology. That isn't to say that directors do not know their way around an editing suite, or which filters to use on the camera. Most do. The best learn. What the director needs most, however, is the insight to understand immediately what the story is about, what passions drive the characters, and what each actor needs in order for him to make those passions real.

When we think back on any situation—in a bar with friends, a bitter row, a day on the beach, a night of love—we see it from our own point of view. As we piece the memory together, the mind selects the most salient and piquant details with camera angles, distances, juxtapositions, close-ups, and long shots in a richly woven tapestry.

This selection of fragments is the same as taking frames of film and, in our heads, cutting movies from our recollections. According to anthropologists, once monkeys learn to use tools—to prise open seashells, for example—future generations are genetically blessed with that knowledge. Likewise, a century after the Lumière Brothers first shot moving pictures, it seems to be an innate human predisposition to be able to piece together the puzzle of a film story and, perhaps more important, to actively take part in its telling by incorporating our own experience and imagination.

Actors develop and refine this art; the director, like a hypnotist, will draw out the appropriate memories to bring a scene to life. You don't have to be an out-of-work father with hungry mouths to feed to play that particular role, as Clint Eastwood showed in *Unforgiven*, the story of a retired gunslinger who crawls back into his old skin in order to put food on the table. Similarly, it's unlikely that in Beverly Hills Sigourney Weaver would have come face to face with an alien bent on genocide (though anything's possible in Beverly Hills) before she starred in *Alien*. Both actors' performances in these films were convincing because these proficient actors are able to dredge up emotions that inform their characters.

The director must know the character he is creating as well or *even* better than the actor; the evolution of the character's story will be part of the pattern painted inside his mind. Shooting schedules by necessity divide scripts into convenient but disconnected chunks that are stuck together when filming is completed. Cinema actors are trained to give realistic performances with minimal preparation; it is considered by many that too much preparation can blunt their edge, the reverse of work in theater, where rehearsals are lengthy and stories are told chronologically.

For example, a woman who stabs her husband and is taken away by gendarmes in a rainy Paris exterior shot, may not get to show what led up to the fatal event until weeks later when the crew moves on to do the villa interiors in sun-drenched St Tropez. If the director dresses the woman in the Paris scene in a clinging gown that becomes diaphanous in the spring rain, it's going to look a whole lot different than if she were wearing an anorak and climbing boots. Are her shoulders sagging, or does she hold her head high? Is mascara running in black streams over her cheeks or are her scarlet lips puckered in a defiant smile? Was her husband a brute and do we feel her pain and relief as she plunges the knife into his back? Or is she a scheming gold digger who deserves the guillotine? The way the audience reacts depends on the scene staged by the director and the performance drawn from the actress.

To return to *Unforgiven*, Clint Eastwood would not have approached the role by trying to *act* the feeling of a man suffering the torments of failure. Rather, he would have allowed the appropriate consciousness to take possession of him. That state would generate the emotionally applicable movements, responses, behavior, and body language, a glimpse into the inner soul where all sensation occurs on a deeper level. It is the art of restraint and suggestion that Eastwood has mastered, a particular achievement as he normally directs himself.

More than the writer who has shaped his theme, plotted his turning points, and set up his surprises, the director would have combed the material for the emotionally charged moments and, through his cast, so reveal the heart of character. An actor well directed will make his feelings so clear that lines in the dialogue mentioning love, despair, jealousy, hatred, and so on can be edited out of the final cut, the telling having been supplanted by the showing, the point made by Frank Cottrell Boyce in the previous chapter, his diamond-cutting analogy for the shooting script being that moment when the last traces of dust are blown away and the sparkling gemstone is revealed.

POINT OF VIEW

A film goes through three stages to reach completion: pre-production, production, and post-production. All carry equal weight and, as the producer will remind his director, it is in pre-production where they can save time and money on production and post. The ticking clock is the perfect symbol for the process: for the producer the ticking clock is a meter ringing up the bills; for the director, the ticking clock is more like a metronome guiding rhythm and pace; for the audience the ticking clock is a ticking bomb that holds us breathless, waiting for the explosion. The director will keep us waiting, building the sense of urgency and the tension.

Typically, the writer would indicate in a script:

The Firefighter dashes like a 100-meter sprinter into the blazing building to save the baby.

But the Mother's reaction, the Fire Chief's reaction, the play of water arcing from the hoses, the size of the flames leaping from the building, the degree to which the staircase inside is turning to ash, when exactly the Mother's reaction and the Fire Chief's reaction are inserted (and the number of times they're inserted), the swelling crowd, the swirling police lights, and the look on the Firefighter's blackened face as he scoops the infant into his arms—all this (along with set design, costume, the music score) is created by the director from the screenplay's brief scene description.

If the blaze is the first scene in a movie (and it's a powerful opening), the way the Firefighter plays it, and the way the director guides him, depend on how future events unfold. It certainly looks like this guy is our hero, the character we want to identify with, but it requires the whole story for us to understand his action, his motivations, whether he's a coward overcoming cowardice, an ego maniac playing to the crowd, a man whose wife has just died *in a fire* and has nothing to live for. Perhaps the Fire Chief is his older brother, or *younger* brother. The fact that we don't know is what makes the scene interesting. Conversely, the director may give the audience superior position, whereby we in the darkened auditorium know something the Firefighter doesn't—*perhaps it is his baby in the cot?*—and we watch with vicarious angst as this is revealed.

Don Roos's 1998 *The Opposite of Sex* opens with Christina Ricci contemptuously flicking a cigarette butt on a coffin as it is lowered into the ground. We don't know who lies in that coffin, but we're already hooked.

21 *The Opposite of Sex*

▶▶ P.68

Each scene is described on the page when the producer hands the script to the director, but the director doesn't just turn the material into film. He interprets it, shapes it, and gives it pace and inner life. Actors, when given a script, tend to read their parts and count the lines. A director dives in and immerses himself in a script; he'll take it home, turn off the cell phone and read it in one take without making notes. He will want to get a sense of the story. He will then go back and read through it again many times, looking for nuance, depth, reversals, and surprises. He will need to engage emotionally with the work in order to create an emotional response in the audience. If the story doesn't move him, he should pass on it, because it will remain flat when it reaches the screen.

If the story does grab him, he will undoubtedly perceive elements differently from the writer. That's when the fireworks begin. Perhaps the female screenwriter is telling the above Firefighter's story from the point of view of the Mother whose infant is trapped in the building. The director may see the story from the Firefighter's point of view, and the entire script will have to be restructured for him to tell the story that way. Imagine *Cinderella* told from the point of view of one of the Ugly Sisters. How does she feel when this pretty, self-effacing waif moves into the family home? It is not necessarily a better story. But if that's the way the director sees it, that's the way it will be done.

Burt Lancaster, after thirty years as a Hollywood leading man, got to direct for the first time and relished being the early bird on set each morning; he enjoyed dealing with "temperamental actors" and their "little problems." At the end of the day he was anxious to pick up the rushes and he'd spend half the night studying them. "When you are a director you are God, and that's the best job in town."[3]

COLLABORATION

Scripts for short films are often burdened with excess characters. The director may see immediately that the cleverly constructed lines given to the Barman in one scene and the Desk Clerk in another can be combined: it will save money and time on an extra actor, gives one actor a better role—a chance to develop that role, and those key lines are still there; the same story is being told.

This is collaboration. The writer has to accept that this is going to happen, and the director has to learn how to oil the squeaky wheel and make the running easy. Rewrites, especially after all the rewrites, are painful and a system has to be established right from the beginning. As Maureen Murray (see Chapter Five: *The Producer*), with her smiley faces and steely cold lines, picks out the best and worst in a script, it is better for the writer, and better for the process, if the director tackles each aspect of the screenplay separately: first structure and plotting, to get the overall *feel* of the piece, before moving on to the finer aspects of dialogue and visual interpretation.

PAUSE

PROBING QUESTIONS

When the director breaks down a script, he will ask himself a number of questions:

1. What's the story actually about?
2. Who is it about?
3. Do we empathize with the main character(s)?
4. Are they likeable?
5. What exactly do these people want?
6. Who is stopping them getting it?
7. Why?
8. Are there surprises, thrills, revelations: is the audience led one way before the opposite is revealed?
9. Is the audience lifted and let down and then lifted again, the peaks and troughs going higher and plunging lower as the story builds?
10. Do the main turning points and climaxes appear for maximum impact and interest?
11. Do we have the elements you'd expect for the genre?
12. Have the principal characters gone through major irreversible changes?
13. Are those changes credible?
14. Will those changes move and affect the audience?
15. Is the underlying theme clearly revealed?
16. Is there a satisfactory ending which gives the audience what they expect, but not exactly how they expected it?

PAUSE

These questions should be applied to the script as a whole before the director moves on to the finer details:

1. What's this scene about?
2. What does this scene achieve?
3. Is this scene necessary?
4. What does this scene tell us about the main character(s)?
5. Do the secondary characters have their own dramatic function?
6. Does this scene have conflict, a beginning, middle, and end?
7. Does this scene contribute to the objectives, development, and revelations of the true nature of the main character(s)?
8. Do the characters behave consistently, and where they are inconsistent is that understood and applicable within the narrative?
9. Do the characters have individual voices, word patterns, or slang?
10. Can verbal exposition be replaced by the visual?

At the script stage, every detail can be investigated, chewed over, pulled apart and put back together again at little or no cost. It's the time to get things right. There are directors who rush into production and try to cover holes in the script once they're on set—but, like the writer who's reluctant to write new drafts, this is a director who the cautious producer will avoid.

Theme (no. 15 in the first list above) is the essence of the script: the fight against injustice (*The Hurricane*), the search for love (*When Harry Met Sally*), the struggle for freedom (*Gandhi*), the quest for personal validation (*All Or Nothing*), fear of the unknown (*Signs*). The Pulitzer Prize-winning playwright, Arthur Miller, would finish a play before he was fully aware of the theme. Once he got the theme, he would jot it down, stick it on the wall above his desk and write a new draft with the theme informing the characters' decisions and choices. There may be more than one theme; John Malkovich's extraordinary, if sometimes muddled, *The Dancer Upstairs* (2002) blends love, injustice, and the struggle for freedom.

GENRE

An independent film, especially one made by a writer/director, is likely to be an exploration of ideas, an individual voice with a specific viewpoint. Most short films fall into this category: it is the time when new filmmakers will be testing the boundaries of their own creativity, finding their voice. If the short conforms to genre—horror, crime, melodrama, *film noir*, science fiction, comedy—the conventions of that genre need to be observed in order to meet audience expectations.

Film stories, whether they are genre-based or not, are commonly rooted in moral issues and contain lessons on how to behave in a changing world with its myriad anxieties and temptations. The conflict between good and evil is as basic to the modern screenplay as it was to the tribal wise men, and people are more likely to be pondering the ethical conundrums of capital punishment, immigration, and abortion on a Saturday night at the movies than they are in their places of worship in the cold light of day.

Writer Steve Biddulph argues that through television, magazines, and other media, children learn values such as "looks are everything," "your sexuality is something you trade for being liked," "money buys happiness," and "friends will come if you have the right stuff."[4] Celebrity, youth, and wealth are the idols we have come to revere. In a splintered society shorn of the ethical cornerstones of traditional close-knit communities, movies for many have practically taken the place of religion, giving filmmakers the role of moral arbiters as well as entertainers: an onerous responsibility.

Every decade is marked by its genre: the musicals of the 1930s were an escape from the Depression; the Westerns of the 1940s saw stories of split families after the uncertainties of the Second World War; the Cold War and The Bomb were reflected in the science fiction of the 1950s and 1960s; new attitudes to sex, drugs, and rock and roll marked the 1970s; while Schwarzenegger and Stallone were emblematic of the cult of the individual in the 1980s—one man against the world: a drinker, fighter, gambler, veteran, often a loser who, deep down, has the best of human qualities and his heart in the right place.

This, too, can be applied to the protagonists of *film noir*, a style that originated in the 1940s and has continued through the decades: *Chinatown* (1974), *Body Heat* (1981), *Blood Simple* (1985), *Pulp Fiction* (1994), *L.A. Confidential* (1997), *The Man Who Wasn't There* (2001); all exquisite, multifaceted contributions to the genre.

Film noir originated with the writers and directors who adapted the detective novels of such authors as Raymond Chandler, Dashiell Hammett and Cornell Woolrich. The common theme is the dangerous if desirable femme fatale who challenges the values of a male-dominated society normally portrayed as decadent and corrupt. Set in a world of small-time hoods and petty, self-seeking officials, the detective central to these stories is an alienated, down-at-heel outsider who maintains a strict moral code while he sets about both solving the crime and dealing with the symbolic temptations of the femme fatale. Whether he succumbs or not, his integrity is never in question.

The Blues Brothers (1980) has the catchphrase "We're on a mission from God." It sounds both silly and unlikely. But is it? John Belushi and Dan Aykroyd are getting their band together for one last gig, with Southern rednecks and a scorned woman with a rocket launcher in hot pursuit. They need money, not for a stake in some nefarious venture, but to save their orphanage. We identify with Belushi and Aykroyd, as we identify with the musclemen Schwarzenegger and Stallone, because the characters they play are inherently honorable and uphold the values of our culture.

In Quentin Tarantino's *Pulp Fiction*, Bruce Willis plays Butch, a boxer instructed by gang boss Marsellus Wallace (Ving Rhames) to overcome his pride and throw a fight. Butch, however, backs himself against the odds, kills his opponent in the ring, and picks up a fat paycheck. He's about to flee with his girlfriend, but she leaves the watch passed down to him by his father at their apartment, which he knows Marsellus's men will now be watching. But Butch can't go into exile without that watch and, in returning to get it, he has to shoot Vincent Vega (John Travolta) with Vega's own gun to survive.

22 *Chinatown*
▶▶ P.68

23 *Pulp Fiction*
▶▶ P.68

24 *The Man Who Wasn't There*
▶▶ P.68

Fleeing again, he literally runs into Marsellus in a car crash. Both are injured and stumble into a gun shop run by neo-Nazis. Butch escapes, but goes back to save Marsellus from the torture scene unwinding in the basement. Why? It is true to his nature. Butch always does the right thing. In the boxing ring, the death was accidental. In his apartment, he shoots Vega in self-defense. He was told to throw the fight, cheat the punters, and swallow his pride. But he remains proud, with the values we admire and to which we all aspire.

During the course of the story, Vincent Vega's partner Jules (Samuel L. Jackson) has seen the hand of God at work in saving him from certain death and decides to give up crime and "wander the earth." Vega not only ridicules this conversion, but has fallen under the spell of Marsellus's wife (Uma Thurman), the femme fatale. As a man bereft of ethics, he is the obvious sacrifice to ensure Butch's escape. Vega is not the only character in *Pulp Fiction* to lack morals, but his demise serves to underscore the theme that, while crime is amusing in the world created by Tarantino and Roger Avary, it still doesn't pay.

The gap between genres has narrowed and blurred—the *Scream* films are slasher comedies; *Chicago* is a crime musical; kick-ass extravaganzas and gross-out comedies will always be crowd-pleasers. But while society grows ever more divisive and complex, the cinema becomes the place where serious issues are explored untainted by the hidden agendas of politics and newsprint. It's something of a cliché to say that fact is stranger than fiction. More to the point, it is through fiction that we are best able to articulate fact.

Director Stephen Frears's *Dirty Pretty Things* was enticing people out of the pubs and into cinemas over New Year 2003, with a story set among the illegal immigrants who toil at night in London's minicab offices, sweatshops, and grubby hotels. With Chitwetel Ejiofor playing a Nigerian who trained as a doctor, and Audrey Tatou as a Turkish asylum-seeker who dreams of going to America, Frears captures a cruel, creepy, paranoid city and exposes the human side of immigration as he grapples with the issues of color, race, religion, and the illicit trade in human organs.

To take a horror film example, in Bernard Rose's *Candyman* (1992) the ghost of murdered black slave Daniel Robitaille returns to seek revenge on a complacent white society that has failed to confront racism. Paul Wells, in his study *The Horror Genre*, describes this as a metaphor on racist culture and the prevailing legacy of slavery.

The monster—essentially a brutal avenger—is once again morally ambivalent because of the apparent justice that motivates him. Here, the arcane, primitive world perpetrates a seemingly justifiable horror, which the contemporary world must confront in order to find understanding and achieve atonement.[5]

ATTITUDES AND MORALS

Cinema is often blamed for creating a moral vacuum with its diet of violence and pornography. But the reverse—not ironically, but typically—is also true. More than contemporary literature, or any other art form, cinema is the place of philosophical and social debate. A serious novel is considered successful if it sells 10,000 copies. A film can reach millions.

That's not to say that the director's job is to come up with quick fixes for our anxieties and problems, to provide morals and meanings. Film's role is not to lead or to teach, but to stimulate debate. A film doesn't need to say: this is wrong and this is how to put it right; it is sufficient to show the audience what is wrong and leave people to make up their own minds. Like the novelist, the director's brief is to set out ideas in new (preferably entertaining) ways and allow the audience to fill in the gaps; the realization being, as often as not, that there are no simple answers to the big problems, but that is life, and film is a reflection of life. Early talkies found scripts in novels and stage plays. Writers are wedded to the written word, and it was directors such as Georges Méliès and William Dickson who first understood that film is a visual art. "Seeing comes before words. The child looks and recognizes before it can speak."[6]

Film, as no other artifact or memento from the past, painting, written text, or photograph, reveals how the world was when the scenes were shot: the architecture, transport, clothes, and the expressions on people's faces. In this respect images, particularly moving images, are more precise and richer than literature. More than the invention of the camera, the movie camera changed the way we as people—our grandfathers and great-grandfathers—viewed and understood the world. For example, an audience in a Kinetoscope Parlor in Chicago, watching one minute of Highland dancing, would have been viewing something that almost certainly they had never seen before; subsequently they had understanding and empathy with an alien world of bagpipes and men in tartan kilts.

As a director develops his skills, he will not only be able to reveal the world in what we see, but in what we do not see. Often, what is most interesting is what happens in the gaps between images, in the moments between moments. This may come from the action the writer has put in his script (be warned scriptwriters: an excess of directions drives directors crazy!) but more likely it is the director's interpretation of the script inspired by the needs and demands of the characters.

Jenny Borgars, former head of the Film Council Development Fund, told Nic Wistreich, in the online film magazine *Film Netribution Network*, that new filmmakers need to study the work of people who have excelled in the profession. Training is only one route to knowledge, and an enormous amount can be learned by giving someone ten great American scripts that have been made into movies. The new director can study the pages, study the shots and see exactly how the transfer to screen is realized.

According to Jenny Borgars, in the United States scriptwriters have learned to allow the reader enough space to fall into the story, rather than trying to give the reader all the information possible. "A writer/director needs to know what to put down on the page in order to get their film sold into the market—before they actually *make* the film," she continues. "That sounds like a crude distinction but it is quite difficult convincing people of it."

While script development is an ongoing process throughout pre-production, the director will also be liaising with the casting director, cameraman, storyboard artist, set director, the props and wardrobe departments, and makeup, each element adding shades and layers to the dramatic effect the director wants to achieve; the story he wants to cast before the public.

The infamy of Buñuel's short films reflected his times: the left–right divide, new attitudes to sex and the Church. Each generation must tell its own stories and as such the director is the thermometer taking society's temperature. He must see everything, be interested in everything, and always seek truth. The Italian director Federico Fellini once said that at school he learned almost nothing except how to observe the silence of passing time, to recognize far-off sounds, rather like an imprisoned person who can tell the sound of the bell of the Duomo from that of San Augustino. "I have a pleasant memory of entire mornings and afternoons spent doing absolutely nothing."[7]

While he was apparently doing nothing, Fellini was meditating on his times, which he captured in *La Dolce Vita* (The Sweet Life), a film so overpowering when it was released in 1960 that critic Andrew Sarris argued that in terms of social impact, "It is the most important film ever made."[8]

25 *La Dolce Vita*
▶▶ P.69

It was the height of the Cold War; Algeria was fighting the French for independence; thousands perished in the Agadir earthquake, and Fellini, his eyes always half-hidden under a black hat, had chronicled the spoiled, confused, aimless lives of those who frequented Rome's Via Veneto: spent writers and bored aristocrats, calculating adventurers, social climbers, and intrusive, star-chasing photographers, from where the generic term "paparazzi" originated.

26 *La Dolce Vita*
▶▶ P.69

When the film was first released, in the cinema lobby a woman in furs waved her fist at Fellini and screamed: "You are putting Italy into the hands of the Bolsheviks." And a man in a dinner jacket spat in his face, the modern equivalent of challenging Fellini to a duel. As the film moved out across Italy, a civil war erupted in the media, church pulpits, in public debates, and in open fights outside movie houses where the police were often called to quell a riot. *L'Osservatore Romano* described the film as disgusting, obscene, indecent, and sacrilegious; *Il Quotidiano* suggested that the film's title, *The Sweet Life*, should be changed to *The Disgusting Life*.

Looking at *La Dolce Vita* today, it is difficult to understand what all the fuss was about. But, as biographer Hollis Alpert explains in *Fellini, A Life*, at the time, while Italians had achieved a postwar miracle, economically and socially, here was a film that implied that the miracle had been reduced to "the shoddy pursuit of materialistic goals and pleasures."[9]

This view was not shared when the film was released internationally because Fellini had held up a mirror to *his* world, to Rome. In the reflection the Italian public saw truth, and it is truth alone that leads us to greater understanding or to clench our fist in outrage.

La Dolce Vita is set among what at the time was becoming known as the jet set, but as a portrayal of contemporary society, with its naturalistic acting style and scenes shot on location, it conformed to the tenets of neo-realism, a trend that moved across Europe like a breath of fresh air and evolved with a liberal/socialist emphasis on ordinary people living tough, often deprived lives.

27 *Cathy Come Home*
▶▶ P.69

When Ken Loach's *Cathy Come Home* was screened on the BBC in 1966, it resulted in angry exchanges about homelessness and social services in the Houses of Parliament and led to the formation of Shelter, with actress Carol White its first figurehead. The BBC drama was aired again in 2006, stimulating public discussion and revealing, sadly, that although some of the worst problems from forty years ago have been alleviated, there is still homelessness and there are still problems in social services. The appetite for films that make us laugh, cry, and think about who we are and the world we live in, has not diminished and accounts for some of the most successful UK movies in recent years: *The Full Monty*, *Brassed Off*, *Billy Elliot*, and *Bend it Like Beckham*. Likewise, in the United States the box office has been ringing out tickets for feature-length documentaries such as former Vice President Al Gore's 2007 Oscar-winner *An Inconvenient Truth*; Nick Bicanic and Jason Bourque's *Shadow Company*, "a thorough and balanced look at the use of private security forces in Iraq [which] raises serious policy questions," according to Senator Ted Kennedy; and Michael Moore's thoughtful polemics *Fahrenheit 9/11*, *Bowling for Columbine* and *Sicko*.

HAVING SOMETHING TO SAY

The need for stories that shed light on the fears and values of the age is as vital—perhaps more vital—now as it ever was and applies not only to features, but to short films as well. I got the impression, talking to short film directors, that the ideals held dear by the likes of Loach and Fellini are undimmed and, if anything, are shining more brightly. Directing, says Cedric Behrel, is first about *having something to say* and learning your craft in order to be able to say it loud and clear.

You must know how to use the cinematic palette to get across an idea, a vision, a character, and do so with an original, unique interpretation of subject matter. We can't expect a director to be an established writer, essayist or philosopher—he is only a vector of such thoughts, he can only be judged on his capacity to express his material with his tools, the cinematic palette of narration, drama and style. For that, he must make sure he gets the best material possible.[10]

Following the signposts of social realism, Behrel's films include the 20-minute *Lush*, the story of a young woman repressed by her ultra-modern, lifeless environment who sets out on a journey of self-discovery; the 10-minute documentary *Who's Afraid of Vanessa SB?* with artist Tracey Emin; and *St Elucias's Island*, the story of 13-year-old Leah who, caught between her abusive mother and the menace of a vicious, small-time businessman must succumb to a terrible fate or find the strength to break free.

Behrel finds a common difficulty for shorts directors is that they become *too* involved in aspects of the film that have little to do with directing: writing draft after draft, dealing with production issues, locations, and so on. "The focus necessary to direct film—and most of all, direct actors—requires such concentration and energy there isn't enough left in you for anything else," he explains, and remembers driving the lighting van on a film school short because the director of photography didn't have a license.

This has a lot to do with budget restrictions and the fact that most filmmakers tend to self-finance their first attempts. Cedric Behrel's advice is to find the most competent people you can and make sure they are placed in key positions: writer, producer, director; the same opinion expressed by Alfred Hitchcock.

"In this spirit I would think it is more important for an apprentice director to have a production manager than, let's say, a camera operator."

PAUSE

▌▌

BEHREL'S GUIDELINES

1. Cut down on locations and try to get the locations close together.
2. Rehearse. Rehearsal time is cheap and it allows you to save time when you shoot.
3. Have post-production in mind before you shoot; what can be done in post-production should reflect the shooting style.
4. If you use stage actors (the norm in the UK), get them to "play it down."
5. Never shoot a script that you are not at least 300 percent sure about.
6. Know what you are doing: don't try and fit a specific format if you are making an experimental film and, if you are making a genre piece, know the rules and history of the genre you're dealing with.
7. Don't expect to earn money from a short.

Behrel believes that on a short film, a director needs to be persistent but flexible, ambitious but realistic. "You must be hardworking and have vast knowledge of every component of filmmaking," he adds. "You need to be able to talk to everyone on set and be open to nuance. You must know the difference between a good take and a bad one and, more important, know what to do about it."

Being "open to nuance" is much the same as being flexible, which was described by Alexis Bicât as "flashes of inspiration."

"After all the care and planning, once you get on set, those flashes are sacred and can come from anywhere: actors or members of the crew, the sun appearing unexpectedly through the clouds. If you are not open to ideas and prepared to reverse your thinking, you will never be a strong director."

Alexis Bicât directed *Noise Control* (discussed in Chapter 18: *Noise Control*) with *Lock, Stock and Two Smoking Barrels* star Nick Moran playing a fighter pilot. "As far as I'm concerned, he's Britain's top indie actor and I have to admit I was nervous going on set the first day," he explains. "But the thing with stars is that they get where they are because they are good actors. They are actually more easy to work with because they are more technically proficient."

How do you get a major performer like Nick Moran in your short? "Just ask: they can only say no. And they may say yes," suggests *Noise Control* writer Terence Doyle.

While the director assumes complete creative control and bears responsibility for any problems or errors that occur, Bicât stresses that it is essential to have a close bond with the director of photography (DOP). He is normally more technically trained and will ensure basic things, such as the film being exposed properly. "The film is preconceived, with each shot and sequence cut in your head, but the DOP will know whether what you want to do can be done and how to do it."

Noise Control DOP Simon Dinsel had never filmed from a plane before and had to familiarize himself with the specially hired kit, an Aaton Minima camera and the Kenlab stabilizer that operates on a series of gyroscopes. Film can run through this small, versatile camera at 48 frames per second, which makes the action appear smoother when its slowed down to the standard 24 frames per second.

"About 95 percent of people who go up in a training jet throw up and Simon did also," says Bicât. "But he kept going and got all the shots. That's what you need when you're making a short on a tight budget: technicians who are prepared to do anything. Like good actors, they are easy to work with."

Though written as a short in its own right, *Noise Control* was planned as a taster for the feature being developed by the same team and, as such, is rich in feature production values. The film was shot on 35mm with digital composite effects (CGI); video to film transfers; Dolby digital sound mix, the twenty-nine tracks of audio mixed down to six.

"It was one of the biggest jobs on a short film ever undertaken, which resulted in us being in post-production longer than *Star Wars* waiting for downtime in CGI houses, audio suites and so on," adds Bicât. "It also doubled the production cost."

Downtime means free time, usually in the middle of the night, something short filmmakers have to consider when they're doing a budget. Was it worth it? After being cut to eight minutes (a TV ten minutes), *Noise Control* was sold to BSkyB and secured cinema release across Wales. "They do say a short is just a calling card for the director," says Bicât, "but as far as I know, all the creatives involved in *Noise Control* have added the film to their CV."
www.parent.co.uk/noisecontrol

PAUSE

STOP

ARE YOU MAKING THE SAME FILM?

Lots of problems in film occur when the people are not making the same film; where there are actors in one film and other actors in a different film, or when the production design is not supporting the costume design, or where the camera's not supporting the production design. The task is how you cohere a group of people without inhibiting their own voice, because, chorally, their voices are more interesting than yours is as a solo voice. As a director you must always remember that everybody doing a job on the film is better at that job than you are.

Anthony Minghella[11]

21 Christina Ricci, ready for anything in *The Opposite of Sex*.
© BFI

22 Jack Nicholson and Faye Dunaway in Roman Polanski's
noir thriller *Chinatown*. © BFI

23 John Travolta and Samuel L. Jackson shooting up LA in
Pulp Fiction. © BFI

24 Billy Bob Thornton in *The Man Who Wasn't There*. © BFI

25 *La Dolce Vita*. Marcello Mastroianni and Anita Ekberg in a rainy street. © BFI

26 *La Dolce Vita*. Marcello Mastroianni and Anouk Aimée in party mood. © BFI

27 Carol White and Ray Brooks in a scene from Ken Loach's moving account of homelessness, *Cathy Come Home*. © BFI

CHAPTER 7

The Editor

Every member of the production staff has a part to play in the finished film (directors Cedric Behrel and Alexis Bicât emphasized their dependence on the director of photography), but the more liberated the filmmaker becomes with new technology, the more important the work of the editor.

After the director has coaxed the cast, cameraman, and crew into realizing his vision from this incoherent, unwieldy footage, the story is reassembled. The director will study every shot in every sequence, but it is the editor who puts the puzzle together. All those miles of footage may contain not one but numerous interpretations of the same story, and it is in post-production where the best way of telling the story is achieved.

It is a tense and exciting moment. Up until this time, the writer could have dashed in for last-minute rewrites, scenes may have been added or reshot; in Oliver Stone's director's cut of *Natural Born Killers* for DVD, punters can stay with the original "and-they-all-lived-happily-ever-after" final scene, or click on to Mickey and Mallory being blown away in a guns-blazing Armageddon. When the film premiered, reviewers couldn't decide if *Natural Born Killers* was a bloody glorification of violence or a witty parody of American values; even the director must have had doubts to have shot alternative endings in the first place. Whether those doubts were aesthetic or commercial is hard to say, but Oliver Stone was fortunate to have the opportunity to experiment with his product in this way. For anyone making a short film or an indie feature for the festival circuit, the hard, make-or-break decisions must be made the first time around in the editing suite.

To help make those decisions, it is essential that the editor is just as familiar with the script as the director, and it should be remembered that few first-time directors will have seen a film being edited before. The director should have got the shots he needed, but if the budget precludes reshooting, errors and oversights will now be discreetly covered. Lighting, wardrobe, and decor will be scrutinized for inconsistencies. Where a director may want to insert whip-pans, rapid-fire cutting, and wild textural flourishes, the editor—like the tutor with a child genius—will exercise calm and constraint.

ORSON WELLES

When Orson Welles was making *Citizen Kane*, he became so fascinated by editing that he organized a removal truck and a gang of stagehands to haul an editing machine into his hotel room. Surrounded by his actors and hundreds of feet of celluloid, he spent hours drinking whisky and learning to juggle film.

He had discovered the Frankenstein element of filmmaking. Sitting at the Steenbeck, it is really possible to assemble your own creature, and give life to it. The sense of power is intoxicating: a slow scene can be made fast, a funny one sad, a bad performance can be made good, and actors can be expunged from the film as if they had never been. To shoot is human; to edit, divine.[1]

Simon Callow, quoted above, writes in *Orson Welles, The Road to Xanadu*, that Welles had discovered that in the editing process lies the ability to create as if you were God, an aspiration very close to the young filmmaker's heart.

Welles's use of sound was a dramatic advance for motion pictures and sound departments at all the studios studied his methods. Sound contributes enormously, but generally subliminally. "Ambient sound and sound effects can transform a sequence with the simplest of means: a clock ticking, a distant dog barking, the wind, the laughter of children. Any or all of these radically alter the sense of time or place in what is perceived by the eye."[2]

In his radio broadcast of H. G. Wells's *The War of the Worlds*, Orson Welles had terrified the nation into believing that Martians had landed. He had mastered the ability to mingle voices with effects and music and was able to apply his acute aural sense to influence the audience. "Hitherto, in film, what you heard was what you saw. In *Citizen Kane*, for the first time, you heard something—a line, a sound—and then saw where it was coming from. The audience's mind is thus kept in a state of continuous curiosity and alertness."[3]

28 Opening of *Citizen Kane*

Welles set out, in *Kane*, to create a documentary style and, with his big appetites (in this case for authenticity), in the *News on the March* pastiche showing the early life of the young Kane, he encouraged Robert Wise and Mark Robson, his editors, to drag the film over the cutting-room floor in order to get the scratched, grainy effect of old newsreels. Paradoxically, viewing *Citizen Kane* today, the stylization and sound effects remind the audience that they are not watching scenes from a bio-doc, but scenes from a movie. Welles had failed in his objective and made a better film as a result.

29 The Director's Chair on set of *Citizen Kane*

PAUSE

REJECTION!

Film festival selectors (and judges) hate being asked why a film has been rejected and normally reply with platitudes. So, don't ask. Analyze your film and work it out for yourself. Here are some tips.

Editing
Poor editing kills the best intentions. If you edit your own film (and there's loads of great software out there to help you do just that) you are likely to fall in love with your own words, the long shot, and the jump cut. A professional editor isn't wedded to the material; he's not aware of the importance of a single shot, or the backstory behind a particular performance. He sees the rough material for what it is, and works with what he has to string the story together into a coherent, precise, calculated film. A 12- or 14-minute film usually works better when you cut it down to 10 minutes.

Length
There is a good reason why festivals like films that are 10 minutes long and under. It fits with the schedules. A 20-minute film means someone else's film isn't going to get shown. That doesn't mean you shouldn't make longer films. You just need to be aware that if you are outside the pattern it's going to be that much harder.

Lighting
A good actor shows the audience what he's feeling and thinking by a blink of the eye, a shrug, a curl of the lips. It doesn't matter how good the performances are—the subtleties and nuances will be lost without bounce boards at least; a few lights on stands better still. If you have inexperienced sparks (electricians), get an experienced director of photography, and vice versa.

Director of Photography (DOP)
The DOP can make or break a short film. If the director is inexperienced, the editor may be able to paper over the cracks, but it needs a skilled eye behind the camera to make sure the shots are there for the editor to work with. A good DOP will talk the novice director out of his crane shots, the MTV jump cuts, the soft-focus close-ups. Rehearse camera movements and lighting, just as you rehearse actors.

Cast
Your mates might be up for it, but although filming can be fun, it's not a joke. In every city there are drama schools and actors' agencies. Get professionals. Bad acting, no matter how good the script, kills the movie stone dead. When you've got your cast, rehearse before you roll the film.

The Script
Rewrite. Rewrite. Rewrite. Don't shoot until you get it right.

Perseverance
Sometimes as few as twenty films are selected from a thousand or more entries. There may be nothing wrong with your film, so persevere, swallow the rejection and send it out again.

There are two distinct schools of thought regarding the editor's art: that it should be hidden, a device so seamlessly woven into the narrative as to appear invisible, or boldly present like a neon light announcing "Motel" on a darkened highway. Joining one or other of these two schools is fundamental to the film's symmetry, its *look*, and many directors will stay with the same editor once a style and a working relationship has been established. Ethan and Joel Coen have kept most of their cast and crew on side through a string of independent gems, from their 1984 *Blood Simple* to the Oscar-winners *Fargo* in 1996 and *The Man Who Wasn't There* in 2001, shot in haunting black and white by British cinematographer Roger Deakins, his *seventh* Coen film—and he's done three more since.

Orson Welles never developed this collaborative chemistry, at least not with his editors. He would appear in the cutting room, usually late, study the rushes, fire off suggestions and down his whisky without offering the jug. Editors Robert Wise and Mark Robson had little affection for Welles, but they respected his knowledge, learned his secrets and, as revenge is a dish best served cold, both escaped the drawn-out controversy that dogged *Citizen Kane* to begin their own careers as directors.

GEORGES MÉLIÈS AND LUIS BUÑUEL

Where Welles had set out to imitate reality, Georges Méliès had, by 1902, come to believe that reality is actually rather dull and it is the manipulation—in other words, the editing of film—that grips the audience. Where his historic *A Trip to the Moon* engrossed the citizens of Paris for its novelty, the first public showing of *L'Âge d'Or* a generation later caused an uproar for completely different reasons. Film had become a political tool. The left-wing press in Paris supported Buñuel's surreal affront to religious and bourgeois values, while right-wing protestors literally broke into the theater and ripped it apart. *Le Figaro* and *L'Ami du Peuple* led the moral panic accusing "Judeo-Bolshevik devil-worshiping masonic wogs" for being behind the film (Marie-Laure Noailles, who in part put up the money, was the daughter of a Jewish banker). With mumblings of "pornography" among government ministers and an official complaint by Mussolini's ambassador, it was duly banned. As Paul Hammond tells us: "The totalitarian battle lines were drawn."[4]

Buñuel would have been well versed in Méliès's work and was aware of the editor's key role. He may have needed Dalí's input on his early scripts, but cut his own films, importing ideas as much from Hollywood as from early French cinema. For example, a scene from Buster Keaton's 1922 *The Paleface*, where the hero is embracing the girl, dissolves into the same scene (still in a clinch) accompanied by the card "Two years later." Buñuel lends irony to the concept in *L'Âge d'Or* by showing a group of men in a room doing nothing in particular, which dissolves into an identical scene with the inter-title "Sixteen years earlier." Likewise, Méliès's comic use of a character falling out of a window in one place and landing somewhere completely unrelated conforms perfectly to the Buñuel–Dalí surrealist vision and was similarly borrowed. The trick, Buñuel knew, was all in the editing.

By the 1920s, film language had developed to a degree that remains virtually intact, the pace of change driven by the fact that, until 1928, film remained silent. In the theater, the playwright can sidestep tricky plot points by having his actors tell the audience what is going on. In good writing, the skill is to *show* not *tell*, and early filmmakers were impelled to use all the elements of *mise-en-scène* to achieve this elementary goal.

D. W. GRIFFITH

To compensate for the absence of words, silent filmmakers, from Méliès in Paris to Chaplin, Keaton, and D. W. Griffith in Hollywood, quickly mastered juxtaposition, parallel action, framing, lighting, camera angle, focus, filters, montage, and camera movement. What the audience sees is governed by the way in which the director presents the film to us. The way it is cut will determine our reaction.

None of these developments, politically or technically, went unnoticed in the Soviet Union. Before the dust had even settled on the Communist Revolution, the Moscow Film School in 1919 was already a hive of intellectual debate and experiment. Lenin, who had lived in exile in Paris, was aware of the part film could make in educating the masses and intervened personally to ensure the wide release of D. W. Griffith's 1916 *Intolerance*, four interlinked stories showing intolerance throughout the ages and climaxing in a race between a car and a train.

A review in *The New Yorker* described *Intolerance* as "perhaps the best movie ever made," and it would be studied in Moscow and in film schools across Europe for its capacity to elicit strong reactions through the subtle crosscutting of images. Griffith had come to see that there is no imperative demanding that film be presented from the point of view of the audience. He made his camera more selective in his examination of depth of field and recognized that the insertion of reaction shots heightened drama. Griffith had thus shown that in editing, the emotional result could be greater than the sum of the visual content. He was, as Cecil B. DeMille put it, "The first to photograph thought."[5]

Griffith began making short films in 1908, created the concept of the star, and trailblazed every aspect of film technique. Frank Capra once commented, "Since Griffith there has been no major improvement in the art of film direction,"[6] and gossip columnist Hedda Hopper recalled the marks made by stars in the wet cement outside Hollywood's Chinese Theater and declared, "Griffith's footprints were never asked for, yet no one has ever filled his shoes."[7]

Flattery from Moscow came in the form of imitation. While filmmaking was developing in Russia, Griffith's two epics, *Intolerance* and the 1915 *Birth of a Nation*, became templates for the director's craft. What Griffith devised was the convention of preparing a shooting script to plan master shots from the camera's ideal position in order to stage the action in each scene. Every shot that completes the scene refers back to the master shot. In this way, he had invented cinema's unique method of treating space and provided the essential elements for editing the manifold elements into cogent sequences.

The Russians understood that truth itself can be manipulated by editing and exploited this capacity to serve the fledgling Bolshevik state. The early

30 Sergei Eisenstein

directors influenced by Griffith included Dziga Vertov, Lev Kuleshov, and Sergei Eisenstein, whose work is studied as much today in film schools as the Russians studied Griffith in the 1920s. Eisenstein's feeling for pace and his subtle touch with actors brought a new level of quality to Russian film drama. Of his many films, he is best remembered for the 1925 *Battleship Potemkin*, particularly the Odessa Steps sequence, the 60-second massacre of innocent civilians drawn out to more than 5 minutes by the frenetic crosscutting of the 150 shots used in the scene. It has been copied many times but never bettered.

The Russian directors were obliged to glorify the State, but if film is the most powerful form of communication ever known, the role of the modern filmmaker is more akin to the wise man in primitive societies, who serves the hopes and aspirations of the community. Every antiwar story, or union struggle, or civilian massacre, is a reminder of man's need to learn tolerance and evolve to a greater state of humanity.

EDITING SYSTEMS

Today, it is more likely that an editor will be working on an Avid Film Composer, an editing system that stores the rushes digitally on hard disk, allowing instant access to every shot that constitutes the entire film. The machine allows the director and editor to study a variety of versions of each sequence before making a selection and, as those sequences are stored electronically, there is no deterioration during the process. Another advantage of the Avid is that both sound and effects can be tried, used, or eliminated at the keyboard.

The writer and director create the material, but the editor's part in shaping the scenes into a film that remains true to their vision is quintessential. Francis Ford Coppola says a film is created three times: first you write it, second you shoot it, third you edit it. The pace, timing, emotional impact, and the scenes that bring a tear to our eye and send icy fingers running up our spine; with music and sound effects, the editor's job is at the very heart of the creation.

Writers put into words truths we understand intuitively and, as his work goes through its metamorphosis to film, the editor is the director's conscience, the little voice that whispers when enough is enough. The finished film is in the editor's hands. Before the Avid, and before sound brought new problems with synchronization, many editors shunned the Moviola editing machines and continued to cut in their open palms, judging pace and rhythm by instinct and experience. Like the midwife whose very hands enter the most intimate of all human activities, that of childbirth, and just as writers speak of their work as being their baby, when an editor has made the final cut he delivers something new and precious into the world.

MARTIN SCORSESE v. HARVEY WEINSTEIN

Movies *are* the culture. In 2003, when *Gangs of New York* finally rolled out into cinemas after twelve months of delay and infighting, the disputes between Martin Scorsese and Miramax chief Harvey Weinstein were already legendary and made the evening news. Scorsese had spent thirty years nursing the project and the budget had spiraled up from $50 million to $100 million. Like the street fighters depicted in the script, the diminutive Scorsese and heavyweight Weinstein slugged it out as the producer tried to prise control back from his director and the director ploughed on obsessively pursuing his dream.

Was the wildly ambitious three-hour epic going to be a masterpiece or a bloodbath for the investors? "I don't know," Scorsese told Alex Williams in a *Guardian* interview. "When I'm making a film, I'm the audience."

Were there problems because the producer and director had a different vision? "No. Marty and I had a very similar vision," Weinstein replied sardonically. "We had Marty's vision."

The exchanges are the stuff of movies and long before *Gangs of New York* even reached the cinemas, acres of newsprint drew us into the event as we followed the on- and off-screen relationship between icons Leonardo DiCaprio and Cameron Diaz, every gesture and suggestion of body language as they walked the red carpet into the premiere in London's Leicester Square captured by phalanxes of cameras and an adoring public. Reviews in the quality press and radio discussions examined the film's grammar, tone, complexion, every hue and mezzotint; at the outset, Scorsese had given director of photography Michael Ballhaus a book of Rembrandt prints to guide the lighting, and he gave Harvey Weinstein a list of eighty films he wanted him to see including the 1928 *The Man Who Laughs*, ironically a silent movie and with the worst organ music, complained Weinstein, that he had ever heard.[8]

Just hype? Or a legitimate response to our major art form? In the final analysis, was *Gangs of New York* any good? Even with $100 million in the kitty and Martin Scorsese in the director's chair, it is only when the film is edited and on view that the question can be answered. And, then, reviewers and cinemagoers are going to differ. That's art.

PAUSE

THE BUÑUEL LAW

Director Juan Luis Buñuel has worked with many of the masters: his father Luis Buñuel, Orson Welles, Louis Malle, Claude Lelouch, and Philip Kaufman. Buñuel has two basic laws regarding filmmaking.

- The first law, and one that you cannot avoid, is that there is no fixed law—no formulas, no wise sayings, nothing.
- The second law is that you don't know anything about a film till it comes out. You can get the best director, the best script and the biggest stars and the film can be a flop … or the contrary, a bad director, bad actors, bad cinematography … and the film is a huge success. Or the contrary. No laws.

PASSION IN PIECES

Scorsese's film cost $100 million; but for the mere price of a Weinstein cigar, about a hundred bucks, editor/director Sam Small not only made his 10-minute short *Passion in Pieces*, but won the Special "Gold Remi" award at the 2003 Houston International Film Festival, and was Special Jury Selected at the 2002 New Orleans Film Festival. All you need is a domestic miniDV camera, a capture card, a cheap PC, and a filmmaker's obsession, he says.[9]

That's just what I needed: an editor with passion.

Passion in Pieces is based on five Shakespearean sonnets, with modern urban settings and characters, and Small's own voiceover. If the most important element in a film is the script, wisely he chose Shakespeare—but even with just such a wordsmith on board, Small believes it is in the edit where you make the film. Be prepared for a shooting/editing ratio of at least 1:50. If you work alone, shooting is a nice day out compared to the lonely weeks and months spent in front of the computer painstakingly nudging tiny clips one frame to the left and right.

A well-planned shoot helps the editing process and before you begin, it is essential to have a good idea of what the finished film will look like. Cool, blue, and slow? Red, disjointed, and fast? Multicolored, madcap, and fun? It may sound obvious, but the director and editor must have the same vision—and a director/editor has to be consistent.

Small advises filmmakers to *shoot everything in sight*. When on set or location, overshoot everything. If you can shoot the scene in yet another angle, then do it. Actors, even if you have procured them for free, always like acting, so do another angle, another lens attitude. MiniDV tapes are incredibly cheap, so buy a pack of ten for one day, and use them. If you only have 15 minutes of footage for a 10-minute film, you are in big trouble.

Live sound is another key element. If you are using an external mic, and not shooting dialogue, then pull the jack and use the inbuilt microphone on the camera. This is almost always a stereo mic and will have excellent digital quality. The sound can be invaluable for patching silent spots with an authentic "buzz" track, and also can be an important cue for overlaying onto dialogue tracks. Editing is a long haul: a day's shoot can produce a month of editing. Rush it and you'll ruin it. Editing live footage is in some ways akin to animation. You must fit bits of dialogue and action together second by second—sometimes a fraction of a second.

Some software can capture a whole miniDV tape and save it in distinct clips on a computer hard drive, although this fills the drive in next to no time. Sam Small prefers to watch all the takes over and over again, and then capture. As you can only use one take, it is best to do so while the scene remains fresh in your mind. Don't be afraid to try music or sound effects as you edit. It may help you to resolve pace and rhythm as you cut your takes. Most computer editing software has hundreds of video transitions and effects, but be wary of how you use them—and never ever overuse them. Always use cut edits and very occasionally allow yourself the thrill of a dissolve or fade to/from black.

The value and importance of sound cannot be underestimated. Silent films always had a soundtrack, even if it was the local librarian playing an upright piano in the community hall. A truly silent film would emulate deafness for an audience and would be very uncomfortable. Half of every film is sound, sometimes more, says Small. If you find that your live sound of rain on a windowpane is inferior to a library sound, then use the library sound. Don't be proud.

In laying down sound on his own shorts, Sam Small has been inspired by Jacques Tati, the French actor and comedian who made totally original short films. To Tati, the screen was a vast canvas populated by absurd people in conflict with absurd structures. Very often a background "buzz" track is louder than the dialogue, suggesting the ephemeral nature of conversation in relation to the natural world and to that of machines. Tati's films never contain live sound. Everything was painfully dubbed at the edit, and he would take hours to find the right car horn or door squeak. For one scene, he was once observed with boxes of glasses, smashing one after the other until it sounded just right. The music often sounds banal, but he spent months looking for suitable music for the effect he was trying to achieve. To Tati everything made a sound, but not necessarily its own.

Under Tati's influence, Small suggests what he calls *casting against type*. Give the audience the music they are least likely to expect. Try a brass band with a sex scene. You might create a sensation, he says. And a final warning to editors: Don't edit to be interesting or clever. Audiences never find *interesting* interesting, and cleverness often looks silly. What people want is to be emotionally moved by your film. If the filmmaker is not moved by what he is looking at, the audience won't be either.

www.passioninpieces.co.uk

ART

The films we remember best live on because of some unique, intrinsic quality that evolves through the skills of writing, directing, and editing film. As cities crumble and empires fall, all that remains through time is man's art. In the architecture of our churches, in paintings on the walls in national galleries, in libraries and museums, what we create is more lasting than man himself. The films cited in the text, *A Trip to the Moon*, *L'Âge d'Or*, *Citizen Kane*, *Intolerance*, and *Battleship Potemkin*, are all carefully preserved and available for our study and enjoyment today, long after the filmmakers have gone. Whether it is that first 10-minute short or the new Coen Brothers movie shot by Roger Deakins, film's ability to change lives and minds—understood by the likes of Lenin and Hitler—is far better in the hands of artists than dictators, and in presenting truth, none plays a greater role than the editor.

PAUSE

ROGER CRITTENDEN'S TEN COMMANDMENTS[10]

1. Read the script *in advance* of cutting.

2. Become familiar with the director's previous work.

3. Read the background material relevant to the film.

4. Meet the cameraman, sound recordist, and other major contributors to the film who might affect your own job.

5. Liaise with the continuity or production assistant for documentation.

6. Make yourself known to the laboratory contact.

7. Choose your assistant carefully for both efficiency and tact.

8. Find out your director's preferred working hours and eating habits!

9. Ensure that the cutting room is properly set up *before* cutting starts.

10. Make sure that reliable maintenance for your equipment can be obtained.

STOP

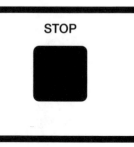

CHAPTER 8

Finance and Distribution

The United States and Britain each have a differing stance toward financing short films, with Australia falling somewhere between these contrary positions. In the US, the attitude is *just do it*. If making movies is your passion, you beg, borrow, or rent the gear, shoot some film and see where it leads you. The industry will come calling when what you're making is good enough.

The global film market is worth hundreds of billions of dollars and grows annually. To get a slice of the pie, the British and Australian governments back their industries in order to compete with the United States. The result is a double-edged sword: people who may never have got the opportunity to make a film can do so with government grants, while in the US shorts made without public money or institutional guidance are often more inspired and individual. Robert Rodriguez is the archetypal American story: unable to get into film school, he raised $20,000 from family and friends and made his name shooting the acclaimed *El Mariachi*. Across the English-speaking world, filmmakers can't help but keep one eye on the vast American market, while in the rest of Europe, short films, features, and television are made principally for the home market and success on the world stage is merely a bonus.

What this all means is that when there's free money available, filmmakers and film funders are locked in an eternal labyrinth. Applying for funds to make short films is the obvious first step, but the cash available is limited and the number of applications overwhelming. Funders face the unenviable task of sifting through a deluge of paperwork and, to help them select which projects are going to get backing, filmmakers with a track record tend to rise to the top of the pile.

That isn't to say that applying for funds isn't a good idea; it is. The process requires tremendous preparation, an edgy script, a compulsive synopsis, the director's statement, or a mission statement, and résumés of key personnel. This demanding combination forces the team to focus on every detail, which is exactly what a project needs whether it gets funding or not. Even with such diligence, it is important to realize that it is still a lottery, ironically so, and a good grasp on realism is the best antidote for disappointment.

In the UK, by far the largest source of finance for short films is managed by the Film Council, the umbrella group set up in 2000 under the stewardship of Alan Parker to end duplication at the various bodies formerly charged with

funding and training. With the streamlining of film subsidy and a multi-million pound investment from the treasury, Parker and his team set out to identify the problems within the film industry and to create a framework for sustained growth in partnership with the private sector, which is largely responsible for film culture and finance. Short filmmakers can apply to the four funds outlined below.
www.filmcouncil.org.uk

UK FILM COUNCIL FUNDS

Digital Shorts

The Digital Shorts program is run by the Film Council's New Cinema Fund in partnership with other organizations. In a complete antithesis to the policy on features, which responds to the marketplace, the inclination with digital shorts is to back experimental and new media projects that exploit film as an art form; it is the training ground for new talent and shorts backed by this fund travel the festival circuit picking up prizes more than cash. Funding is organized through the London Film and Video Development Agency and ten regional bodies (contact details are listed in Chapter 25: *Useful Addresses*). Each region supports eight or so digital shorts which must adhere to the following criteria:

1. Budget—No more than £10,000.
2. Duration—No more than 10 minutes, including credits.
3. Format—All films must be shot using digital technology.

Cinema Extreme

Film Council's New Cinema Fund and FilmFour jointly fund Cinema Extreme, a scheme designed to push the boundaries of cinematic storytelling. From 2006, the scheme has been operating as a development program incorporating a rolling commission process, through which the New Cinema Fund and FilmFour commission a minimum of four films; hopefuls are asked to consider the following:

Types of Film We Are Looking For

1. *Think about features*. This scheme is for people who can already show the beginnings of vision and are a step away from making the next distinctive and groundbreaking new British feature film.
2. *Think about story*. Think about what makes a great short film, but equally think about how this film shows the vision that you would bring to a feature. What kind of stories do you want to tell? What kinds of stories are missing from British cinema? What kind of voice and vision do you want to have as a filmmaker now and in the future?
3. *Think about audience*. Think about what works with an audience sitting in a darkened room and who that audience might be. Think about what has become overfamiliar in short films and try something new. Think about how to engage an audience in your world on screen. Surprise and excite us.

Cinema Extreme is a director-led scheme and all films must be produced by individual producers through a UK-based production company. The Film

Council are seeking participants who are either: (a) a writer/director; (b) a director with a writer who can hook up with a production team or company suggested by the Film Council; (c) a director with a fully developed script who can team up with a writer and producer or production company suggested by the Film Council; (d) a writer/director or director and writer team with a producer or a production company attached. A key focus of Cinema Extreme is to incorporate a level of diversity in both the projects and the filmmaking talent attached which corresponds to the UK Film Council and FilmFour's respective diversity objectives.

Completion Fund

This is a £50,000 fund to support short films that have already been shot but lack the funds to finish. Maya Vision International is responsible for shortlisting and selecting the films in consultation with the New Cinema Fund and will oversee all aspects of the completion process to contractual and physical delivery.

The Completion Fund is for short films that will have a final running time of less than 12 minutes (exceptional shorts of longer duration may be considered). The film will need to be edited to a rough cut or beyond and be available for viewing on DVD (or VHS). The main elements (producer, writer, director, location, story) will be substantially British, and when completed the film will be capable of being fully cleared for cinema, television, Internet, and festival exhibition throughout the world.

First Light

The First Light fund supports 8–18-year-olds with their debut digi-shorts.

In common with all UK Film Council activities, First Light aims to make an impact upon social inclusion and cultural and ethnic diversity objectives. "First Light is establishing itself as a major initiative to help young people get their first films made and make contact with film organizations in their region," explains John Woodward, chief executive officer of the Film Council.

Another scheme set up by the Film Council in 2005 was the installation of digital equipment in 200 cinemas to broaden access to movies shot digitally by reducing the need for companies to distribute films on costly 35-mm prints. How successful the scheme has been is difficult to assess, although the experience of Paul Andrew Williams with his $80,000 first feature, *London to Brighton*, wasn't that encouraging. After winning prizes at festivals in Edinburgh and Dinard, *London to Brighton* was named best UK Feature at London's Raindance Festival. Instantly acclaimed as one of the best British films in recent years, the film was released in fifteen cinemas in December 2006; five weeks later it could only be found it one London cinema and five more in the provinces. As Rachel Cooke pointed out in *The Observer*: "Perhaps it is time to follow the French and make it the law that cinemas devote a proportion of their screen time to the homegrown."[1]

PAUSE

FILM FINANCE CORPORATION OF AUSTRALIA

The Film Finance Corporation (FFC) of Australia is the principal agency for funding film and television and operates to ensure that Australians have the opportunity to make and watch their own screen stories. With offices in Melbourne and Sydney, the FFC only funds projects with high levels of creative and technical contribution by Australians, or projects certified under Australia's Official Co-Production Program.

Since its inception, the FFC has funded more than 1,000 projects with a total production value of $2.5 billion; recent box office successes include *Jindabyne*, *Wolf Creek*, and *Little Fish* as well as classics *Lantana*, *The Man Who Sued God*, *Rabbit-Proof Fence*, *Chopper*, *Shine*, *Strictly Ballroom*, *The Adventures of Priscilla: Queen of the Desert*, and *Muriel's Wedding*.
www.ffc.gov.au

COMPETITIONS

The number of competitions for first-time filmmakers is growing, and the Internet is the best resource for finding them. Broadcasters tend to buy in most of their limited supply of short films, and then from established sales agents, but the BBC and others do finance the occasional season of new shorts and supply submission details by post and on the net. The BBC also puts short films online. Borough councils that want to attract feature projects to their area will have a film officer in the culture department and some give small grants for short films to local filmmakers, though normally for worthy rather than artistic causes.
www.bbc.co.uk/filmnetwork

PAUSE

PRIZE FILMS

Filmaka is a short film network designed by established filmmakers to discover emerging talent. Run by Tim Levy of Future Capital Partners Limited, Filmaka is a twice-monthly subscription-based worldwide competition that offers filmmakers the facility to enter short films online with a prize of $3,000, plus the chance of making a feature film.

Films are judged by a panel of award-winning jurors including: John Madden (director, *Shakespeare in Love*), Paul Schrader (writer, *Taxi Driver*), Neil LaBute (writer/director, *Nurse Betty*), Zac Penn (producer/writer/director, *X2*; *X-Men: The Last Stand*), Colin Firth (actor, *Love Actually*), Bill Pullman (actor, *Independence Day*), Deepak Nayar (producer, *Bend It Like Beckham*), Laure Bickford (producer, *Traffic*).
www.filmaka.com

APPROACHING COMPANIES

Funding schemes and competitions come and go; if those detailed in these pages have since vanished, others will have replaced them. But it doesn't matter how many competitions and grants there are, there will still be thousands of applicants for each film that receives seed money. Being turned down does not necessarily signify that projects are faulty; they may be ahead of their time. Art is subjective. Most artists need to experiment through trial and error before they do their best work, and one must wonder how many great artists there would have been had they only been given the chance.

Self-financing is taking that chance: it is the route chosen by Luis Buñuel, Alexander Salkind, Christopher Nolan, and many filmmakers—men and women so driven by their vision to shoot movies that they grabbed destiny and a camera in their own hands and went out and did it. Self-financing requires passion and perseverance, kind, trusting friends and parents, the nerve and the ability to inspire others, small businessmen met on trains (as was the case with Salkind), or the local rich guy who fancies seeing himself on the silver screen.

A small company—or better an alliance of small companies—may be persuaded to put up some money in order to see their logo on the credits and publicity material, a mention in the local paper, a link on the website. Larger companies only show interest if there is something clear and definite in it for them. Tiffany Whittome, producer of the 15-minute *Homecoming*, ran a product placement company before forming Piper Films, and in her experience, if you want a name brand to put up the budget for a short film, you have to understand the marketing strategy of that brand. "You need to have a conversation with them before you even start writing the script, you have to work with the brand right from the conception. If they feel that they are in control, they are more likely to agree to the venture."[2]

The ideal situation, she adds, is when you cast a famous actor and the actor is willing to be associated with the brand: beer, alcohol, a clothing line, something that works within the context of the story. "But, again, you have to be in discussions as soon as the actor is attached, and be flexible in changing the script to accommodate the brand," she says. "Sometimes the big car companies, like BMW, put up the entire budget for a film if there is a way that they can use the film for their own purposes."

Some companies are more generous with goods than cash; they may supply a vehicle for a specific scene, or bowls of potato chips and crates of booze for the wrap party. "Just call the company that does their marketing, or call the brand directly. Tell them the scenario, that you'll credit them on the film, and they will have the pleasure of being associated with supporting the independent films industry," suggests Tiffany. "Perhaps even throw in association at festivals or screenings—especially if it's a drinks brand

CRUCIAL QUESTIONS

The qualities needed for raising money have already been covered in Chapter 5: *The Producer*, and if film funders don't call you in the middle of the night promising to back your opus, then the producer and writer have to sit down with their script and ask themselves some crucial questions:

- How much is the film going to cost?
- How much can we raise?
- Is there a market for this film?
- What is the USP—the unique selling point?
- Would I pay to see this film?
- Or will the making of it be an end in itself?

If the answer to the last question is yes—that the intention is to have some fun and gain experience—the goal, when the film is shot, has already been accomplished. On the other hand, if the aim is to sail the film into the marketplace, it will require sufficient finance to achieve the quality that will ensure distribution. With a feature, it is advisable to have distribution in place at the same time as finance; in fact, a distributor will ordinarily be one of the components that makes up the package. Short films, while less expensive, are more risky because it is the finished product that goes to the distributor.

EXPOSURE

There is an ever increasing number of outlets for short films, and the best of them will pick up fees when they are shown. But the principal reason for making shorts is for the filmmakers to get exposure and that entails applying to festivals and entering into competition. Those that are good enough will win the plaudits and the teams behind them will be another few rungs up the ladder when they go out again in search of finance. Short films have gained a new respectability and are worthy of being considered a genre, but the ultimate goal will normally be to reach a wide audience and in the long run that can only be achieved with a feature.

One writer/director who has built her career in this way is Glasgow-born Lynne Ramsey. The Film Council put development cash into *Morvern Callar* (2002) with Samantha Morton and Kathleen McDermott, but only after her critically acclaimed debut feature *Ratcatcher* (1999), and her three distinctive short films, *Kill the Day* and *Small Deaths* (1996), and *Gasman* (1998). *Small Deaths* won the Prix du Jure at Cannes and when *Gasman* won the same prize two years later, people began to take notice. Lynne's shorts are moody, atmospheric pieces where shadowy, shifting worlds are seen through the clear, vivid eyes of children and innocents. She has found her own unique style, her voice, and in her idiosyncratic vision funders see an originality they want to support. Lynne Ramsey's short films can be found with her features on DVD.

BIG FILM SHORTS

Big Film Shorts is a California-based shorts distributor serving as sales agent and consultant for film bookers and programmers. The extensive catalogue contains scores of short film favorites as well as winners from festivals such as Sundance, Telluride, and Cannes. In the American tradition, Big Film takes shorts from across the genre regardless of length, format, and national origin.

Big Film Shorts, 100 S. Sunrise Way #289, Palm Springs, CA 92262, USA. Tel. +1-760-219-6269.
www.bigfilmshorts.com

INTERNET DISTRIBUTION

YouTube, Google Video and PutFile
Internet distribution has changed radically since the founding of YouTube, the largest archive of short films on the planet, and its rival broadcasters Google Video and PutFile (see Chapter 2: *A Brief History of Short Films*).
www.youtube.com
www.video.google.co.uk
www.putfile.com

These file-sharing Internet distribution sites are free and allow anyone in the world to make short films and show them to the world. There is, as a result, a deluge of short films; the majority, it has to be said, of inferior quality and dubious content, but traditional short films distribution sites continue to play a valuable role in screening *filmmaker* shorts and more often than not concentrate on niche areas of the market.

Reelplay
Reelplay is targeted at acquisition executives, investors, and industry professionals; there is also a step-by-step guide to creating and editing a website, which is then hosted on Reelplay's online marketplace.
www.reelplay.com

Filmfestivalspro
Filmfestivalspro has festival details and opportunities to make online acquisitions.
www.filmfestivalspro.com

The Film Centre
The Film Centre is an encyclopedia for the short filmmaker with cameras and kit for sale, jobs for crew, breaking news, and a year-by-year list of short films.
www.filmcentre.co.uk

Shooting People
Shooting People has changed from a free to a subscription site, but is still probably the best starting place for short film enthusiasts and for indie features. "An essential part of filmmaking," according to Mike Figgis.
www.shootingpeople.org

STREAMED SHORTS

Sites come and go, but some are now established and offer useful tips for those studying the market before shooting their films.

In-Movies and Brit Shorts
In-Movies and Brit Shorts are UK locations with a wide-ranging fare of homegrown shorts.
www.in-movies.com
www.britshorts.com

Ifilm
Ifilm, based in the US, is streaming more than 6,000 short films, with articles and festival information. Ifilm touched three-quarters of a million hits with its short film *405*.
www.ifilm.com

Atom Films
Atom Films receives about fifty films monthly in the UK (four times that amount in the US) and is constantly on the lookout for "fiction and animation with a strong narrative structure and good production values, favoring dark comedies with an off-the-wall sensibility." The Ardman *Angry Kid* animations have knocked up more than one million hits.
www.atomfilms.com

Rights
Atom has its rights structure worked out: they offer producers an advance against percentage of gross sales for a seven-year license period. That is not typical across the board and arrangements vary greatly. There are sites that pay small fees, particularly if there is a star in the cast, while others by contrast charge producers for showing their material. Some Internet distributors, however, demand international rights, which include theaters, TV, and video; there are problems with piracy and copyright, and while legal issues remain unresolved, filmmakers would be well advised to read the small print before they sign away rights.

PAUSE

31 Propeller Studios

32 Propeller Studios

33 Propeller Studios

P.102

AS SEEN ON TV

In the first twelve months following its launch in February 2006, Propeller TV broadcast more than 600 short films.

Screening on Sky 195, Propeller is a not-for-profit channel with a regular Short and Sweet slot, and apart from being the only broadcaster with a dedicated strand for shorts, it is the only UK satellite television channel showing 100 percent original programming.

Short and Sweet has a cult following among film fans. Viewers get an up-to-the-minute roundup of film gossip and film reviews, and it shines a spotlight on the talent behind the best short films. The channel reaches more than 8 million homes in the UK and 70 million across Europe.

Propeller shows shorts making their debut as well as those that have toured the festival circuit. According to Propeller acquisitions chief John Offord, the channel has a strong following among industry professionals and gives filmmakers the chance to get their first broadcast credit and all that can lead to: an agent, securing new commissions, and a boost to DVD sales.

Send films to John Offord
Propeller TV
c/o Screen Yorkshire
46 The Calls
Leeds LS2 7EY
UK

www.propellerTV.co.uk

SELF-DISTRIBUTION

Self-distributors can create a buzz on a dedicated website with film clips, behind the scenes footage, interviews, and photo stills. A site open to feedback can respond to support and suggestions, which in turn will be a useful tool in the marketing campaign and the production of a press kit. A hard copy press kit is another prerequisite and should contain the story synopsis; cast and crew lists with their experience and brief biographies; production details including the running time and print format; the details of the producer, director, and writer, with interviews; and good-quality still photographs that can be used for festival programs and sent to the newspapers.

While webcasting expertise is constantly changing and improving, short films are the ideal medium to get the legal and technical issues straight in preparation for the time when watching features over the net becomes commonplace. It is unlikely that this will ever be a serious challenge to a night out at the movies, but experimental and documentary features, with facilities to order copies on DVD, will have a greater opportunity to find an audience. Producer Scott Meek told *Screen International* that the notion that independent films with an independent spirit, made as an act of self-expression, necessarily have to open with prints and advertising in conventional cinemas "is actually a bit like us clinging on to silent cinema at the beginning of sound."

In the UK, there are more than 300 film societies and while aficionados meet to pore over the virtues of early Eisenstein or the deeper significance of Hitchcock's *Psycho*, they may be persuaded to warm up the debate with a short. Film clubs meeting in colleges and cafés from Sydney to Chicago offer another route to exhibition with short films being screened, together with interviews with industry players and networking sessions.

The New Producers Alliance (NPA) was set up in the UK as an open-access, self-help organization in 1993 under the leadership of Alex Usbourne and Jeremy Bolt. Based in London, it became an educational charity in 1995 and a dozen years on has 1,000 members and affiliated groups in many parts of the country. Combined with the weekly e-magazine, networking, film nights, business breakfasts with broadcasters and production companies, there are regular master classes in development, pitching, packaging, financing, and distribution. With support from the Film Council, the NPA's Nine-Step Training Program offers members a recognized qualification and NPA executives are in demand as consultants and lecturers. In April 2004, the NPA launched a members' short film competition. Each month a film is selected for screening before the feature at the monthly screenings, and from those twelve, the winning film gets the red carpet treatment at the Cannes Film Festival.
www.npa.org.uk

PAUSE

DISTINCTIVE FILMS

Shorts International was set up to distribute "great short films" and manages the world's largest and most diverse short film catalogue, with more than 2,000 high-quality shorts. Shorts International supplies some 120 broadcasters worldwide, across every platform and medium. They are looking for your distinctive films, so let them know that you are out there.
www.shortsinternational.com

SCREENING ROOMS

For those who have chosen the self-financing route from the beginning, they can stay on the indie trail using the professional services provided by screening rooms or preview theaters. The purpose is to sell the film to sales agents or distributors, and filmmakers give themselves a better chance showing their work on a big screen on 35mm with Dolby sound and the cast on hand to lead the charm offensive. It is also a good time to invite the press and lay on some wine and nibbles for the cast and crew, who have no doubt made the short on deferred payments. Numerous screening rooms are situated in London's Soho and charge in the region of £100 an hour, a two-hour session allowing a 10-minute short to be shown several times. Theaters vary in size, seating up to 100 and as few as twenty.

It would be remiss here not to mention *The Guerrilla Film Makers Handbook* by Chris Jones and Genevieve Jolliffe, a 600-page tome published by Continuum Press. "Invaluable insider information that gives you everything you need to know to make your movie," wrote Matthew Vaughn, producer of *Lock, Stock and Two Smoking Barrels*.
www.livingspirit.com

Another useful volume for filmmakers looking for cash, which has the self-explanatory title *Get Your Film Funded, UK Film Finance Guide 2003–2004*, by Caroline Hancock and Nic Wistreich, is published by Shooting People Press.
www.shootingpeople.org

GREAT SITES

A trio of sites that should be on every movie maker's list of favorites are the British Film Institute (BFI), the American Film Institute (AFI), and the Australian Film Institute (AFI)—the latter two sharing the same initials. These three organizations offer a variety of services particularly useful to those starting out in the industry.

BFI

Established in 1933, the BFI has the largest film archive in the world, a vast collection of film stills and posters, and leads the field in film restoration and preservation. In February 2003, with digital expertise from Hewlett-Packard, the BFI opened Mediatheque on London's South Bank with the facility for the public to view hundreds (and later to be thousands) of historic films, everything from the VE Day procession to Roger Bannister running the first four-minute mile. The BFI runs the London Film Festival, the National Film Theatre on the South Bank, and the IMAX Cinema.
www.bfi.org.uk

AFI (USA)

The AFI, formed in 1967, is the preeminent national organization in the United States dedicated to advancing and preserving film, television, and other forms of the moving image, and "promotes innovation and excellence through teaching, presenting, preserving, and redefining the art form." With New Media Ventures (NMV), AFI has developed digital filmmaking coursework, student monitoring and teacher-training programs in the AFI Screen Education Center and for online film studies. The Institute sits on an eight-acre site in the hills overlooking Hollywood and is guided by four primary missions:

1. Training the next generation of filmmakers.
2. Presenting the moving image in its many forms to a national and international public.

3. Preserving America's great movie heritage.

4. Redefining the moving image in the new digital era.

`www.afi.com`

AFI (Australia)

Founded in 1958, the AFI is Australia's foremost screen culture organization and is responsible for producing Australia's annual AFI Awards, the country's premier film and television awards.

As a producer of the industry's night of nights, the AFI plays a central role in the way in which the Australian film industry is known and understood, both locally and internationally, and is crucial to the definition, business, and culture of the Australian film, television, and other moving image industries.

`www.afi.org.au`

PAUSE

▮▮

MEMO FROM THE BFI

The BFI offers the following advice:

• Get online—from production information to sales, distribution, exhibition, marketing, and publicity—the Internet in an invaluable resource for filmmakers.
• Have at least one very strong production still. This will be used endlessly.
• Have all clearances (especially music clearance) in place before approaching buyers.
• Make sure you allow enough time to get the film print right before your first exhibition opportunity.
• See as many films as you can, both contemporary and from the history of world cinema. Check out shorts on the Internet.
• Information is power! Find out all you can about the industry by reading the weekly trade press (*Screen International, Variety*, etc.).
• Working at any level in the industry will gain you valuable experience. Unpaid expenses-only work experience placements are a way in.

The British Council

Another key organization is the British Council. The easy-to-use website of the Film Department of the British Council has a comprehensive funding list for short films, scriptwriters, animators, and documentary-makers, not only based in the UK, but in Europe, and from co-funding partners across the Continent. New filmmakers will find legal and financial advice, as well as a wide-ranging section on training and careers. The catalogue of British directors is a useful tool for new producers (directors need one feature or three shorts to be included); there is an index of British films, features, and shorts, a status report on British films in production, a directory of film and video festivals, and a listing of all films released in the UK. For anyone new to film, the British Council is a good place to start.

`www.britfilms.com`

GETTING YOUR FILM SHOWN

In the early 1980s, best-film Oscars were picked up by Richard Attenborough for *Gandhi* and David Puttnam for *Chariots of Fire*. At the 1982 Academy Awards ceremony, *Chariots of Fire* screenwriter Colin Welland lifted the gleaming statuette above his head and announced the onerous words:

"The British are coming."

Trouble is, they never arrived. Up until then, before the feature was shown in cinemas, it was normal to screen a short film, the finance granted to distributors through the Eady Levy. The fact that distributors, rather than the producers, of short films got their hands on the grant had long been a bone of contention, although as if yielding to the auguries of Orwell's *1984*, Margaret Thatcher's government withdrew the levy and most tax breaks for film production that year. The film industry remained in the doldrums until Cool Britannia appeared a generation later and revived the business through the Film Council, although yet again filmmakers saw one of their principal funding limbs yanked off when Gordon Brown, in the 2004 Budget, withdrew tax breaks through the Sale and Leaseback scheme introduced in the 1992 and 1997 Finance Acts.

This quick, painful history lesson was learned by Kim Leggatt and Douglas Miller after they were backed with lottery money in 1997 to make the acclaimed *Princess* with Brian Cox. They had grown up seeing short films with the main feature in movie houses and their dream was to see their short on exhibition at the local cineplex. They were to discover that apart from taking films on the festival circuit, there was no practical route into television, in the UK or abroad, and showing shorts with features had become a dim memory that cineastes, like old soldiers, recalled as if from a golden age gone and long forgotten.

With the determination it had required to get lottery cash in the first place, Leggatt and Miller set out to revive this lost tradition. They had some success with *Princess* and learned another valuable lesson: to get shorts in the cinema they have to be just that: short, in order not to conflict with either advertising or the four or five screenings a day the exhibitors need to attain from the main feature.

During their two-year battle to get their film seen, they became a font of information for other aspiring short filmmakers and set up the Short Film Bureau (SFB) in order to concentrate on distribution. They moved their operation from Brighton to London with fifty films on their books, and formed valuable relationships with Channel 4, the BBC, Sky and broadcasters across the world. They began putting short films on airlines, did one deal to show films at Burger King, and more cinema chains are again showing warm-up shorts before the main feature.

Leggatt and Miller steered a fresh course into feature distribution in 2003, and Dawn Sharpless, SFB's former co-head of sales and acquisitions launched Dazzle, a new initiative for the sale, distribution, and exhibition of short films. Dazzle is what Dawn calls a "selective, bijou company." After spending the last several years watching shorts, running the film club Peeping Tom's, and working in Paris for Buena Vista, among others, Dawn Sharpless knows what she wants to put in her catalogue and the buzzwords are "quality" and "originality." "If a film engages me then I will work with the filmmakers and do everything I can to help them. It's not a financial question: I don't think, yeah, this film is going to make a lot of money. No. I have to love it. Comedy and light drama are an easy sell, but that's not necessarily what I'm looking for."

Dawn receives dozens of spec films a month. On average, fewer than five of them are worth seeing more than once; about one a month makes it into the catalogue. The best films, or at least those that Dazzle take on, still tend to reach Dawn after doing the festival circuit. For a short film to make cinema sales, it needs to be 10 minutes maximum and, again, comedies sell best. Dazzle distributes a wide range of material, from 15-second digital micro movies to 35-mm mini-masterpieces. The criterion for becoming a Dazzle film, says Dawn, is very simple: they have to be good.

www.dazzlefilms.co.uk

MAKING MONEY

Now, how about the money: are short filmmakers going to make their fortune?

Dawn Sharpless shook her head and waved a warning finger. "Filmmakers ask: How much am I going to make? But that's not really the question. What they should be asking themselves is: How can I get shown? How can I make sure my little darling gets screened? If you make any money, you should see that as a bonus."

Licensing fees vary: Sky at the time of writing pays £500, irrespective of length, for a three-month license, allowing them to show a film as many times as they wish. Channel 4 pays $130 a minute for a three-year license. Some cable companies offer as little as $50 a minute. From that, Dazzle takes a commission of 40 percent and earns its money by first helping the filmmaker get his film commercially finished, helping to clear music rights and then reselling the films as many times as they can.

One of the biggest costs can be acquiring music rights. Young filmmakers want to use current stars to create the mood they imagine, but the cost of clearing Fat Boy Slim or the White Stripes can be more than the entire cost of making the film. "They come to me with this kind of soundtrack on their films and say, 'Don't worry, no one will notice.' But they will notice. If you make a film for your own amusement and show it to friends, no one will bother you, but if you want to see it screened on TV and in the festivals, you have to be professional and do everything the right way."

Dawn suggests using original music. Composers just starting out in their career will often, at little or no cost, be willing to sit down with the filmmakers and create the music they have in mind, even the music they admire by their rock heroes. "But don't get too close to the original, or you'll still end up facing Madonna or Eminem across the courtroom."

In Dawn's opinion, short films in the UK are falling behind those in the US and Europe and advises filmmakers to get an education by going to every screening possible. "There are festivals all over the country; the Soho Rushes festival is free, so there's no excuse. Learn the techniques, study what makes a good story—and only then should people be thinking about making a film."

Thanks to the pioneering work of the Short Film Bureau and Dazzle's timely arrival, more exhibitors are screening short films with features; some (though woefully few) cinemas schedule shorts nights, showing several in one evening; and there are more TV slots on HBO in the United States, Canal Plus in France, in Japan, on oil rigs, and on numerous airlines.

SHORT CIRCUIT FILMS

Another initiative to get shorts shown with features is Short Circuit Films, backed by the Film Council and set up to create a network across the UK. As Alan Parker made clear at his first major presentation to the film industry, a sustainable industry will need distribution-led companies in order for British films to carve out their share of the $60 billion a year world market. "In the immediate future, we are going to have to compete on the basis of skills, even more so than costs, so we need to rapidly expand the quality of our skills base because it is the life-force that will protect the UK's ability to make film."[3]

Expanding that skills base will mean that ongoing support for short films, and enterprises such as Short Circuit, will ensure the work is seen. Under this scheme, the print and British Board of Film Classification (BBFC) costs are paid by Short Circuit for completed films of no longer than 10 minutes, which are submitted with a 35mm negative or internegative. Selected titles are offered to distributors to be attached to an appropriate feature on anything from one to fifty prints, Short Circuit striking the prints and sponsoring the PR.

Producers will be expected to deliver prints to cinemas well in advance of screening and be present for the technical check when the print is prepared for projection. Prints are occasionally damaged during projection, and the producer should check the print before it goes out to another exhibitor. As part of the Film Council's education program, Short Circuit also organizes one-day seminars on short film marketing and distribution.
www.shortcircuitfilms.com

ZOO CINEMAS

One group dedicated to showing shorts with features is Zoo Cinemas, with venues in London at the Gate, Ritzy, Phoenix, and Everyman, and the Cameo in Edinburgh. A couple of hundred films a year reach them and selection is made on individual strengths and the likely capacity of a short to engage the audience and establish the tone for the feature. It is important, if you want to be part of the film industry, to keep up to date by reading the trade press, as suggested by the BFI; if you are making a short be on the lookout for a feature that complements it. Release dates and confirmed cinemas for all new movies are available from the Film Distributors' Association (formerly the Society of Film Distributors—see *Useful Addresses*).
www.picturehousecinemas.co.uk

To get short films into Zoo Cinemas, or any cinema (and many festivals), they must be supplied on 35 mm, unless the cinema is equipped with digital technology. This will oblige filmmakers to decide on format when they are drawing up a budget. The cost of renting 35-mm kit can be as much as the cost of buying a proficient camcorder, but then the overall cost will be much the same if the tape is then transferred to film.

There are three main film formats:

- 35mm—this is the most expensive. The camera comes with bulky equipment that requires a team to shift it around on set and a multitude of lenses that can create the entire spectrum of mood and effects. It captures a clean, precise image and, with the exception of the 70mm IMAX format, for the purist, there is no other way to make film.

- 16mm—the format gained in standing after its wide use in television and, although it lacks the gloss of 35mm, it is still used for serious productions. A slightly larger picture area can be obtained with Super 16; it is used by Ken Loach, who casts non-professional actors and shoots miles of film to capture natural performances; it was also chosen by the team behind *Lock, Stock and Two Smoking Barrels*.

- 8mm—the Super 8 and Real 8 mm are formats for those learning their craft.

The alternative to film is tape, used in a variety of DV, miniDV, DigiBeta and HD. Tape has many advantages: it is more cost-effective to produce rushes, and films can be edited before being transferred, if required, to 35mm

Cinematographer Mark Duffield[4] told an audience at a New Producers Alliance session on formats and technologies at the London Film School that he believes high-definition video (HD) will eventually supersede film and it is better to embrace the change than ignore it. Both forms, he says, have their own "interesting aesthetics" and the loyalty to film merely buys into the historic language of cinema.

Duffield shot the independent feature *Butterfly Man* on 35mm on location in Thailand and won the 2003 cinematography prize at the Slamdunk Festival—the alternative to Sundance. He has shot numerous short films using various formats and has come to see that a lot of so-called good cinematography is more to do with good set design, costumes, and lighting. If that is in place, the rest follows.

"Of course there are differences: film is a chemical process, video uses pixels—it's like painting in oil or acrylics," he said. "People think if they shoot on 35 mm they will have a masterpiece. But high-definition video is constantly improving and very soon you won't be able to tell the difference. Like shooting in black and white, film will one day become a specialist tool, not the norm."

He explained that digital grading—or *timing*, as it's known in the United States—is starting to revolutionize the way films are going to appear to the audience and how we now have a palette of millions of colors and tones to help us achieve "a look." Perfect examples, he pointed out, are *Amelie*, *Sex & Lucia*, and *xXx*.

"Shooting on film or tape needs the same discipline, the same care with lighting, the same preparation, and if this is all done, when the tape is blown up to 35mm, it will be the quality of the product that matters, not the way that you got there."

PAUSE

MOVIEOLA

Movieola lays claim to being the first digital TV channel devoted exclusively to short films—"A feature film experience in a fraction of the time" is this Canadian broadcaster's motto. Movieola packs in a full daily program of festival winners, classics, films under 60 seconds and 40-minute dramas, comedies, cartoons, documentaries, and the late-night Vidiots Show with films appropriate to the hour.
`www.movieola.ca`

PITCHING

When the film funders do call, it is not always to announce that there's a check in the post. On occasions, it is to invite the producer—sometimes with his director—to pitch the project to development chiefs, a skill requiring the same verbal dexterity as the street trader hawking perfume outside Bloomingdale's.

Pitching has a long tradition in Hollywood—deftly satirized in Robert Altman's 1992 *The Player*—and what happens in Hollywood crosses the globe with the certainty of the tide. With executives drowning in a sea of words, memos, outlines, new scripts, second drafts, text messaging, and the machine gun spray of e-mail, a verbal pitch is an efficient way for filmmakers to get their message across to potential funders in as short a time as possible—often as little as three minutes, the so-called "elevator pitch."

At film festivals, a more generous 10-minute pitch is common. Producers will suffer repeated rejection, but it at least gives them a chance to hone the pitch, as well as the concept, until they do find interest—or conclude that the idea just isn't going to hack it after all. One problem for producers is that ideas are sometimes "in the air" and while what they are pitching may be completely original to the writer, it may already be yesterday's good idea to the rushed exec behind the desk.

After attending the formats session under the chairmanship of short filmmaker Alexis Varouxakis, I went along to the NPA's crowded pitching and development night later in the year, where independent producer Daniel San (*Understanding Jane*) hosted a panel discussion with screenwriting tutor Phil Parker, independent producer Phil Hunt (*Fast Food*), Parallax producer Sally Hibbin (*Land and Freedom*; *Carla's Song*; *Liam*) and Film Council executive Himesh Kar.

They had all been through the mill both pitching and hearing pitches, and they didn't always agree on how to approach the process, but if there was a common denominator it was this: *don't* tell the story—get people interested in the idea, the lives of the characters, and the hurdles they face.

"What really matters is the power of the concept," stressed Himesh Kar. "If you can get people's eyes to light up, you've got them. If they want to know more, they'll ask, don't worry."

"Make your story grounded in reality," advised Phil Hunt. "When a story comes from the real world, or grows from a life experience, it's something everyone can identify with."

Kar was nodding thoughtfully as he spoke. "Be careful, though," he added. "Pitches that come from people who say it's a personal story, that they have lived this life, it can be interesting, but I often find it off-putting. I strongly believe in the force of the idea. That's what affects me."

What they did agree on is the need for research: "If you know about the guy you're talking to, it is less intimidating. It will be easier to find out if you have things in common," said Sally Hibbin. "Find out what people are looking for. Speak to assistants and secretaries. They are the first point of contact. They often have an overview and will know if you are wasting your time—or worse, wasting the time of the person listening to your pitch."

They dismissed the suggestion from a member of the audience who asked whether a $50 note in a birthday card for a secretary was a good way to reach the boss. Kar turned his thumbs down. "Absolutely not. There's a bullshit detector that goes off when people try and manipulate the system or exaggerate, when they say they have credits when they don't, or they have stars attached when it's just a wish list. If the person you're pitching to is interested in the idea, the first thing he'll do is go on the web and check the Internet Movie Database to check your credits. And if you say you have a star on board, he'll ring the agent. Everyone knows everyone in this business and if you're making your way in, you have to be honest and plainspeaking. That's the way you earn respect."

As an experienced producer with Ken Loach and a dozen films to her credit, Sally Hibbin has come to rely on the Six Degrees of Separation theory. If you really need to reach an actor or an actress, there is always someone who knows someone and you follow the trail until you get to him or her. In the end, actors want to work, and if they are right for the role, and if the project interests them, they'll want to be involved.

For those setting out in their career, it is not going to be as easy as that. In a former incarnation, Himesh Kar represented writers and directors at the William Morris Agency and in his experience, agents and their assistants are very cynical. They have seen it all and heard it all and they are always on their guard. "In the end, it's very difficult to get talent involved unless you already have the money."

Phil Parker makes the point that it is often more important, in the early stages of a filmmaker's career, to find allies than to find money. If you are able to get an executive producer attached to a project, it may help a lot more in the long run, first to complete the package, and then to find finance. "A pitch rarely gets your film financed, a short or a feature, but it may get your foot in the door. It may seem strange, but most people in the film industry are amazingly generous. There is a core of people willing to be mentors. They are bombarded with projects and whether or not they decide to help you will really depend on the way you approach them."

Danny San, chair for the event, points out that if you are going into the film business, you are there for the long haul. You will tend to meet the same executives again and again. You will get to learn what people are looking for, how to approach them—and when to approach them. "You have to be so passionate about a project that even if everyone turns it down, you are still passionate. That passion is infectious. It will get you noticed."

PAUSE

THE PITCH

How exactly do you approach a pitching session? Phil Hunt outlines his own 10-minute plan:

1. Introductions and greetings: give your full name, company name, and a business card. Don't expect people to remember you, even if you have been invited to pitch a project.

2. Tell them what you are going to talk about: a short film, feature, documentary, TV series.

3. Clarify exactly what you want: development money, funding money, to read a script, to read a new draft.

4. Briefly outline your credentials and achievements.

5. Give them a chance to ask you questions.

6. Present the main elements of the story, the characters and conflicts, and why you believe this story is unique. *Do not* tell the story. Describe the target audience, any similar films, and how much money they took.

7. Give an idea of the budget, funds attached, if any, and potential sales. Point out the benefits to the company you are pitching to.

8. Summarize important aspects of the package: cast, director, department heads.

9. Leave supporting material: synopsis and/or script, details of the package.

10. Thank the exec for listening to you, shake hands and go.

The Finer Points

Danny San points out that there are grave dangers in taking a colleague to a pitching session. "If there is not a unified vision, they will know straight away," he adds. "I find it best to go alone the first time and, if I am called back, I will take the director with me. Whichever way, you should practice a pitch like an actor with his lines. Collar friends and pitch a film like you were telling a true story. You have to get so familiar with the subject, you can tell it in 30 seconds or in 10 minutes, and retain the same essence."

In the same way that the $50 in the birthday card ploy is ill advised, the panel counsels against overpackaging projects, filling pages with pictures or graphics. Many ruses have been tried. The producer Paul Trijbits (*Brick Lane*; *The Wind that Shakes the Barley*) admits to having once delivered a horror script to a production company in a miniature coffin. But while this might be mildly amusing, the script will have to stand up to the hype.

Parker drew everyone's attention to the importance of the written outline or synopsis, which is crucial to supporting the verbal pitch. His advice is that it should be no more than four pages long, and better still just one or two, and suggests dividing it into four brief sections:

> **1.** A premise statement, setting out the characters and what the story is about.

2. A description of the needs or dilemmas faced by the central characters.
3. A section that deals with the central crisis of the drama, leaving enough space for the executive to get involved—don't reveal the plot.
4. A statement that this will be this type of film, this will attract this type of audience—something totally positive.

Finally, he explained that the major weakness he comes across is that projects are rarely what they claim to be. "A film has to be unique *and* familiar, a mixture of both, and that is very hard to achieve."

DUŠAN TOLMAČ

To return to financing short films from public funds, the competition is tough, but filmmakers do come through the process and I spoke to Dušan Tolmač about his experience after being awarded £9,000 by the Film Council to shoot *Remote Control*, his digital short (6 minutes 40 seconds) about a middle-aged couple fighting over their TV remote control.

As part of the award, Dušan attended workshops in script development; he took part in directing sessions with professional actors; there were lectures on the changes in digital technology and conferences with industry experts. The training sessions took place concurrent with the shooting of the film; Short Circuit, as stated above, handling distribution.

"There doesn't seem to be any secret about getting finance. It doesn't matter how many short films you have made, you can still get turned down. Tastes and views change on an almost daily basis," he says. "I have been working with the same team for three years and it was vital for the award to have the team in place; it means you are taken seriously."

Dušan believes that the secret of a good short film is honesty. "You have to be true to yourself and true to your depiction of human situations," he explains. "The beauty of cinema is that the same piece can mean ten different things to ten different people—as long as it is underpinned by an essential truth, it will work for each one of those people on a variety of levels. If you approach the film honestly, the format and length and genre are secondary."

Although Alan Parker is convinced that training is the best medicine for the industry, Dušan Tolmač has come to a different conclusion. He has seen what he describes as "genuinely dreadful films" making it to the screen purely based on the persistence or connections of the filmmakers involved. "There are too many films that have nothing to say," he points out, and reiterates the words of director Juan Luis Buñuel: "There are no formats, no short cuts. If films are made from the heart, with sincerity, it shows on the screen and involves the audience."

Dušan made his first short film in 1998 and, after several shorts, pop promos, and TV commercials, he is hunting down finance for his first feature. "People say you have to learn your craft. I don't really believe that. I have never read a book on screenwriting, and I never learned to direct. People try to formularize the process, but it's not about formulas, it's about communication. As I've already said, it is your emotional input, your veracity, that will make a film work."

When he shot his first short, he remembers being so involved with getting the crew and locations organized that he walked out of the tube in Notting Hill on the first day and suddenly panicked. "I had no idea what I was going to do, but you go on set and just do it; you let it happen. Of course," he adds wryly, "It's important that the people you're working with know what they're doing."

STOP

31 Propeller Studios

32 Propeller Studios

33 Propeller Studios

PART

III

Getting it made

CHAPTER 9

Crewing

Thanks to the profusion of Internet directories, finding crew, wherever you happen to be in the world, has become effortless. Knowing who is good at their job and who isn't comes from experience, but most technicians will have a showreel and producers can make their choice based on a study of these visual CVs. Anyone without a showreel is either going to be an old hand known by reputation, or a complete novice waiting to get his break as an assistant in one of the crafts.

The Film Centre was launched a decade ago and maintains a comprehensive database of people working, or wanting to work, on independent productions on both sides of the camera. The center provides a hire service for cameras, lights, grip, and sound equipment, including owner-operators. There are useful tips and the extensive catalogue of short films is predominantly British, but with growing representation from the United States and the rest of the world.
www.filmcentre.co.uk

Film Centre's founder, Boyd Skinner, says the popularity of the site is down to its easy navigation, and the fact that it's free! "There are various sites with crew listings, even the Internet Movie Database has a directory, but you can be more creative and try the local media colleges," he suggests. "Students are grateful for experience in work placement positions, especially outside the classroom, and if you find a genuinely interested lecturer, he'll probably be keen to give his students a chance at crewing. At the very least, it's a good place to find runners."

Skinner advises producers to find a good all-rounder who knows all the various disciplines. "Most small productions fall down for lack of good organization, or when the *creatives* don't have a strong point of view. So your producer/production manager/art director, often rolled into one, needs to be a good organizer/people-mover, but not necessarily with a film/video/media background."

If you can afford to get one key member on the crew, who would it be? Sound, lighting, director of photography?

"I'd still plump for a technical person with some experience, usually the cameraman, provided he doesn't run the show, and it's a plus if he has editing experience. But … horses for courses; it goes without saying a proficient sports cameraman isn't necessarily going to be the first choice if you're shooting drama. In fact, my ideal person would be an editor with production experience! He would know the shots and coverage you need, and roughly how to achieve it. He is the best judge of whether you actually got the shot, if it will cut, if you need another angle, or whether you can move on. These are all the director's decisions, of course, so one would hope then this is actually the director's background."

There are a number of reasons why experienced crew and well-known actors lend their time for little or no wages to new filmmakers making shorts; actors like to act, but more than that, there is a feeling on a film set that you are part of a family and film people openly embrace new members joining that family.

On Terence Doyle's short film *Noise Control* (see Chapter 18: *Noise Control*), Nick Moran joined the cast for two solid reasons: he enjoys making shorts and he got the chance to fly a fighter plane. On *Greta May* (see Chapter 21: *Greta May: The Adaptation*), veteran grip Pete Nash joined the crew because he had worked previously with director of photography Jean-Philippe Gossart; he believes the young cameraman has a big future (I tend to agree) and will want to work with him again when he's shooting features. Pete Nash brought an air of professionalism to the team and was quick to remind producer Sacha Van Spall that while he wasn't working for union wages, he did expect hot food "and that doesn't mean pizza." Laying tracks and lifting dollies is hard, demanding work and a film crew functions at its best with decent grub. On *Greta May* we paid the crew a nominal sum, but maintained union standards and the hot food that was prepared three times a day made a substantial hole in the budget.

Another commonly used system of payment is deferrals: crew and cast may be paid a small sum, or nothing at all, but receive anything from 100–200 percent of the union rate once the film goes into profit. Needless to say, few short films go into profit, but deferrals may be useful for filmmakers making the jump from shorts to a low-budget first feature.

New sites for crewing are constantly appearing. A few established ones are listed below.

UNITED KINGDOM

Shooting People
London-based Shooting People is "the voice of independent filmmaking." This Internet information exchange network has 30,000 members and grows by 100 new members a week. It is a key place for indie and shorts filmmakers to meet other shooters, find collaborators, and follow the triumphs and travails of members as their films enter the marketplace. Membership costs £30 (UK); $40 (US).

The distribution label Shooting People Films was launched in 2006 with the aim of giving independent filmmakers greater control over distribution. The label has released two documentaries, *Unknown White Male* and *KZ*, and two collections of short films on DVD, *Best v Best* (Volumes 1 and II), with award-winning shorts from around the world. These are essential watching for anyone making short films today.

"Shooters" receive e-mail updates daily. There are regular parties, screenings, and Q&As with patrons such as Anthony Minghella, Richard E. Grant, and Christine Vachon. The Mobile Cinema travels the highways from New York to LA showing short films made by members. "Shooting People is a necessity for anyone who works, lives and breathes independent film!" Morgan Spurlock (*Supersize Me*).
www.shootingpeople.org

Talent Circle
In true low-/no-budget indie style, Talent Circle was launched without funding in 2003 and has grown into an essential service for the UK film community. Jobs postings, training opportunities, and industry news online appear in tandem with offline screenings, networking events, seminars, trade shows, film festivals, and parties. "Our membership consists of directors, producers, actors, writers, crew, editors, music composers—and we could go on, but basically if your talent could help get a film or production made at any stage, then this site is for you."
www.talentcircle.co.uk

Film-TV.co.uk
Film-TV.co.uk was set up as a showcase for film and TV professionals wishing to continue developing their skills, rather than new entrants to the industry. That said, crew with a year's experience can join the directory. There is a guide to getting your foot in the door in film and TV with tips and stories from members, and for crew, the all-important job vacancies.
www.film-tv.co.uk

UNITED STATES

Media-Match
The Hollywood-based Media-Match is an online directory containing résumés of more than 25,000 film and TV professionals. There's a message board, job vacancy listings, and a handy piece of hardware that allows producers to set their own search criteria, using a combination of job type, program type, specialty, credits, experience, and location.

Media-Match serves European as well as US productions and works with all the major studios as well as the BBC, Granada, Hat Trick, the Playboy Channel, and Disney. Freelancers can add photographs to their details and once a week they receive an e-mail with details of which companies have checked out their résumés.
www.media-match.com

FilmStaff.com
The production team at FilmStaff.com claims more than 300 feature film and television credits—from low-budget independent projects to films directed by Steven Spielberg. Film production and television production listings are updated daily, as well as jobs on commercials, music videos, theater, and interactive projects.
www.filmstaff.com

IMDbpro

The Internet Movie Database—IMDb—lists just about every feature ever made and every short that has made it to the festivals. Once people are listed on IMDb, they feel that they've made it.

A new innovation is IMDbpro, providing professionals in the business a contact listing for crew and cast; it lists 65,000 executives and producers, 10,000 production companies, films in production, and film release dates. The service costs $12.95 a month, and is worth every penny according to Fred Baron, executive VP at Twentieth Century Fox. "An invaluable information resource. I rely on IMDbpro every day."

`www.imdbpro.com`

AUSTRALIA

The Film and Television Institute

Based in Freemantle, the Film and Television Institute is arguably the oldest screen resource organization in Australia. It provides a complete crewing service, widely used by Australians, but also overseas production companies taking advantage of the country's generous allowances to filmmakers and long months of guaranteed sunshine.

Supported by the Australian Film Commission, the FTI provides a full production service, hires out equipment, and contains (at the Adelaide Street offices) a 121-seat cinema, video editing suites, an animation center, digital labs, training rooms, studio space, and office accommodation.

`www.fti.asn.au`

STOP

There are two location musts on budget shorts:

- Have as few locations as possible.
- Keep the locations close together.

That doesn't mean that the story needs to adapt to the locations, but if the same story can be told by combining or cutting locations, so much the better. Take another look at Quentin Tarantino's *Reservoir Dogs*. There's a lot more talking than action. Most of the action takes place in an empty warehouse. But the odd glimpse of the outside world moderates any sense of claustrophobia.

GRETA MAY

To return again to my short film *Greta May*, in the original short story, the stranger, Richard, gives Greta his telephone number on a tube train. Getting permission to shoot on the Underground is straightforward. London Transport has a film division for that purpose. But is the train setup essential?

Later in the story, we see Greta rehearsing on stage in the theater. On a scouting expedition, we looked at the Battersea Arts Centre. Not only did it have a theater space we could use, as the story has a theatrical background, the foyer was actually a far better place for the first meeting of the two main characters. It was a bonus that the arts center is in an old town hall with a regal, if faded elegance and a pair of sweeping marble stairs that would have been perfect for a Fred Astaire/Ginger Rogers movie. Being a local authority concern dedicated to promoting the arts, the rental cost suited our budget and the production company's third-party indemnity covered the insurance.

Now, without changing the story in any way, not only were we able to shoot two scenes in the same location, but the sound of Greta's hollow footsteps in the cavernous foyer was able to reflect her inner feeling of emptiness, an accidental homage to the library sequence in Orson Welles's *Citizen Kane* (see Chapter 12: *Sound Design*). The arts center had toilets (an essential!) and a café where we put some money through the till at breakfast and lunch.

Another shot required Greta to study magazines outside a newsagent's. We went to the shop nearest the house where we were shooting the interiors.

By luck, the proprietor had once allowed his premises to be used by the BBC and his brush with that eminent institution meant that our request touched on some nostalgic nerve. He negotiated a £50 fee for the two hours we needed to get the shot and was on hand in case we needed any extras. People like the movies and even on a small production, they are often keen to help. It goes without saying that a thank-you letter with a copy of the DVD will make life easier for the next low-budget producer seeking a location.

INTERIORS

Another important consideration is having enough physical space to shoot. If you've got a girl in the shower, à la *Psycho*, along with the actress, you're going to have to squeeze into the bathroom the director of photography with his camera, a tripod at least, and perhaps a grip to dolly the camera; the sound engineer and boom operator; the gaffer with his lights; wardrobe with a gown ready to wrap the starlet; the clapper boy to shout "Action" and, of course, the director—and let's hope he doesn't have the same girth as the majestic Mr. Hitchcock. It is easier to make a large space look small than to operate in a small space surrounded by kit and crew.

If a film has a lot of interiors, you could try asking a real estate agent if he has an empty property; he may be persuaded to let you have a short-term lease. The property will give you a variety of rooms for wardrobe and makeup, a base for the kit, and a challenge for the set designer who, like a painter with a blank piece of canvas, generally prefers to begin his creation with an empty space. As the example above shows, shooting in bathrooms is particularly difficult (producers should try and get them written out of the script), and if the scene is crucial, you might try asking the management at a hotel if you can hire a room for a day. Emblazon the hotel's name on the credits and they may even let you have a room for free.

The great illusion in movies is to make the audience believe that what they are seeing on screen is authentic. The audience is a willing party to the illusion, and what matters is the *sense* of veracity and the power of the story itself. In *Perfume*, which is set in France, the Barrio Gótico in Barcelona becomes Paris and the old quarter of Gerona stands in for the pretty town of Grasse in Provence. What may come as more of a surprise is that several principal scenes in Michael Winterbottom's emotional rollercoaster *Welcome to Sarajevo* were shot in London, a tough assignment that required all the skills of Mick Ratman,[1] a veteran location manager and chairman of the Guild of Location Managers.

34 *Perfume*
▶▶ P.116

EXTERIORS

Sarajevo is an Austro-Hungarian city with sturdy stone buildings from the Grand Epoch at its heart and a fringe of rundown 1960s tower blocks rising in the distance. "If you search London, you can find exactly the same," Ratman explains. "You just have to be creative." This means dressing the set: covering street signs and road markings, or paying the local authority to remove them. Ratman elaborates: "You then add your own street names and markings as necessary. If it's a period film, you lay down false cobbles or straw. The location manager looks at the details, consults books of reference, and steeps himself in the period and place where the film is set."

Mick Ratman has location-managed five features and numerous shorts. His advice is: if you can afford a location manager, bring him in as early as possible. The location manager studies the script, breaks it down into locations, then breaks the locations down into the number of scenes there are in each location and how many days are needed. "You cut your cloth to suit your budget," he adds. "If you want to shoot in St Paul's Cathedral, it's easy enough, but it will cost a fortune. A location manager may well suggest doing an establishing shot of St Paul's, then shooting the interiors in a lesser-known church that won't cost any more than a donation to the roof fund."

The location manager is employed to save the production money, but just as important is his role of ensuring that the crew behaves responsibly and leaves each location with the providers happy to welcome back other productions in the future. A code of practice can be found at the Guild of Location Managers' website.
www.golm.org.uk

PAUSE

MICK RATMAN'S SEVEN-POINT LOCATION GUIDE

1. Don't be too ambitious.
2. Plan everything: every shot; every take.
3. Don't undervalue the importance of storyboards. The more time you spend planning, the easier the shoot.
4. If you have a good idea, you have to check it through, plan every detail, and make sure it really is a good idea before you shoot.
5. Try to find one location that can be shot to look like several different locations.
6. Get an experienced location manager who can advise creatively—not only on locations, but on the way the director wants to shoot each scene. A location manager who has been in the job for a while knows what has to be done and how to do it.
7. Look outside the envelope!

PERMISSIONS

It is the producer, production manager, or location manager, if you have one, who will generally seek permission, where necessary, to shoot on location and it is his responsibility to provide the owners or local authority officers with a basic Location Release Form. These can be downloaded free from various sites on the Internet; there is an example of a British form below.

From: <name of company and address>
To: <name of owner of premises and address>
Dated: <date>

Dear <name of owner of premises>

Name of film (the "Film"): <name of film>

This letter is to confirm that we may film at your property which is known as _____ (the "Property") from <start time to finish time> on <date> together with a setting-up period of _____ hours and a clearing-away period of _____ hours.

It is therefore agreed as follows:
1. That our personnel, props, equipment, vehicles, and artists employed on our production are allowed onto the Property for the purpose of setting up and filming on the dates and for the periods agreed.
2. We may return to the Property at a later date if principal photography and recording is not completed on the dates agreed.
3. We have notified you of the scenes which are to be shot on or around the Property and you confirm and agree that you consent to the filming of these scenes.
4. We are entitled to incorporate all films, photographs, and recordings, whether audio or audio-visual, made in or about the Property in the Film as we may require in our sole discretion.
5. We shall not make any structural or decorative alterations to the Property without your prior consent. In the event that we do want to make alterations and you agree, we shall properly reinstate any part of the Property to the condition it was in prior to those alterations.
6. In consideration of the rights granted in this letter we will pay you the sum of <£amount> on <date>
7. You agree to indemnify us and to keep us fully indemnified from and against all actions, proceedings, costs, claims, damages, and demands however arising in respect of any actual or alleged breach or non-performance by you of any or all of your undertakings, warranties, and obligations under this agreement.
8. This agreement shall be governed by and construed in accordance with the law of England and Wales and subject to the jurisdiction of the English Courts. Please signify your acceptance of the above terms by signing and returning to us the enclosed copy.

Yours sincerely,
Signed................................

Form provided by E. M. Media, the Regional Screen Agency for the East Midlands, UK.
www.em-media.org.uk

STUDIOS

If you have won the lottery, rather than merely received a lottery grant, or you have wealthy parents or sponsors, you may choose to shoot in a studio. Building a set allows you to shoot at any angle, put up walls and knock them down again, throw televisions through glass windows. And you don't have to worry about the weather. Studios provide space for a production office, wardrobe, makeup and hair, catering, workshops, and a props area. You can often save money shooting a feature and, if you're working on a budget short, you can at least take the tour (in Hollywood, the studios guarantee a nostalgia-fest recreating the memorable moments from *Jaws*, *Alien*, *Titanic*, and *Indiana Jones*). In the UK, Pinewood, Elstree, and Ealing have facilities to rival Hollywood. Back in the real world, Brighton has a studio attached to the film school, and in Liverpool, from about £1,400 a week, you'll be following the footsteps of Samuel L. Jackson, Robert Carlyle, Emily Mortimer, and Meat Loaf, who crowded the stage in studio one to film the interiors on *The 51st State*.

SCREEN AGENCIES

In the UK there are more than a dozen screen agencies backed by the Film Council. The agencies help filmmakers to find locations and make contacts with the local authorities and police. It is perfectly legal to shoot in public areas in the UK but, if you are trailing cables over sidewalks and may potentially create an obstruction, the police and local authority must be informed, and the producer will need to show proof that he has valid insurance. Many film and TV police dramas are shot in London and producers will need prior permission to shoot exteriors of police stations and other police facilities. You will also need permission to dress your actors in police uniform and for anyone to carry weapons, even if they are dummies. For a fee, a Rent-a-Bobby will remain with the crew to manage crowd control.

Film agencies also provide information on other essentials such as toilet facilities and parking.

www.ukfilmcouncil.org.uk
www.met.police.uk
www.filmlondon.org.uk

If you are shooting in an area you don't know, the regional screen agencies will put you in touch with a location scout who will set up recces during pre-production. A location manager will do the same job and also, if required, deal with contracts, negotiate fees, and stay with the crew throughout production to ensure the smooth running of the shoot. He will be knowledgeable about the practicalities of a film crew descending on a location in his area and can save a production time and money by knowing what it is and isn't possible to shoot.

PAUSE

LOCATION WORKS

Looking for a medieval castle? Or a replica Guantánamo?

With its online library of 1,500 locations across the UK coupled with a location-scouting and management service, Location Works is probably the largest and most comprehensive location resource in the UK.

Location Works is a service for film, television, photographers, and events, and works with budget productions as well as full-on features.
www.locationworks.com

THE LOCATION MANAGERS GUILD OF AMERICA

The Location Managers Guild of America (LMGA) was founded in 2003 as a nonprofit, nonunion-affiliated organization with 400 members in California and scores more across the United States. With its comprehensive list of members, available locations, and legal requirements for shooting film in the United States, the LMGA provides a complete location service for local and overseas production companies.

The LMGA works closely with the California on Location Awards—created in 1994 and known as the Cola Awards, which honors location professionals and production companies for their work on location in California.
www.locationmanagers.org

DIRECTORIES

Contact information for location personnel and location libraries can also be found in a number of directories including *The Knowledge*, *Kemps* and *Kays*, which are available in hard copy or online.
www.theknowledgeonline.com
www.kftv.com
www.kays.co.uk

LOCATION LIBRARIES

There are numerous commercial location-finding companies and libraries in the UK. Some libraries hold location photographs of the entire country; others specialize in a particular region or type of location, private homes, period properties, industrial sites, and so on. Locations may be grand country houses and castles in Scotland, but likewise more modest or eccentric properties, cottages, flats, lofts, and tree houses are also listed.

There is a fee for this service, but that may be offset where libraries act as agents and negotiate a fee with the owner of the location; owners listed in libraries are familiar with the disruption that occurs when film crews descend on their property. With a library's help, a deal concerning a location can often be signed and sealed just days before shooting begins.

FILM INSURANCE

The moment the producer starts to assemble crew, he will have to insure the production. There are many specialist companies listed in *The Knowledge*, *Kemps* and *Kays*, and there is useful advice at the Film Council's website (all domains above). Film insurance is highly specialized, each production carrying different risks. The types of insurance needed and the level of premium will vary from film to film—but it is the law, whether you are in Los Angeles or Leeds, that all productions must be insured. At its most basic, your insurance should cover sickness, accident, death (of crew, cast etc.), physical loss and damage to equipment and assets, employer's and public liability.

Producers will need to supply contact details of their insurance company should it be required by equipment houses, local authorities, or studios. The cost of insurance on a short? It can vary greatly depending on the number of days, and the size of the cast and crew, but you will need to think in terms of several hundred pounds and, just as you need to cut deals with the facilities houses, you can try the same with insurance companies. If you need advice and you have a location manager, talk to him.

STOP

34 *Perfume* film poster.
© BFI

Casting

A short film is a puzzle, by its very nature often more complex than a feature. Even when the script has been tuned, the locations sorted, and some cool deals have been cut with the facilities houses by the producer, the puzzle will remain muddled without due care and attention being given to casting. It is unlikely, although not out of the question, that you will have a star name in your short film, but finding the right actor for the right role is the key piece that holds all the pieces of the puzzle together.

A director of photography shooting his first film has undoubtedly been a focus puller and camera assistant. Sound designers serve an apprenticeship as sound editors. The sparks must survive the deadpan wit of the gaffer before he is let loose on the panoply of lights. Just as the craftsmen know the tools of their trade, trained actors, who can get into the skin of a character, will find the soul of a part and give more than the director expects. Dustin Hoffman as Michael Dorsey in the 1982 *Tootsie* is so desperate for a job that he summons up all his power and expertise, cross-dresses for a casting and lands a female role in a soap opera that makes him/her famous.

Casting often comes at the end of the long, laborious task of getting the script right, the director working alongside the writer, or the writer/director producing new drafts under the watchful eye of the producer. While the writing process continues through one draft after another, the director will also be working on a variety of other equally important details: the shot list with the director of photography, and the storyboards, alone or with an artist; he'll be seeking out locations, thinking about costumes, and liaising with the art department. After months, even years, of talking about the film, when it starts to happen, everything happens at the same time and if casting suffers during the last-minute rush to production, so will the finished product.

The same care that goes into the script has to be applied to casting and, once the cast is in place, the director needs to ensure that each actor understands the dreams, foibles, and motivations of the character he is going to play. The director must give clear, simple directions that are consistent and easy to follow. He must establish a trusting relationship that will get the most from rehearsals, and he needs to know how to jazz up poor performances before shooting begins. A first-time director must learn how to be firm without being a bully—if he wants a football-playing six-footer to weep like a child, he will know exactly why and will inspire the tears from his actor. All aspects of *mise-en-scène*—set, costume, music, sound—contribute to audience pleasure and participation in the film, but it is the actors who hold our attention every moment they are on screen. Memorable performances occur as if by magic when the director casts the right actors for the roles, when he feels completely comfortable with those actors, and when the actors feel comfortable with each other: what they call screen chemistry.

A director learns directing from doing it, but knowledge is power and the director will have more authority on set when he does his research. In *Directing Actors,*[1] Judith Weston describes directing film as a high-stakes occupation—"the white-water rafting of entertainment jobs," and adds, "For many directors, the excitement they feel about a project tightens into anxiety when it comes to working with actors." In this practical guide, Weston explains exactly what actors want from a director, what directors do wrong, how actors work, and the director/actor relationship.

PAUSE

IN THE SPOTLIGHT

Spotlight was founded in 1927 with 236 artists; it was the same year as *The Jazz Singer* brought the silent era to an end. Based in the heart of London in Leicester Square, the service was formed "to give professional performers the best and most efficient exposure to casting opportunities."

There are now has more than 30,000 actors, actresses, child artists, presenters, stunt artists, and dancers listed in the print version of *Spotlight* and Internet directories. As the industry's leading casting resource, Spotlight is used by most TV, film, radio, and theatrical companies in the UK, and serves to connect actors, agents, and producers worldwide.

• Spotlight Interactive was voted Best UK Internet Directory in 2003.

• During 2005, an average of 23,000 artist searches were performed on the website each week, with almost 60,000 viewings of individual CVs.

• A weekly average of 130 casting breakdowns were sent out to agents via The Spotlight Link in 2005, with more than 26,000 artists submitted weekly for an average of 400 individual roles.

• Spotlight is a subscription service starting at £60 for three months.

www.spotlight.com

CASTING DIRECTORS

The ideal way to cast a film is to join Spotlight (see box), or use a casting director who gathers a portfolio of CVs and glossy 10 x 8 photos. Casting directors are the go-between between actors and their agents—and little-known performers will have an agent straight out of drama school if they are serious about the business. If you have a role for 7-year-old identical Chinese twins, a casting director will know exactly where to look to fill those roles.

Once the casting director has found suitable actors, he will liaise with the production company in setting up auditions. In fact, the first audition is often with the casting director, and actors need to give a convincing performance before they are even sent to auditions. The casting director wants to provide the absolute best person for the role because that reflects on his skill and justifies his fee. The cost of employing a casting director varies greatly and many will assist in casting a short film gratis if they believe the filmmakers are eventually going to make a feature, showing support for talent as well as it making long-term commercial sense.

Where do you find a casting director? Tap the words into your search engine and press "enter."

ACTORS' AGENCIES

Short filmmakers can approach actors' agencies directly. Agents will suggest suitable talent if they like the script and believe that the exposure will both enhance their client's career and give him a useful addition to his showreel. The more work their clients do, and the better roles, the more valuable a commodity they become. Agents will normally negotiate a fee that, while reduced for budget filmmakers, pays for the agent's time and shows the actor he is working with professionals. Agents take on a client for the long term, each part building a career that is rewarding for the actor and economically viable for the agent.

For those working on a low-budget film in the UK, a useful organization is CastNet, a free service providing online CVs, photos, and showreels. Producers can contact the agency directly to receive "intelligent, immediate suggestions for your production," explains CastNet's Danny Richman.[2] "We will contact all actors on your behalf, schedule castings and let actors know of the outcome. Once we have made suggestions it is then up to the director or casting director to make the final shortlist and selection."

PAUSE

THE DANNY RICHMAN GUIDE TO CASTING

1. Allow sufficient time to see a wide selection of actors for each role and include time for callbacks to confirm your original shortlist. Do not leave the castings until a few days before you intend to shoot.

2. Make sure that you use a reputable casting service to advertise your breakdown. Ensure that actors subscribing to the casting service are required to have trained at an accredited drama school and have at least three professional credits on their CV. Use a casting service that only allows submissions from actors that meet the precise requirements of your breakdown.

3. Research the drama schools with the best reputations and attract the highest number of applicants. If an actor has graduated from a drama school such as RADA, LAMDA, or Central (in the UK), he will already have completed a rigorous and competitive audition process indicating a probable high level of talent.

4. When preparing your breakdown, try to be as specific as possible and provide as much detail as you can about the character and his situation in the film. Good actors are attracted to interesting roles that closely match their playing range and characteristics. A description of "Jim, 25–30, male" will attract only the most desperate and least experienced of actors.

5. Let actors see your script prior to the casting. If they have read the script and have expressed an interest they are far more likely to show up on the day of the casting. It will also give the actors the maximum possible time to prepare for the role.

6. Make sure that you are well organized and provide actors with all relevant information about the logistics of the casting and what they will be required to do on the day. Behave professionally at all times and never ask actors to attend a casting at a residential address or hotel.

7. Try not to keep actors waiting unnecessarily at the casting and ensure that refreshments and toilet facilities are available.

8. Make the actors feel comfortable and in a supportive environment. Allow sufficient time for them to have several attempts at reading.

9. Give the actor guidance during the casting. Even if he has given an excellent reading, ask him to read it differently to test his ability to respond to direction.

10. If the reading contains dialogue, ensure that there is a third party present to read the other character(s). Do not attempt to do this yourself, as you will find it far more difficult to view the actor's performance objectively.

11. Never direct actors to read with emotive instructions such as "Happier," "Angrier," "More flirtatious" etc. This type of instruction will only result in a contrived performance. Use verb-based direction such as "Thrill her," or "Destroy him" and make sure the actor realizes how much is at stake for the character in the chosen scene. If there is little at stake for the character, then you have not chosen a suitable scene for a reading.

12. If you have no intention of casting the actor, do not go on to ask him questions about his availability. This will only give the actor the false impression that he has a strong chance of being cast.

13. Always let the actors know as soon as possible after the casting whether they are being considered or will not be considered for the role.

www.castingnetwork.co.uk

CHAPTER 11
CASTING

PAGE
121

I asked Danny Richman what general advice he would give new filmmakers regarding casting.

Danny Richman (DR): **New filmmakers frequently devote far too little time and attention to the casting process. An underdeveloped script and poor selection of actors are the two areas most likely to result in a poor-quality film. It is vital that filmmakers understand the qualities that make a good actor, how to determine an actor's ability from his CV, and be able to spot an actor who may give a reasonable audition but fail to deliver on set.**

Clifford Thurlow (CT): **Do producers come to you with fixed ideas, and if so, how do you help them make sure they get the right person for the part?**

DR: **There is a huge community of actors available for even the most low-budget film productions. Filmmakers should have clear vision of the roles they are trying to cast. The only exception is where the role requires an uncommon ethnic background, children, or those aged over 60. These categories of actors can be far harder to source for a low-budget film offering little or no payment.**

CT: **Do you try and balance the cast: if there were two female leads, for example, would you go for a blonde and a brunette?**

DR: **Although the primary consideration should be the quality of the performance, audiences will often visually identify a character on the basis of very obvious physical characteristics such as a blonde female. If both of your main female characters are blonde, this may cause some confusion when they appear in different scenes.**

CT: **Do you find some actors are better adapted for stage than screen?**

DR: **Many drama schools have traditionally focused more on stage performance than screen. Some actors may therefore graduate from drama school with little idea of how to adapt their performance for the camera. It is important to look at an actor's CV for evidence of screen work and to film the audition to ensure that he is able to adapt his performance.**

CT: **How can you help short filmmakers specifically?**

DR: **Many filmmakers may have had the experience of advertising their requirements on a casting website or in a casting publication only to find themselves inundated with applications from entirely unsuitable, inexperienced, or poorly qualified actors. CastNet uses a unique process to ensure that every actor is entirely suitable for a specified role, has confirmed his interest and availability for the production and has achieved a high standard of training and professional experience. This can save stressed filmmakers an enormous amount of wasted time and expense in finding the right talent for their production.**

CT: Do short filmmakers have unrealistic hopes?

DR: If they did not have unrealistic hopes, they would probably never have chosen to pursue a career in filmmaking! They should, however, ensure that their short films are realistic in what they are trying to achieve and are not overly ambitious in terms of cast, location, and special effects. Most new filmmakers fail by trying to do too much, too soon, rather than just telling a simple story, truthfully and economically.

CT: Are short films a good place for actors to hone their screen skills?

DR: Many actors may be participating in a short film solely to gain material for their showreel. Actors gain the most by working on a well-organized production, with an efficient crew and talented director who understand how to work and communicate with actors. Unfortunately, these are few and far between in the world of short filmmaking and in most British film schools far too little time is devoted to working with actors.

THE CASTING SOCIETY OF AMERICA

A one-stop shop for casting in the US is the Casting Society of America, the premier organization of casting directors in film, TV and theater. It has more than 350 members represented not only in the United States but also in Canada, the UK, Australia and Italy.

CSA was founded in Los Angeles in 1982 to establish a standard of professionalism and to provide its members with a support organization to further their goals and protect their interests. With less than forty members during its first year, the monthly newsletter helped grow the organization and drew into its ranks many of the top casting directors in the industry. The creative contribution of casting directors is recognized by the Academy of Television Arts and Sciences and since 1989, casting directors have been awarded Emmy statuettes in various casting categories.

What can the CSA do for producers?

"We are diplomats; we are counselors; we are negotiators," says Mary V. Buck, former CSA president. "We are teachers; we are artists and visionaries. We are a key element in the creation and success of every theater, film, and television project ever made."

www.castingsociety.com

PAUSE

STOP

THE MYSTERY OF THE MISSING EARRINGS

The title role in my 10-minute short, *Greta May*, requires the actress to go through a range of costumes as well as of emotions. Three agencies sent forty actresses to three castings and the standard of performance was extremely high.

This was a role an actress could really sink her teeth into and the actresses were pulling out all the stops to try and get it. One actress appeared looking scruffy and depressed and seemed perfect for when Greta is in her dejected state.

The actress called that night to say she had forgotten her earrings. She had some fresh ideas about the character and asked if she could attend another audition to try them out. She arrived dressed to the nines as the optimistic Greta May, slipped on her earrings and gave an upbeat performance.

I didn't cast that actress because I had a clear mental image of who I was looking for (in the script notes I'd written: twenty-five, vulnerable but with a steely core of self-preservation). The actress wasn't quite right for the role, but I admired her determination and kept her photo and CV on file.

CHAPTER 12

Sound Design

The sound designer and composer are not the same thing, and rarely does the same person do both jobs. The composer writes music. The sound designer is responsible for all aspects of a film's audio track, from the dialogue and sound effects recording to the rerecording of the final track.

Before the turn of the twentieth century, William Dickson was experimenting with sound (see Chapter 2: *A Brief History of Short Films*). His sound version of the Kinetoscope was called the Kinetophone and, to the continuous one-reeler peep show, viewers could hear a soundtrack through two rubber ear tubes.[1] A long way from MTV, but that's where it all began.

Dickson continued to experiment with sound at the Edison laboratories and by 1913 had devised a system to synchronize the picture on screen with sound played on a 5½-inch celluloid cylinder record. This was achieved by connecting the projector at one end of the theater to the phonograph at the other, using a long pulley. Edison financed nineteen talkies over a two-year period, but the system never worked that well, the film and the record were often out of sync, and Edison finally abandoned sound to continue making silent films.

THE BEGINNING OF SOUND FILMS

The Jazz Singer—starring Al Jolson and released by Warner Brothers in 1927—is generally considered to be the beginning of sound films, although it was Orson Welles, a generation later, who grasped the full potential of sound and introduced a variety of new innovations. With his long experience in radio, he came to film knowing instinctively that the soundtrack could play an equal role in film narration and give balance to the three-legged stool of dialogue, music, and visuals: footsteps on the stairs, a key turning in a lock, a ticking clock, or a ticking bomb. In a Welles film, for the first time, sound was used to warn the audience of what to expect before the visuals—an expectation that was then confirmed or, in counterpoint, the audience was surprised with the unexpected.

When Welles came to make *Citizen Kane* in 1941, his use of light and shadow drew on the Expressionistic styles of filmmakers in Germany and Russia, but it is the intricate multilayered soundtrack that tells us more about mood and ambience—the hollow echo of footsteps in the monumental library, the boom of a steamboat landing, and after Kane strikes his wife Susan in a tent on the beach, over the icy silence that follows a woman is heard laughing hysterically in the distance.

Welles developed what became known as the lightning mix. In linking montage sequences by a continuous soundtrack, he was able to join what would have been rough cuts into a smooth narrative. For example, the audience witnesses Kane grow from a child into a young man in just two shots. As Kane's guardian gives him the famous sledge and wishes him "Merry Christmas," we fade to a shot of Kane fifteen years later, where the phrase is completed: "and a Happy New Year." In this instance, the continuity of the soundtrack, not the images on screen, creates a seamless narrative structure.[2]

THE BIRTH OF SOUND DESIGN

35 *Apocalypse Now.*

⏹ ⏩ P.128

Although after Welles sound men began to play a prominent role in post-production, the term "sound design," to cover all non-compositional elements of a film, only came into being when it was coined by Walter Murch[3] during his marathon twelve months in the sound studios working on *Apocalypse Now*, which won him his first Oscar in 1979. We can recall Colonel Kilgore's classic line, "I love the smell of napalm in the morning." Of course, we can't *smell* napalm in the cinema, but our senses are pricked by the cold, gnawing whirr of helicopters, the sound allowing us to *feel* the presence of napalm. Similarly, Tom Tykwer's 2007 film of Patrick Süskind's *Perfume* is a story about the world's greatest originator of scents. The visuals alone could not convey the sensation of fragrances wafting on the air, but the sound of liquids pouring from glass vials, unguents heating in cauldrons, and the extravagant intakes of breath taken by Ben Whishaw as the murderer Jean-Baptiste Grenouille allow us to imagine the secret perfume he is creating.

To return to Walter Murch, although he is best known for *Apocalypse Now*, it was his work on *The Conversation* that had first elevated the status of film sound to a new level, recognized by his first Oscar nomination in 1974. Gene Hackman, as Harry Caul, is a surveillance expert who can record any conversation between two people anywhere. Caul's obsession with taping, analyzing, and interpreting sound is part of his being and in the intense, fixated Caul it is easy to imagine Walter Murch looking back from the reflection in the mirror.

The term "sound design" came originally from the theater, but in film Walter Murch established the fact that the sound designer played a creative role equal to that of the editor, director of photography, and art director, and the credit duly appeared for the first time on *Apocalypse Now*. Coppola's 2001 *Apocalypse Now Redux* has forty-nine extra minutes added to the cut, and if you pump up the volume on your DVD player, you get a pretty good idea of Murch's contribution to the finished film.

Murch assisted in reconstructing an old print of *Touch of Evil*, producing the sound designs Welles had noted in the shooting script before technology was up to realizing them. Murch's achievements in sound were fully recognized in 1997 when he came away from the Academy Awards with a double Oscar for editing and sound on *The English Patient*.

SOPHISTICATED SOUNDTRACKS

Before stereo, film sound was of such low fidelity that only dialogue and occasional sound effects were practical. The greater dynamic range of the new systems, coupled with the ability to *place* sounds to the sides and behind the audience, required more creative decisions and sound professionals to make the most of the improved technology.[4]

The sound designer's role can be compared with the role of supervising sound editor; many sound designers use both titles interchangeably. The role of supervising sound editor, or sound supervisor, developed in parallel with the role of sound designer. As the demand for more sophisticated soundtracks on film grew, supervising sound editors became the head of large sound departments with a staff of dozens of sound editors, and were expected to realize a complete sound job with a fast turnaround. It is far from universal, but the role of sound supervisor comes from the original role of the sound editor, that of a technician required to complete a film, but having little creative authority. Sound designers, on the other hand, are expected to be creative, and their role is a generalization of the other creative department heads.

Just as the Internet has changed short film distribution, the web has streamlined the work of sound designers. Rather than trawling through record stores and sound libraries, or creating their own effects, the designer has a virtually unlimited choice of crisper, more "believable" sounds at his fingertips. On my short film *Greta May*, I sat in the editing suite at True Media in Soho's Golden Square with Tony Appleton listening to thousands of doorbells and telephone ringtones and trying to decide what would fit the *noir* mood of those moments. We had a perfectly acceptable location recording of a taxi door closing and the taxi pulling away. We listened to dozens more on the computer speakers and when we found one that sounded a fraction better, we grabbed it without shame.

Computer technology has similarly revolutionized music composition and a sound designer, particularly on a short film, will often assist the composer on the electro-acoustic portion of the composition.

STOP

35 *"I love the smell of napalm in the morning."*
Robert Duvall as Colonel Kilgore in *Apocalypse Now.* © BFI

CHAPTER 13

Music and Post-Production

Sound plays a vital part in the overall feel of a film, but it is music, more than anything, that brings out the emotional heart of a scene and the director has to learn to leave *space* for music in order for it to be a part of the storytelling process. Music sets mood and atmosphere, it creates tension, and contributes in a subtle way to showing the audience about the desires, fears, and even the nature of the characters. In Sergio Leone's 1969 *Once Upon a Time in the West*, with its sprawling twelve minutes of credits, composer Ennio Morricone uses a different instrument for each of the larger-than-life protagonists and, even before we see them on screen, we get to feel their presence with just a few notes whispering through the score.

An action-packed movie may need racy music, but a film with undertones and subtext requires a score that is more multifaceted, creating expectation more than thrills. In the 1970 *Five Easy Pieces*, we meet Jack Nicholson as a construction worker and only later do we discover that he is railing against his musical, middle-class family. When he goes home to visit, the score switches from contemporary to classical, and when Nicholson sits at the piano to play, he brings his two worlds together by hammering out Chopin's haunting *Prelude in E Minor* like a piece of ragtime. The metaphor is understated and not everyone will get it, but for those who do, it adds another dimension to the story and provides a deeper level of appreciation.

Most film scores are written in the style that the audience expects from the genre: the evocative cellos in a horror flick, the jazz in *film noir*. But in a short film the director may want to go against type and do something more original and adventurous. Composer John Williams wrote a romantic score reminiscent of Strauss for John Badham's 1979 *Dracula*, adding a feverishly sexual tone to Frank Langella's performance as the ravenous Count.

There are two distinct categories of music in a film: incidental or featured music, which is not "heard" by the actors; and background music—music they do hear and needs to be arranged to fit the feeling and location: a nightclub, an elevator, the song on the taxi-driver's radio; the music is never random but will be part of the emotional texture underpinning the scene.

MUSIC RIGHTS

People making their first short film, especially students, may be tempted to borrow music from their favorite bands. With music download programs, it is almost too easy. But be warned: music copyright is complex and acquiring rights is generally expensive, often more than the entire budget of a short film. Clearing music rights for festivals (where copyright owners know that no profits will be made by the filmmakers) may cost just a few hundred pounds, but if the film ends up a winner and you get the chance to show it further afield—on television, even streaming on the Internet—the rights issue will come up again. Getting music rights isn't difficult. The Mechanical Copyright Protection Agency (MCPS) keeps details of who owns what, and in many cases administers the negotiations and collection of money for rights.

MCPS also handles library music and there is an astonishing amount suitable for every mood and genre. This, too, costs, about £100 for a minute of music. Details at:

www.mcps.co.uk

PAUSE

THREE TYPES OF MUSIC RIGHTS

- **Composition:** This applies to the composer and lyricist. The music is normally licensed to a music publisher and the copyright runs out seventy years after the death of the last writer involved in the piece.

- **Recording:** Recording companies normally own the recording rights and those rights expire after fifty years.

- **Performance:** An artist's performance on a piece of music is also protected by copyright (so you can't just take clips and put them in a documentary). Record companies normally protect performer's rights, but it is sometimes necessary to get the performer's permission, as well as that of the recording company, to use clips.

WORKING WITH A COMPOSER

If buying in copyrighted music is too expensive, the indie route is a wise alternative, in every sense of the word.

When writing music for film, the composer is not entirely free to follow his own muse, but has to tune into the narrative structure. The composer writes the score, but influenced by the style imagined by the director who will, most likely, turn up at the studio with a bunch of CDs and vague memories of the films that enthused him to become a filmmaker in the first place. It is up to the composer to find the mood, the tempo, the essence, and arrange a score that is both original and, magically, the theme music to the director's dream. After the script rewrites, shooting, and editing, it is the final part of the collaboration that is filmmaking, and the composer really is the key piece that makes the Chinese puzzle slot into place.

If the director doesn't have a fixed notion of the music, the composer can be more creative and come up with something exciting and experimental. Just like the writer, director, and director of photography, the composer on a short film will often have more freedom to play with the aesthetics and it is only with this freedom that great new concepts can be explored. When the collaboration between director and composer creates a powerful piece of music on a short, there is a good chance that it will continue through further shorts and into features; to give one example, David Julyan scored Christopher Nolan's short *Doodlebug* in 1997, his breakthrough feature *Following* in 1998, the director's Hollywood debut *Memento* in 2000, and three films since.

A film score is so central to a film that it offers a real challenge and filmmakers working on a budget need not be nervous about approaching a composer with a request. He can only say no, and he may say yes. By the same token, composers who want to break into film should send out demos to small production companies, contact film tutors at colleges, and network.

IN TUNE WITH SPENCER COBRIN

36 Spencer Cobrin

Composers may have come through years of study in the conservatoire or, alternatively, from the hard road of rock. Spencer Cobrin belongs to the latter category. With three films in three genres behind him—a short, a feature, and a prizewinning documentary—he has a pretty good idea of the role the composer plays when working with experimental and inexperienced filmmakers.[1]

Cobrin had no formal training, except he did learn to read music as a child when studying the trumpet. He played drums in several bands in the London clubs and was asked to audition for Morrissey, the controversial ex-vocalist from The Smiths, when he set out on his solo career. This, as he says, "came totally out of left field; such is the magic of life." He worked with Morrissey for seven years, "an emotional rollercoaster to say the least."

During the long hours on the road, Cobrin began writing music, which led to the publication of several co-writing projects with Morrissey. When his tenure with Morrissey came to an end, Cobrin started his own band, wrote music and licensed songs to independent features in the UK and the US. His film breakthrough came in 2004 when he "pitched" on the short *Alice and Kitty*, a fictionalized drama based on the true story of Kitty Genovese, who was murdered in New York. The following year, he wrote the score for *Send In The Clown*, a feature comedy about a boy who wakes from a coma and pursues his childhood dream of being a clown, to the disappointment of his father. His documentary debut came in 2006 with *My Child: Mothers of War*, a film about the mothers of American soldiers fighting in Iraq.

PART III
GETTING IT MADE

I asked Spencer where he started when he was scoring a short: was it the script or the film?

Spencer Cobrin (SC): By the time a filmmaker or producer reaches out to a composer, the film has more or less been assembled, unless he brings in someone at the very early stages, which I believe is kind of rare, but there are no hard and fast rules. So in my case it's the film, not the script that is the starting point. If I were to base the score on the script I think I would find that misleading, first because by the time the film has been shot it's probably been through several significant changes, and second, I'm writing to the moving picture, not the written word. On the other hand, I do like to read scripts as it's fascinating to see how the words on the page are made manifest, but that's more of a directorial intrigue than a compositional one.

Clifford Thurlow (CT): What part does music play in a film?

SC: Music is the glue. It's like an invisible actor: it describes the narrative in sound, guiding viewers from one point to the next, leading them along the narrative's path. Music adds emotional intensity and impetus. It can describe characters and their psychology, it creates moods, defines geography and the time period; it does so much. I would say the addition of music, if it can at all be quantifiable, probably makes up 40 percent of a film. The effect it has with the picture is really incredible. Music plays a very significant role: even if its role within a dramatic piece is a subtle one, it nonetheless can't be diminished.

CT: Do you have a different approach with a short and a feature?

SC: I don't think so, as a short is a condensed version of a longer form; I suppose it depends on the film itself.

CT: If the director has a fixed idea about music, do you accommodate that, or convince him/her that you have a better plan?

SC: Obviously the director, especially if he has written the script too, has a much clearer and deeper understanding of what it is he wants than someone coming in cold and seeing the piece for the first time. It can also be a case of trial and error. To get inside the head of the director is very important. There could be things that may not be directly apparent at the initial screening, so it's a good idea to give yourself time to watch the film, study it, and absorb as much as possible of what it is the director is aiming for and then to give it your fingerprint—that is after all why you are on board in the first place. Maybe the film will have a temporary track that has the kind of feel or direction they are looking for, but that can be misleading as it may not necessarily bring out what is inherent in the film. It's interesting to see how, by trying out different pieces of music, it can alter the feel of the drama and by doing so give scenes a completely different meaning.

CT: Is music useful to cover gaps in the story, places where the director perhaps has not been able to elicit the right emotions or performances from the cast?

SC: Music has the power to bring to the fore emotions in varying degrees so that if a performance is lacking a certain something, music can certainly help support, enhance, and reinforce what might otherwise be missing.

CT: And it follows—can the music be intrusive?

SC: Oh definitely. It's important to strike the right balance, otherwise it may feel that there is too much music, which might suffocate the story, or conversely, not enough could leave it a little thin on the ground and you lose impetus. Music doesn't have to be everywhere.

CT: On a practical level, how do you go about writing the score?

SC: What's the story and who are the characters? What does the director want to bring to the film by way of music? Getting the tempo and pacing right is the cornerstone of making the music fit snugly. There are other factors, such as how to play a scene. Do you want to hit certain points in the performance or dialogue to emphasize the drama, or play through the scene? Diegetic sound can also spark ideas as well as improvising, intuition, and just sheer grit.

CT: Has technology changed music scoring?

SC: Yes, absolutely. Not just how music is created, but what kind of music and sounds can be created and manipulated. I haven't crossed any thresholds myself as I started writing solely in the digital realm.

CT: What relationship do you have with the sound designer?

SC: So far I haven't worked with a sound designer. That would be interesting, though, as these two fields are closely linked—sound design is used on the same level as music. The sound design I have done within my own work, though, is actually conceived of as part of the composition itself, as opposed to seeing it as a separate entity.

CT: Is it possible for filmmakers with little musical experience to create their own music?

SC: I think everyone has the potential to do anything, really. So in that case, anyone can create music, anyone can make a film; but more to the point, will it be any good? If you've slaved over a project for as long as it takes to make even a short film, would you want to risk blowing it by potentially adding something that might compromise all the hard work you've poured into it?

CT: Finally: list the three absolute essentials that music must do on a film.

SC: I'm no professor but I would say: to set the mood/tone, support/enhance the narrative and performances, and to bring a sense of finality/conclusion.

CREDITS

While the director works with the composer, the producer should be thinking about how he is going to exploit the film at festivals, in competition, at film clubs, and with sales agents. He will be compiling a press kit (there's an example in Chapter 21: *Greta May—The Adaptation*) and working with an artist on a poster design and artwork for a DVD cover. The film has to stand up, but every detail adds a layer of gloss and professionalism to the package.

During pre-production and production, the director has so much to do that he rarely gives any thought to the credits; getting the film wrapped is a Herculean task in itself. But credits are, or at least should be, part of the storytelling process (think of the *Pink Panther* movies) and should prepare the viewer for the style and genre of film they are about to watch. The area of credits is one that makers of short films often overlook, as Matthew Konz at Leapfrog Entertainment knows all too well (see the box below).

PAUSE

BORING CREDITS

Watching the quantity of short films that I do, I am disheartened at how boring and similar opening credits tend to be. So many films consist of a simple white font on a black background—usually Arial or Times New Roman. This is one of the main areas of neglect in short filmmaking. Choose a font which suits the story, there are thousands available for free download on the Internet, and try to be more creative with opening credits.

Try integrating opening titles into the story and the opening shots of your film—it is actually quite rare for short filmmakers to overlay text on top of an image—most openings of short films jump between footage of the film and black screens with white text, which is almost ubiquitous and, from my point of view as a programmer, really boring and uninspired.

Ideally, you should be putting the credit style under the same level of scrutiny that you place the story. First impressions mean a lot, and the font choice, size, movement, color, and style of your credits can lift the opening of your film immensely.

Matthew Konz

www.leapfrog-entertainment.com

STOP

CHAPTER 14

Trade Unions

When filmmakers of short films and low-budget films first make an acquaintance with trade unions, they may find themselves in a dilemma. Few people attracted to film are going to be against a worker's right to be in a union and be protected by that union. But here's the crux of the dilemma: they often wonder what this could possibly have to do with them. *We're just trying to make a movie, for heaven's sake.*

Unions, however, play a vital role in filmmaking, not only in fixing rates for their members, but in setting hours, conditions, and safety. One of the major reasons for a new production company to sign agreements with unions, actors' guilds, and writers' guilds is to be able to hire their members for a production. But here's another side of the dilemma: only films with industry backing and the appropriate budget can afford the wages those unions have negotiated.

The unions recognize that short films and low-budget features are ideal training grounds for technicians and actors entering the industry, and have responded by creating a variety of agreements to fit the scarce resources of independent filmmakers. Some low-budget films are actually no-budget films and, while it wouldn't be admitted in those union offices, union bosses tend to turn a blind eye when their members are moonlighting on an indie film. It is to everyone's advantage that the film gets made. On the flip side of the coin, if unions get the impression that their agreements are being flaunted, or their members are being exploited, they will seek an injunction and close down the production.

It is not unusual, on a short film, that those financing the project (usually a combination of writer/director/producer) will want to put the production on a professional level and will raise sufficient funds to pay the cast and crew at least a nominal sum. A 10-minute short requires an optimum four-day shoot (at 2½ minutes of usable footage in the can a day, that's still a challenge for novice directors and crews); the payment of £100 or $150 per day for the four days is typical, a modest amount, but when everyone on set is paid equally it inspires a team spirit, a sense that everyone is just as valuable and important as everyone else.

New filmmakers should be aware of what the unions do and how they may be able to help, rather than hinder, a production. Like flour to the baker, research is the filmmaker's first ingredient. A good place to learn more about unions, wages, and rights is filmmaking.net, which has a lively message board with questions such as: "How much should I get paid as…" and both experts and fellow contributors respond with their views and comments.

Pay is an important factor, although as Benjamin Craig at filmmaking.net points out, "If you are a high school student considering whether working in the film industry will be a financially rewarding career, then you are looking down the wrong path. If financial security is your primary career driver, you should consider law, accounting, medicine, or another stable industry with a well-defined entry path. You don't become a filmmaker for the money!"[1]
www.filmmaking.net

There are scores of trade unions and guilds for every branch of the profession: writers, editors, cameramen, musicians, etc. Below is a list of key organizations that new filmmakers should be aware of.

UNITED KINGDOM

BECTU

The Broadcasting Entertainment Cinematograph and Theatre Union (BECTU) represents permanently employed, contract, and freelance technicians primarily based in the UK who work in broadcasting, film, theater, entertainment, leisure, and interactive media.

The union negotiates pay, conditions, safety, and contracts with employers for its 27,000 members, publishes the magazine *Stage, Screen and Radio* ten times a year, provides a script registration service, and operates Skillset—see box on page 138.

The Freelance Production Agreement between BECTU and Pact (Producers' Alliance for Cinema and Television) sets out minimum rates of pay for freelances across film and television production.
www.bectu.org.uk

Equity

Equity is the only trade union representing artists from across the entire spectrum of arts and entertainment. Formed in 1930 by a group of West End performers, Equity quickly spread to encompass the whole range of professional entertainment with a membership drawn from actors, singers, dancers, choreographers, stage managers, theater directors and designers, variety and circus artists, television and radio presenters, walk-on and supporting artists, stunt performers and directors, and theater fight directors.
www.equity.org.uk

MU

The Musicians' Union (MU) was founded in 1893. It maintains links to orchestras, music colleges, and various musical resources for its members. The union helps track down stolen instruments, protects copyright, and sets fees. Short filmmakers who want to put Babyshambles or Bruce Springsteen on the soundtrack will need to add several thousand pounds to their budget and

may want to consider using original music by an up-and-coming composer. The MU is happy to advise.
www.musiciansunion.org.uk

UNITED STATES

WGA
The Writers' Guild of America (WGA) protects writers, settles disputes about credits in the film industry, and collects millions of dollars in residuals for its members. The WGA is the leading screenplay registration service in the world, taking in 55,000 pieces of literary material each year. The service costs $20 ($10 for members) and provides legal evidence in fraud, theft, and plagiarism cases. Unlike most organizations representing writers (*the lowest man on the film totem pole*), the WGA is a powerful body with a bite as fierce as its bark.
www.wga.org

IATSE
Renamed in 1995 as the International Alliance of Theatrical Stage Employees, Moving Picture Technicians, Artists and Allied Crafts of the United States and Canada (IATSE), the union set up shop in 1893 as the National Alliance of Theatrical Stage Employees. Projectionists were the first film technicians to join the union's ranks and the membership now comes from all the crafts in film and TV production, as well as product demonstration, conventions, casinos, audiovisuals, and computer graphics.
www.iatse-intl.org

SAG
Up until the 1940s, actors signed contracts that bound them to the studios. The Screen Actors' Guild (SAG), formed in 1933, struggled for almost a decade to finally bring the contract system to an end. SAG represents 120,000 working actors in film, television, commercials, video games, music videos, and other new media. SAG has devised low-budget agreements with indie filmmakers and upholds strict regulations regarding scheduling. Contracts vary and filmmakers may be required, for example, to use a certain number of union members on a production "whether they are needed or not."
www.sag.org

AUSTRALIA

MEAA
The Media Entertainment and Arts Alliance (MEAA) in Australia represents people working in the media, entertainment, and arts industries. The website provides information on working in these industries and has a list of wage rates and conditions, upcoming events, and membership information.
www.alliance.org.au

PAUSE

SKILLSET

Skillset is the Sector Skills Council for the Audiovisual Industries (broadcast, film, video, interactive media and photo imaging), an organization that provides UK-government- and EU-sponsored film courses, media careers advice, and guidance for professionals already working in the industry.

With £5 million of government funding, in 2005 Skillset set up seven academies offering new courses (including the first ever film MBA), summer schools, work placements, master classes, bursaries, online learning resources, and a talent scout program to help develop the brightest and the best.
www.skillset.org

STOP

PART

IV

TITLE

Interviews with filmmakers

CHAPTER 15

Daniel Mulloy[1]

- 2007 **Son** (in production).
- 2007 **Dad**—best director Orense, best director Sapporo, premiered at Sundance.
- 2006 **Antonio's Breakfast**—best short BAFTA, best short Aspen, best short Indianapolis, best short Kansas, best short Newport, Youth Jury Award Clermont-Ferrand, Onda Curta Award, premiered at Sundance.
- 2005 **Sister**—best short BAFTA Wales, ARTE Award Hamburg, Tamashi Award Japan, best short Concorto, best short Pol-8.
- 2002 **Dance Floor**—best newcomer BAFTA Wales.

37 Daniel Mulloy on set (left)

■▶ ▶▶ P.144

38 Daniel Mulloy working with children

■▶ ▶▶ P.144

Daniel Mulloy studied fine art at the Slade School in London and came to filmmaking by chance. At nightclubs in his early twenties, he was often appalled by the way some clubbers treated the bathroom attendants. It was a subject he wanted to explore, but oil and canvas in this case was too limiting a medium. He got hold of a video camera and, without training, shot a short film about the life of a Nigerian woman who looked after the bathroom in a club.

It was 2002 and *Dance Floor* won the BAFTA prize for best short film. He followed this "surprise success"—his words—with *Sister*, winner of the BAFTA best short in 2005, and *Antonio's Breakfast*, the 2006 best short at BAFTA and Clermont-Ferrand, and selected at Sundance. At the time of writing, *Dad*, made in 2006, is winning prizes from Spain to Japan, and he is working on his fifth short, financed by Sony.

It's an impressive record. Tall and slender, a former athlete, Mulloy seems almost embarrassed when I ask him to reveal the key to making a great short film.

Daniel Mulloy (DM): There's no money in shorts, so filmmakers can be experimental. I don't mean technically, with clever angles and wild cuts—that only draws attention to the process. I mean you can experiment with where you take the audience emotionally. More than a feature, where there are so many other concerns, including other people's money, short films can be intimate, personal, concise little gems that show a unique perspective, moments from someone's childhood, or their favorite food. They don't need to deal with grand subjects and are often most successful when they tackle simple themes that everyone can in some way relate to.

I believe it helps if you have something to say about the world. You can't just put a lot of emotive ingredients together—like people living in poverty, or children being mistreated, and expect to have a great film. The film needs veracity. It has to be your understanding and your connection to the material. You travel the world and there is a Zeitgeist with certain films that have an appeal to people everywhere—and all those films, in my experience, have one thing in common: they all have integrity. The films can be comic, ironic, dramatic; but it is the passion behind the story, the feeling the viewer is left with, that lifts the film. For me, this seems to be a common factor in what makes many films popular with audiences.

When Mulloy gets an idea for a new short, it is usually a simple scenario. *Antonio's Breakfast* is about a man looking after his elderly father. It could be set anywhere in the world and he tells the story from his viewpoint, a British citizen who has grown up in London.

DM: Little things that seem insignificant can be life-changing and hold the germ of a story. It is finding beauty in the mundane and expanding on it, digging into its essence. In a short film, what I try to do is explore experience, my own or other people's, and translate that experience into a brief glimpse of someone's life.

Clifford Thurlow (CT): Should films contain a message?

DM: I have tremendous respect for filmmakers who tackle difficult subjects. It's not easy and the results are often disappointing. Directors have massive power because they are able to talk to the audience through the first person, almost one to one. They should not abuse that power by relinquishing responsibility. If a film encourages debate it serves a valuable purpose, but it's not your job to spoon-feed people with your message.

CT: What is the main mistake made by new filmmakers?

DM: I think it's concentrating on style. Too many shorts look like pop videos. People get obsessed with format. They want to shoot on 35mm rather than video. It is the emotion that's captured, not what it's captured on. When you are putting something into the public arena, a film, especially a short film, should express something you think is worth being expressed.

Filmmaking should be fun and, in Mulloy's opinion, it is up to the director to "lead from the front" and make sure everyone enjoys the process.

DM: All the people surrounding the director are there to make sure his or her vision is realized. The director is responsible for how the finished film is going to play, but he/she cannot make the film without the goodwill and hard work and talent of those that he/she has chosen to collaborate with.

Mulloy in his films has, until his current production, avoided using music.

DM: **Music is such a powerful tool. It can so easily tell the audience what to feel and, if you are learning the craft of filmmaking, it seems more appropriate to stick to the language of film. It's the same with technical feats and great camera movements. They really aren't necessary and a great treat to savor for feature-length films.**

Like many filmmakers, Mulloy finds writing a new script an intense and emotional experience.

DM: **When I have an idea, I think about it for a long time; try and work out what I am trying to say. When the idea is solid in my mind, I go to the British Library when it opens at ten and stay there at the desk until six. For the first two hours it's very quiet and you can plan out what you are trying to do, then I just write the draft straight through.**

One problem he sees for first-time filmmakers is that they often take too long to make their film, and then wait too long before they make their next film; Mulloy found this himself, taking three years between *Dance Floor* and *Sister*.

DM: **Don't stop after one. Carry on making films. You learn the process by working. It is a continuing process. If you are going to be respected as a filmmaker it will most likely come from having a body of work.**

Daniel Mulloy's shorts are a masterclass in low-budget filmmaking. They can be found on the Sister Films website.
www.sisterfilms.co.uk

STOP

37 Daniel Mulloy on set (left).
Photo by Emma Critchley

38 Daniel Mulloy takes a
risk to work with children!
Photo by Emma Critchley

Jack Pizzey, Documentary Filmmaker[1]

39 Jack Pizzey

 ▶▶ P.148

A middle-aged man sits on a train gripping a bottle of Nembutal pills in his fingers. His features are immobile. He stares out the carriage window as the landscape turns gray in the setting sun.

Sitting opposite the man is Jack Pizzey. A young navy officer, he has been trained to recognize the signs of men under stress and how to deal with it. He knows, too, that Nembutal is a potent tranquillizer.

When Pizzey draws his fellow passenger into conversation, the man tells him that everything he has ever done has gone wrong. His life isn't worth living. When they arrive in London, he's going to swallow the pills and end it all. Pizzey persuades the man to seek help and takes him to St Mary's Hospital, close to Paddington Station. He is shocked to discover that as the suicidal man hasn't actually taken the tranquilizers, they will do nothing to help him.

Pizzey sits there until four in the morning trying to convince the man that there is always a solution to life's problems. The man, obviously unconvinced, puts the bottle to his mouth and swallows all the Nembutal pills. Pizzey raises the alarm and the nursing staff finally go into action: "Oh, now we'll *have* to treat him." They race the man into theater to pump the pills back out of his stomach.

Jack Pizzey was outraged by what he saw as a heartless way of dealing with a suicidal patient and, ultimately, an inefficient use of public money. During his weekend leave, he wrote a feature article about what had happened, phoned all the newspapers, and his piece appeared the following week in the *Guardian*.

Pizzey had found his calling. He was shortly to leave the navy; he joined the training program at the BBC, and has made more than 100 documentary films since. "The lesson I learned from meeting the man on the train is that you must follow your instincts and idealism," he says. "You must question what you believe is wrong—and try to put it right."

Not long after completing the BBC training course, Pizzey found himself with a camera crew in the headquarters of a major pharmaceutical company in Basle, interviewing company bosses on charges that they had organized a cartel to keep the price of the vitamin C artificially high. One of their own executives had reported them to the European Court, which had fined them, but then the drug company victimized the whistle-blower to the point where he was prosecuted for treason by the Swiss government; the charges were dropped, but the man's wife committed suicide and he left his homeland never to return. Pizzey conducted the interview surrounded by the drug company's lawyers and, when he brought the story back to London, the BBC's legal team had to go through every frame and every word before they would screen the film. Pizzey reflects: "This is grim, meticulous work, but when you believe what you are doing is worthwhile it gives you a high and you can't imagine doing anything else."

Pizzey quotes the dictum of Lord Reith, the former director general of the BBC: the corporation's mission is to Educate, Inform, and Entertain. To pin down all three, says Pizzey, requires "the talent"—a protagonist who can carry the story, and the antagonist(s) who are preventing the protagonist from getting what he wants or needs or deserves. "Writing a story is about structure and rewriting. A documentary is about research," he explains. "Spend as many days and weeks as it needs to find someone who has a story to tell, or a wrong to be righted. One person leads to another; one thing leads to another. Even if you know nothing to begin with, you learn the subject through your research."

Like fiction filmmakers, Jack Pizzey believes in the maxim: Don't tell me. Show me.

"The non-commentary documentary always works best for me; stories that the people who are involved tell in their own voice. These stories come from the heart. They have passion and immediacy," he adds. "A non-commentary documentary is more difficult, but it *shows* the audience what is happening without a voiceover *telling* them. If you do need a voiceover, it is always best to use someone involved in the story—the director perhaps. Even if you can get David Attenborough, unless he is connected to the film, the commentary will be detached."

Pizzey advises documentary-makers to do the recce themselves. "You must meet all the people you are going to use in the film. You must get to know them. If they know you, and learn to trust you, they will open up and give you what you want on camera," he says, and adds: "But when you get to filming, whatever you've planned, be open to what actually happens and how you may use the surprising and accidental."

He gives the example of a time when he was co-directing and presenting a co-production with the BBC and an Israeli broadcaster. They were on a small plane flying over the Middle East. Pizzey was sitting beside the aisle doing a piece to camera—what in Israel and the United States they call a "stand up." A passenger pushed between him and the camera, so Pizzey stopped. "My co-director was stunned: "Jack, that's reality," he told me. "You just carry on. The film is more real when it is not poised and posed to the camera."

The incident taught Pizzey a valuable lesson, which he took with him in a more precarious career as a freelance. One of his first commissions was from ABC in Australia, to make eight 60-minute documentaries which he called *Sweat of the Sun, Tears of the Moon* (an Inca phrase for Gold and Silver) covering the history and politics across the length and breadth of South America—which he did after six weeks of intensive Spanish and which served him well enough to later interview King Juan Carlos of Spain for BBC 2.

"We were filming one time in a small pueblo high in the Andes in Ecuador, when suddenly the houses started shaking around us. Everyone was shouting *"Temblar, temblar! Earthquake!"* I glanced at the cameraman; he shrugged, and we carried on filming," he says. "I had already learned my lesson from the Israeli director—you have to be open to what's happening: reality works best when it's real."

Looking back, Pizzey believes he was lucky to get on the training program at the BBC. He did bring to the course other life experiences, but what tilted the balance was that article in *The Guardian*. "I think these days, if you want to get into the business, you have to make a film. If fifty people go for a job and six of them have made a film, they are the ones who are going to get an interview," he muses.

Pizzey advises making a film of 7–10 minutes that tells a structured story with a central point, and has a believable protagonist and an unambiguous conclusion.

"We look to documentaries to right wrongs," he adds. "But it is also a pleasure and a privilege. A film is the best toy you can be given to play with. The editing process it is pure magic. When you put one image against another, you get eureka moments and that's thrilling."

For most of his career, Jack Pizzey has made campaigning documentaries, but with his fondness for the arts, he has set up Films for Artists, a company that does just what it says on the label and makes films for and about artists. **www.filmsforartists.com**

JACK'S FAVORITES

During his career, Jack Pizzey has received four BAFTA nominations and won numerous prizes for his films. In the selection below are some of his personal favorites.

- *Viva Nica!* A 50-minute film about Nicaragua's campaigning artists, writers, and singers on the barricades. Channel 4.
- *Sweat of the Sun*, Tears of the Moon. Eight 60-minute documentaries covering South America for ABC. Winner of the Australian Logie Award.
- *King Juan Carlos*. A 60-minute BBC 2 interview.
- *Hussein the Survivor King*. A 60-minute BBC 2 interview.
- *Peking to Paris*. Twenty 30-minute films following eighty-five antique cars around the planet. The History Channel and Sky and Star's Travel Channels.
- *Slow Boat from Surabaya*. Six 50-minute travelogues. A&E and Discovery, ABC, and BBC 2.

STOP

39 Jack Pizzey

PART

V

TITLE

Scripts

CHAPTER 17

Broken

40 DVD cover

Broken is a 20-minute film written and directed by Alex Ferrari and produced by Jorge F. Rodriguez. The full script appears at the end of this chapter.

- Budget: $8,000.
- Running time: 20 minutes.
- Shot: on miniDV.
- Festival screenings: close to ninety, with many prizes.
- Three hours of special features on the DVD and six commentary tracks.
- Reviewed and interviewed by over 250 international press outlets and entertainment websites.

What's the film about? Here's what it says on the DVD cover:

A gun blast, a flash of light, and a young woman awakens to the comfort of her own bed. Bonnie Clayton has it all, a great relationship, a challenging career, and the burden of a dream that grows more vivid and disturbing with each passing night. But when Bonnie is abducted by a sadistic stranger and his colorful entourage, she discovers that the key to her survival lies within the familiar realms of her recurring dream.

When Alex Ferrari and Jorge F. Rodriguez shot *Broken* as a promo for a feature, they rewrote the rule book and showed filmmakers and Hollywood studios what could be done on a tight budget with total commitment. With their 8,000 bucks and, it has to be said, a lot of dedicated assistance from amigos, actors, and crew, they shot a calling-card masterwork with the gloss of 35mm and the look and feel of a big-budget flick such as *Sin City* or *Batman*. *Broken* explodes onto the screen and through twenty nerve-jangling minutes we are dazzled by more than 100 visual effects (FX) created not in a digital post-production studio but, incredibly, on *an Apple computer*.

Dispensing with the standard 10-minute-and-under imperative, some ninety festivals selected *Broken*, including the influential Los Angeles International Short Film Festival. The filmmakers traveled the country picking up awards, networking, and selling DVDs of the film, which they show with more than three hours of behind-the-scenes footage and how-to tips from the team. As Jorge Rodriguez explains, "You have to learn that 50 percent of the creative process has to go into marketing and promotion."

Horror is one of the most successful genres in filmmaking and from the DVD extras we encounter the art of creating scars, tattoos, shotgun blasts, burnt eyes; there's even a useful recipe for making "brain matter." Just as important: there are insights into acquiring and using weapons, stunt work, the rehearsal process, and insurance. Rodriguez gives advice on producing shorts; Ferrari explains how to make DV look like film, and why shooting on miniDV can be the most economic and effective; Angel Barroeta has some useful ideas on indie cinematography; and Megan Graham goes step by step through the ways of attaining high-quality makeup special effects at little or no cost.

Broken was made by Rodriguez's Fortuity Films and Ferrari's The Enigma Factory. To date they have sold close to 5,000 DVDs through the production website WhatisBroken, Amazon.com, and at comic-book fairs, earning back the initial investment and putting this $8,000 short film into profit. Comic-book fairs? The book, *The Art of Broken,* was published in March 2007. It has 100 pages of illustrations of visual effect breakdowns, sets, on-set photographs, character designs, and storyboards by artist Dan Cregan, Ken Robkin, and director Alex Ferrari.

Broken is the perfect example of how to exploit every aspect of a project, how to push and keep pushing, and how to find new angles and give a short film legs. After making the film, marketing is fundamental: it is the gasoline that drives the car. Ferrari and Rodriguez went everywhere and wrote to everyone, including Roger Ebert on the Chicago SunTimes: a kind word from the celebrated film critic is enough to launch a thousand careers. This is what he had to say:

41 Concept art
⬛ ▶▶ P.156

42 Concept art
⬛ ▶▶ P.156

Broken is essentially a demonstration of the mastery of horror imagery and techniques, effective and professional. Looking forward to Broken: The Feature.[1]

Rodriguez is busy doing just that, developing *Broken* with the working title *Soulless,* along with a slate of feature projects, while Ferrari took some time out to take part in Steven Spielberg's *On the Lot* show, launched in spring 2007 on Fox. Out of 12,000 entrants, Alex Ferrari made the top 100, who were then set the task of making a 3-minute short from scratch in seven days, to compete for a $1 million development deal with Dreamworks.

CONVERSATION WITH JORGE RODRIGUEZ

How do you make a great short film? Rodriguez shares his thoughts.

Jorge Rodriguez (JR): **First off, you have to have a clear purpose of what you are trying to accomplish with your short. Are you doing it for experience? Is it a vehicle for a larger project, and so on. After that, it is all about the planning. What kind of budget do you have? And how can you take the majority of that budget and get it up on the screen? Most important, it's about surrounding yourself with a team of people who share your vision and desire to see your project cross the finish line.**

Clifford Thurlow (CT): **What was the development process on the script of** ***Broken*****?**

JR: Alex approached me with a short script that he wanted me to read. I liked the story and began working on the dialogue and giving it a bit of my own spin. He had a clear idea about where we were going to shoot and what we had at our disposal there, so it was just a matter of constructing the story around what we had at the location.

CT: You had lots of great actors and obviously a good crew. How did you assemble these people?

JR: The talent was acquired through open casting calls in our area as well as working with smaller local talent agencies. Over the course of two weekends, we had over 350 people show up for the parts we were casting. We just had to find the right combination of talent and attitude that worked for us.

CT: And the crew?

JR: Florida is home to some of the best and hardest-working crews around. For some positions it was just a matter of calling the people we already trusted and checking their availability. With other positions we put the word out and met with dozens of people until we found the skills we needed.

CT: *Broken* is very high-energy. Did that come from the atmosphere on set?

JR: The script was filled with tension and energy that was definitely palpable on set. Everyone from cast to crew had a level of anticipation, a kind of "How the hell are we going to pull this off in five days?" vibe. We had lots of setbacks, but the mood on the set was always positive. It was my job to make sure that everything ran as it was meant to and that Alex didn't have to worry about anything but directing the movie. We had a lot of fun and a real sense of accomplishment when all was said and done.

CT: You managed to make this film for $8,000. How is this possible?

JR: When you know you only have $8,000 you don't create a budget for your film, you back into it. Reverse budgeting is a skill every indie filmmaker learns one way or another. You can't stick a round peg in a square hole. What you've got is what you've got, and if that means you have to production-design, stunt-coordinate, and do the catering yourself, then that's what you do. You also find people who can multitask. In one case I trained our set PA to become the prop master and gun wrangler. He rose to the job and handled it brilliantly. Even my wife Michelle was coordinating craft services and supplies from her hospital bed just hours after giving birth to our third daughter, Jessica. You do what you have to do to get the job done and you don't keep score.

CT: You shot on miniDV. Is this a good camera for short filmmakers?

43 Costume design
◼ ▶▶ P.156

44 Costume design

45 Poster designs
◼ ▶▶ P.156

46 Poster designs
◼ ▶▶ P.156

47 Poster designs
◼ ▶▶ P.156

JR: The DVX100A gave us the ability to not only shoot with two cameras on our limited budget, but also to get a great look using its 24p technology. Another reason is that in the post-production process you can obtain the filmic look desired. It is a great camera not just for its cost and availability, but for its ease of use. The media is cheap, the rental is cheap, but in the final product you can get a professional appearance and, in the right hands, it can look a lot like film.

CT: So would you say the miniDV is the best format for shooting low-budget shorts?

JR: Depending on your budget and your resources. MiniDV has an easy learning curve as well as an ease of access. It is a great tool to cut your teeth on.

CT: The locations were stunning. How did you get these places?

JR: We shot on location at AG Holley State Sanatorium, one of the oldest standing sanatoriums left in the entire US. The facility is mostly abandoned, although it is still staffed and carries a census of about thirty to sixty tuberculosis patients, mostly people who are HIV-positive, who populate one private floor of the main hospital building. We were allowed the use of the entire facility with the exception of the infected floor. We negotiated a reasonable rate to rent the facility for pre-production and production, and got insurance to cover us and them for the time we were there.

CT: How long was the shoot?

JR: Five days; but just before we were scheduled to shoot, the facility, as well as the rest of South Florida, was hit by a massive hurricane. The buildings withstood the storm but suffered extensive damage: enough damage that we had to postpone the shoot for two weeks. By the time we were ready to go in again, we were informed that during the week we would be shooting, the facility would be used as a federal aid station. We said no problem, but little did we know that for the next five days we would be sharing a usually abandoned site with 200,000 people. Considering the massive traffic jams, the late starts, the later nights, and the condition of the facility, it was amazing that we got the whole thing shot in the original five days.

CT: What part did the music composition play on *Broken*?

JR: Mark Roumelis's contribution through *Broken*'s score and sound design was one that gave the project a genuine authenticity and provided the audience with a glorious feast for the ears.

CT: What advice would you give to someone wanting to get into the film industry today?

JR: Be clear on what you want to do, and be prepared to take the long way around to get there. It takes more than just talent to get somewhere in the industry. The world is filled with talented people who didn't have the balls to hang in there. Another route is to become a student of the business side, not just the creative. You need money to make movies: learn how to get it, and get to the people who have it, then dazzle them with all your wonderful ideas. Fill your quiver with as many arrows as you can, so that when the opportunity presents itself you are prepared to take advantage of it. And another thing: be kind to everyone you meet, because those people you meet on the way up will most likely be up there soon as well, and if they are not you will most certainly see them on the way down.

CT: *Broken* looks like a promo for a feature. Was that the intention?

JR: Always. It was only meant to be shown as a part of the package for the feature script, but after people saw the trailer it took on a life of its own. That is when we decided to put together the DVD and Alex came up with the ideas of all the extras for the DVD.

CT: I asked Alex Ferrari about his directing style. How does he like to work?

JR: Fast! I like to move the camera a lot. I'm a technical director so I love to move the camera and compose the shot. Every shot is storyboarded before I walk on set. It's the Hitchcock in me. My major influences for *Broken* were Robert "The Man" Rodriguez and David "screw the studio" Fincher—among others. Those guys make films their way and do it with a great amount of style and control. *Se7en* and *Fight Club* are on my top five of all time, and almost all of Rodriguez's films as well. Also, comics like *Sin City* and *100 Bullets* had an influence. They have fun telling stories ... this is supposed to be fun. If not, we would get real jobs. Also, I admire Akira Kurosawa, Marty Scorsese, Steven Spielberg, Sergio Leone, and Quentin Tarantino.

CT: The FX on *Broken* are exceptional. What hardware did you use?

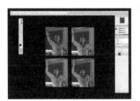

48 Screen Capture

▶▶ P.156

JR: Sometimes I look back and forget how I got there. I just play around A LOT with the tools. Many independent films do not take the time to design their stories. I did not want to fall into that trap. It also took about thirty-five hours of rendering all the filters to get the final look for *Broken* (on an Apple G5 2Gb dual-processor, with 4Gb of RAM and 1 terabyte of storage). I was an Avid editor for over six years, but when I was introduced to Apple's Final Cut Pro, I was hooked. The power this little program has is amazing. It gave me the ability to open my own post-production facility (Numb Robot) and for the price—$1,299—there is nothing on the planet that can come close. The transfer modes that Final Cut Pro has are amazing. I'm able to get very unique looks that you could never get on an Avid. It's like having Photoshop for a moving image. I also love the speed and scalability of the program. For a little bit of cash you can have Final Cut Pro editing HD footage and you can scale up at your own pace. Also, since Apple purchased Shake, we can transfer files with the greatest of ease. Bottom line: even if we get $20 million to make the feature version of *Broken*, it will be edited on Final Cut Pro ... NO DISCUSSIONS!

www.whatisbroken.com

Int. Abandoned Medical Facility (large room) Concept Art

Int. Medical Institution (Hallway) Concept Art

41 Concept art.

42 Concept art.

46 Poster designs from film stills no. 1

48 Screen capture

43 Costume design

45 Poster designs from film stills no. 2

47 Poster designs from film stills no. 3

TITLE

Broken

Story by Alex Ferrari
Screenplay by Alex Ferrari and Jorge F. Rodriguez
Produced by Jorge F. Rodriguez

FADE IN:

1 INT. ABANDONED MEDICAL FACILITY - EVENING 1

Petrified eyes fill the frame. We pull back to discover a young woman leather-bound to a vintage wheelchair, only wearing a "Dabbit" (an old Looney Toons-type cartoon) nightshirt.
A gun barrel is aimed at her. The trigger is pulled and a bullet ERUPTS out of the gun.
Every detail of the bullet's exit from the gun is seen.
Sparks fly as the bullet SLICES through the air toward its target.
Just as the bullet is about to find its victim, we slam into an ECU of her face. She lets out a HELLISH cry.

2 INT. BONNIE'S APARTMENT - BEDROOM - NIGHT 2

The woman wakes from her nightmare. Her eyes are an unnatural blue but they slowly change to a realistic brown.
Her back is soaked with sweat. She was the woman in the dream and it's not the first time she's woken up like this.
The alarm clock is flashing 3:15 a.m.
The bedroom is well manicured. Clothes and shoes are laid out for her work day.
BONNIE CLAYTON, a young twenty-something woman, gets up and sits on her bed wearing only her "Dabbit" nightshirt.
She reaches over to her night table and grabs a pill bottle marked "for sleep." Then she pulls the last pill out. She places the bottle back on the night table and we see a frame with pictures of her and her boyfriend Christian.

3 INT. BONNIE'S APARTMENT - KITCHEN - NIGHT 3

She stumbles in the dark toward the kitchen and stubs her toe as she navigates her way to the fridge. She cracks it open. Nothing but health food, soy this, and tofu that.
The light from the fridge slightly illuminates the darkened living room. She is not alone; the light exposes the boot of someone who is sitting in the living room, watching her.

She grabs the soy milk and moves over to the counter. As she is about to drink from the carton, someone starts playing a HARMONICA in the living room.
The sound startles her and she almost chokes on the pill, which she now has coughed out. She drops the milk carton and spills the milk on the floor. Slamming her hand on the counter...

> **BONNIE**
> Jesus Christ! Christian. You scared the shit out of me. When are you going to stop sneaking up on people?

She turns and sees a silhouette of a man sitting in her boyfriend's favorite chair. She grabs a towel and starts to clean up the spilled milk.

> **BONNIE (cont'd)**
> Was your trip cut short?

> **DUNCAN**
> No ... but your trip is about to begin.

Bonnie jumps out of her skin. She slips and falls on the milk as she tries to get up. She attempts to flip the kitchen/living room light on but things are not going her way.
DUNCAN is a thirty-something man who is wearing an outfit as unique as his harmonica. The man has style. He is calmly sitting in the living room with his face lost in the shadows.
Half a glass of red wine sits on the end table. He smiles lewdly at Bonnie as he notices her nightshirt.

> **DUNCAN (cont'd)**
> Long time no see, little girl.

A chill runs down Bonnie's spine. She slowly crawls against the wall toward the doorway.

> **DUNCAN (cont'd)**
> I wouldn't ...

Then she makes her move and jets for the only exit.
Before she can reach the door Bonnie is FRONT-KICKED IN THE FACE by an imposing redheaded woman, MARQUEZ. Bonnie's head is whipped back as blood flies out of her lip and mouth.

> **DUNCAN (cont'd)**
> ... do that.

Marquez sweeps her legs out from under her and Bonnie slams onto the floor. Still dazed, she looks up, Marquez is over her and the last thing that Bonnie sees is her fist.

TITLE SEQUENCE: B R O K E N

4 INT. ABANDONED MEDICAL FACILITY - ELEVATOR - EVENING 4

The sound of a BLUES HARMONICA fills the air. The door of an old freight elevator opens as a vintage wheelchair exits.
BONNIE has her arms and legs bound by leather straps to the wheelchair.

4A INT. ABANDONED MEDICAL FACILITY - HALL - EVENING 4A

Her mouth is duct-taped. She is completely unconscious as she is pushed by Marquez down a long hallway.
Once used to care for tuberculosis patients, the corridors of this abandoned hospital are now overgrown with out-of-date medical technology and bear the scars of a fire that licked through the entire facility.
Patterns of permanent shadow decorate the walls and rooms of this medical graveyard.

4B INT. ABANDONED MEDICAL FACILITY - ROOM - EVENING 4B

Bonnie is rolled into a cavernous room, where DUNCAN sits calmly with his back to her. He is the source of the evening's soundtrack.
Marquez walks over to him and whispers in his ear and he stops playing. He makes his way over to Bonnie. His face is cloaked by the shadows cast across the room. He inspects her for a moment, then pinches her nose with his hand.
She wakes with a gasp, trying to breathe air. Her eyes are still blurred from being knocked out by MARQUEZ.
Duncan speaks. His voice has a hypnotic quality to it.

                    DUNCAN
              (eerie Mr. Rogers vibe)
            Rise and shine.

He begins to circle Bonnie, walking in and out of the light, much like a tiger circling its prey before devouring it.
Now fully awake she finds herself strapped down and her mouth taped shut. As she FIGHTS for air you can see the tape on her mouth going in and out.

                 DUNCAN (cont'd)
            Relax darling.

For the first time we see Duncan's face, which is decorated by a deep scar running from the front of his cheek to the back of his ear. Bonnie is repulsed.
He notices that she doesn't seem to recognize him.

                 DUNCAN (cont'd)
            Do I look familiar?

Bonnie shakes her head, no.

                 DUNCAN (cont'd)
            Does anyone in this room look familiar to
            you?

Duncan's motley crew, six men and one woman (Marquez) in all, start to come out from the shadows.

SNAKECATCHER: A killer with Aztec roots. A tribal tattoo decorates his arm as he swings his cane.
GABRIEL: Duncan's large and silent clean-up man. An old case sits by his feet.
SHA-MON: His outfit is as flamboyant as his personality. He's wearing alligator couture as his .45 dances in his hands.
RUNT: A large gentleman wearing a pair of Uzis. The bulldog of the bunch; when cornered he usually blasts his way out of situations.
PENANCE: Ex-missionary from South America. He sits quietly behind Duncan.
UKYO: A bald Buddhist with issues. Sanskrit protection tattoos are engraved in his head. He stands behind PENANCE, waiting.
All of them give her a knowing look. Bonnie looks around and shakes her head, no.

                    DUNCAN (cont'd)
          Then we have a problem.
               (beat)
          Marquez, inform management.

Marquez nods and quickly leaves the room.

5 EXT. ABANDONED MEDICAL FACILITY - EVENING 5

The sky is lit up by lightning cracking open the dark veil of night as a storm rolls in.
Another flash reveals a MAN wearing black walking rapidly past an old air conditioning unit the size of a small space station. A FAMAS F1 assault rifle is in his hand; an impressive piece of weaponry.
He jumps some pipes and heads for an old maintenance door, which he breaks open with little trouble and makes his way into the hospital.

6 INT. ABANDONED MEDICAL FACILITY - EVENING 6

Duncan moves closer and slowly runs his hands through her hair. Then, quick as a rattlesnake, he savagely rips the duct tape off her mouth.

                    DUNCAN
          Better?

She takes in a few mouthfuls of air as her lips and mouth begin to burn.

                    BONNIE
               (almost hyperventilating)
          Please ... let ... me ... go.

                    DUNCAN
          I can't do that.

Bonnie is searching her mind for answers to this whole thing. A nervous smile comes across her face.

                    BONNIE
               (hysterically)
          This is a joke? Right?
               (beat)
          Right!

> DUNCAN
> Yeah, it's all one big joke
> (beat)
> ... and you're the punchline.

Marquez walks back into the room. She smiles at Bonnie as she whispers into Duncan's ear.

7 INT. ABANDONED MEDICAL FACILITY (OTHER SIDE OF ROOM)- EVENING 7

Moving like a cat, the man in black makes his way through the room.

8 INT. ABANDONED MEDICAL FACILITY - EVENING 8

His face turns serious.

> DUNCAN
> Thank you.

He turns to Bonnie and begins to circle her again as he pulls the harmonica out of his coat pocket.

> DUNCAN (cont'd)
> (sarcastically)
> Bonnie, right? Well Bonnie, do you know what this is?

She nods her head, yes.

> BONNIE
> It's, it's a harm ...

He cuts her off.

> DUNCAN
> Marvelous little thing really. It completely transformed the face of Western music.
> (To himself)
> Why can't I come up with something like this?

Bonnie feels that the right leg strap of the wheelchair is loose and starts to discreetly tug on it.

> DUNCAN (cont'd)
> Anyway, the reason I'm so fond of this awkward little tin sandwich is because like you, its complexity lies within its simplicity.
> (beat)
> Dozens of little reeds working together to make the perfect note.

He blows into it.

>   DUNCAN (cont'd)
>   Perfection attained ... Or is it?

He takes the harmonica and slams it violently on the wheelchair. Then blows again. This time a distorted note, sounding like nails across a chalk board, leaves the wounded instrument.

>   DUNCAN (cont'd)
>   Perhaps a reed has split.

Duncan begins to fiddle with the harmonica as he moves closer to Bonnie.

>   DUNCAN (cont'd)
>   When something like this happens, we have
>   a choice to make. One can either ...

Takes the harmonica and runs it down from Bonnie's face and shirt using the harmonica as a scalpel.

>   DUNCAN (cont'd)
>   ... open her up. Checking every ... single
>   ... reed ... till we find the broken one. Or
>   you simply ...

Pulls away from her, drops the harmonica on the floor and crushes it with the heel of his boot.

>   DUNCAN (cont'd)
>   ... replace it.

Duncan hugs her head in a lovingly sick manner and strokes her hair.

>   DUNCAN (cont'd)
>   Management is no longer concerned with
>   your ... lack of progress. Now they just
>   want "you" ...
>   (whispering)
>   ... replaced.

9 INT. ABANDONED MEDICAL FACILITY (OTHER SIDE OF ROOM)- EVENING 9

The man quietly screws a scope on his assault rifle and takes aim. We see the crosshairs on Duncan.

10 INT. ABANDONED MEDICAL FACILITY - EVENING 10

Bonnie's scared shitless.

>   DUNCAN
>   But let me let you in on a little secret.

Duncan is about to whisper in Bonnie's ear when a large man in a Kangol beret bursts through the door.

> **GUARD**
> Duncan, the men have ...

Without missing a beat, Duncan pulls out his hand cannon and nails the guard in the head. Blood squirts onto Bonnie's face as the man slams against the wall and drops.
The other associates barely move; some even smile. GABRIEL quietly opens the case next to his feet and pulls out a rubber smock and gloves.

> **DUNCAN**
> I detest interruptions.

He puts them on and walks toward the new stiff. GABRIEL grabs his feet and pulls him out of the room.

> **DUNCAN (cont'd)**
> Thank you Gabriel.

11 INT. ABANDONED MEDICAL FACILITY (OTHER SIDE OF ROOM)- EVENING 11

The man's crosshairs switch to the back of Bonnie's head.

12 INT. ABANDONED MEDICAL FACILITY - EVENING 12

Bonnie's face is SLACK-JAWED, frozen in fear. Duncan cleans off the small squirt of blood with his hand.

> **DUNCAN**
> (whispers)
> Where was I?
> (beat)
> Ah yes. Everyone here — even the fellow wearing that ridiculous little hat — came here for a reason and one reason only: to kill you.

Takes the gun and rubs the eyes of her Dabbit shirt.

> **MARQUEZ**
> Duncan we don't have time for ...

Duncan cocks his weapon, abruptly ending any objection Marquez may have had. She retreats slowly into the shadows.

> **DUNCAN**
> Now me on the other hand, I came for two things.

Duncan moves the gun slowly down Bonnie's shirt. Her fear is being replaced by anger.

>   DUNCAN (cont'd)
>   To get one last look at your eyes ...

He takes a deep whiff of her hair. His breath stutters in excitement.

>   DUNCAN (cont'd)
>   ... and to give you a little something to
>   remember me by ...

Duncan moves in close. Bonnie stops breathing and pulls back.

>   DUNCAN (cont'd)
>   ... you know, return the favor.

A smile, razor-thin, curls the corner of his lips as he begins to breathe down her
neck.

>   DUNCAN (cont'd)
>   (whispering)
>   I love this part.

Her pupils constrict and her eyes change to a vivid shocking blue.
Then, like a whip, she SLAMS her forehead hard into his face.
Blood erupts from his mouth. No one else is going to touch her tonight, not if she
can help it.
The men move in; Duncan waves them off. He grabs his mouth and wipes the blood.

>   DUNCAN (cont'd)
>   Look at those baby blues. This bitch is
>   furious. I just had to see it for myself.
>   (pause)

Bonnie says nothing.

>   DUNCAN (cont'd)
>   And now that I've seen them ...

He draws his weapon and points it right at Bonnie. That's all this situation
needed.

13 INT. ABANDONED MEDICAL FACILITY (OTHER SIDE OF ROOM) - EVENING 13

Muffled fire shoots out of the man's weapon.

14 INT. ABANDONED MEDICAL FACILITY - EVENING 14

At the sound of the trigger, Bonnie flinches from a sharp pain in her head. She feels
the action before it happens.
Just as Duncan is turning to see what is happening, the first bullet hits him in the
leg, and the other slices his cheek and rips through his ear, sending him flying into
a group of barrels and out of commission.
The bullet that hits Duncan in the ear now punctures PENANCE, standing behind him,
spits out of his back, and tears through a large mirror, shattering its pieces all

over the floor.

The darkness of the cavernous room cloaks the sniper as what is left of the crew fire blindly toward the far side of the room.

14A INT. ABANDONED MEDICAL FACILITY - UKYO DEATH - EVENING 14A

Before UKYO can react, another group of bullets puncture his body. His protection tattoos were no help to him today.

14B INT. ABANDONED MEDICAL FACILITY - RUNT DEATH - EVENING 14B

RUNT turns the room into the Wild Bunch; he aims blindly and starts to spray the room. THE MAN changes his focus and takes RUNT out. Gun smoke thickens the room.

14C INT. ABANDONED MEDICAL FACILITY - MARQUEZ PT #1 - EVENING 14C

MARQUEZ notices where the last shots were fired from and grabs an old surgeon's lamp. Faster than a snake spits, she whips it toward the action, slamming it on and exposing the cause of the evening's excitement.

She pulls her hand cannons from her back holsters and opens fire. There is no wasted movement.

THE MAN returns fire and hits the lamp, sending sparks out, burning MARQUEZ's face. She falls and takes cover behind a loose wall in the middle of the room.

14D INT. ABANDONED MEDICAL FACILITY - SNAKE DEATH - EVENING 14D

SNAKECATCHER jumps into action and starts to blast away.

THE MAN fires and shoots the gun out of SNAKECATCHER'S hand.

THE MAN is out of bullets and tosses the rifle.

He rolls on the floor, jumps up and opens his cane to reveal a sword. He whips the sword at THE MAN.

The sword just misses THE MAN and lands four inches from his face. As SNAKECATCHER is about to pull another gun from his back, THE MAN grabs his side arm and takes him out.

14E INT. ABANDONED MEDICAL FACILITY - SHA-MON/ GABE DEATH - EVENING 14E

SHA-MON comes out from behind a wall and grabs BONNIE'S wheelchair and uses it for cover as he fires. THE MAN pulls out his hand gun but can't get a clear shot.

GABRIEL comes back into the room, guns blaring.

THE MAN changes his focus and pins GABRIEL down by the gate door. SHAMON tosses BONNIE'S wheelchair over to GABRIEL for cover as he finds new accommodations.

The bullets crisscross each other. Bodies are flying everywhere. Bonnie is smack in the middle of a John Woo film.

GABRIEL slowly walks over to where SHA-MON is and uses BONNIE as cover. THE MAN is empty. He fired his last bullet. GABRIEL gives BONNIE a look. She returns the favor but also bites down on his shooting hand as he yanks it back.

SHA-MON comes out. In a blink, THE MAN pulls out two surgical steel knives, which he whips in one motion at the men.

The knives SLOW DOWN as they pass Bonnie's head; she turns and sees her reflection

and a strange insignia carved in the blade.
The knives ramp back to speed and nail both GABRIEL and SHA-MON in the neck and rip out the back. The knives stick in the wall behind them. They fall faster than Pauley Shores's career.

14F INT. ABANDONED MEDICAL FACILITY - MARQUEZ PT #2 - EVENING 14F

MARQUEZ sees her comrades go down and loses her mind. She jumps out and begins to shoot, her hand cannons raging against the weaponless MAN.
THE MAN runs quickly for SHA-MON'S gun, which is lying next to his dead body. He dives and grabs the gun, whips around and fires a bullet at MARQUEZ, who is still screaming and has just run out of ammo. The bullet flies right into MARQUEZ's mouth and explodes out of the back of her head as she drops hard.

14G INT. ABANDONED MEDICAL FACILITY - DUNCAN'S RETURN - EVENING 14G

He is now behind Bonnie's wheelchair. Feeling the coast is now clear, he starts to move toward her but is stopped in his tracks by the sound of clapping.
Duncan rounds the corner, bloody gun in hand, taunting the MAN.

> DUNCAN
> Bravo kid, B R A V O.
> (pause)
> They said you were dead.

The MAN in disgust tosses the gun aside and slowly gets up, hands raised.

> CHRISTIAN
> They talk a lot, don't they?

> DUNCAN
> Guess that makes them liars.
> But then again, aren't we all?

The legrest strap of the wheelchair is almost completely loose now. The Man gets up from the ground and walks unarmed toward Bonnie and Duncan.

> DUNCAN (cont'd)
> You can take the mask off now.

THE MAN takes his mask off to reveal CHRISTIAN, Bonnie's boyfriend.

> DUNCAN (cont'd)
> And while you're at it, set the sword down
> too, Samurai.

Christian smiles, surprised that Duncan remembered.

> DUNCAN (cont'd)
> You didn't think I'd forget, did you?

He slowly reaches behind his head, pulling out a STOCKLESS SAWED-OFF SHOTGUN from his back. As he places it down, we see the word "KATANA" engraved on the barrel.

> DUNCAN (cont'd)
> Kick it over here. I taught you better than
> that.

"KATANA" slides over to Duncan's boot. He picks it up off the floor, looks it over and cocks it with one hand.

> DUNCAN (cont'd)
> I always hated this thing. It has no style.
> No panache.

Duncan taunts Christian by placing the shotgun along the side of Bonnie's face.

> DUNCAN (cont'd)
> Much too crass to use on such a delicate
> face.

> CHRISTIAN
> Come on man, this is business. Stop making
> it personal.

> DUNCAN
> Oh, personal ...

Duncan shoves KATANA down Bonnie's shirt.

> DUNCAN (cont'd)
> ... hold this, will you?
> (pause)
> You know my therapist says the exact same
> thing.

He starts to run his hand down the gun and her shirt.

> DUNCAN (cont'd)
> ... can't let go of the past, can't move on.
> I need closure.

Duncan's breath stutters as he steps back aiming the gun at Bonnie. Her look expresses the anger and hatred that she has for this man.

> DUNCAN (cont'd)
> Which reminds me.

Without warning, Duncan fires a shot. Bonnie flinches and realizes she is still alive. But over her shoulder, Christian falls to his knees. A smile dances across Duncan's face.

> DUNCAN (cont'd)
> (To himself)
> I'm starting to feel better already.

The man's thigh is torn open and blood flows from the gaping wound. He painfully strains to get up, but can't. He looks up and sees Duncan's barrel now aimed at

Bonnie.
Duncan stands back and aims his gun at the side of Bonnie's face.

> ### DUNCAN (cont'd)
> Now, don't move. I wouldn't want to kill
> you.

A piece of broken mirror dangles and twirls, reflecting the scene. It breaks loose and falls, causing Duncan to turn for a split second.
Bonnie rips the leg of the wheelchair completely loose, and slams her body back into the chair, simultaneously pushing off with her foot. Seeing this, CHRISTIAN grabs hold of the chair, SLAMMING it to the floor.
Her leg kicks the gun out of Duncan's hand.
Christian falls over Bonnie and grabs KATANA, which is still resting in her nightshirt, and zeros in on Duncan as Bonnie sees the man's face for the first time.

> ### BONNIE
> Christian!?

Christian pumps a shot into Duncan's chest, which sends him flying back into the pieces of broken mirror. His body lies motionless.

14H INT. ABANDONED MEDICAL FACILITY - CHRISTIAN - EVENING 14H

The man limps around and places the wheelchair upright.
Her eyes widen as they return to normal at the sight of her lover.

> ### BONNIE
> But how ...?
> (relieved but confused)
> Honey, what the hell is going on?

> ### CHRISTIAN
> Shh.

Christian looks back; he thinks he hears something.

> ### CHRISTIAN (cont'd)
> We don't have much time.

> ### BONNIE
> (screaming)
> Time? What the hell are you talking about?
> Get me out of this thing!

Christian covers her mouth with his hand. He moves the hair covering her face away and looks into her eyes. They exchange a look only two souls in love are capable of.
He passionately kisses her. For her it's a kiss hello; for him a kiss goodbye.
He pulls away as he hears the sounds of glass breaking and footsteps outside come closer.
Christian limps over to the gun on the floor, which he dropped in the firefight.

CHRISTIAN

I did all I could to protect you, but now
I'm out of options.

He takes a small case from his back pocket, places a strange blue bullet into the gun and slowly turns, raising the weapon to Bonnie.

BONNIE

Christian, what are you doing?

CHRISTIAN

Trust me Bonnie, you're better off forgetting the whole thing.

He takes aim.

BONNIE

God, I just want my life back!!!

CHRISTIAN

I'm sorry honey, but it was never your life to begin with.

He fires. The strange bullet ERUPTS out of the gun toward Bonnie. Every DETAIL of the bullet's exit from the gun is seen.
Sparks fly as the bullet SLICES through the air toward its target.
The bullet RIPS into her arm; we SLAM into an ECU of her face as she lets out a HELLISH cry.

15 INT. MENTAL INSTITUTION HALLWAY - NIGHT 15

We snap back from the HELLISH cry to reveal Bonnie being injected in the same arm by a nurse. Two huge orderlies are trying to restrain her. She begins having convulsions.
We are now in a mental institution and Bonnie is a patient.
She gets pulled up from the floor, kicking and screaming. When she sees her psychiatrist, she loses her mind.

BONNIE
(frantically yelling)

Who are you? Where am I? I loved y ..!
(turns to the doctor)
You bastard! You—you did this to me!

ORDERLY #1

We were walking her back to her room and she just snapped Doc.

NURSE

We found this next to her bed.

The nurse has multiple blue pills in her hand. The doctor turns to Bonnie. She is still mumbling incoherently.

>   **PSYCHIATRIST**
>   (To Bonnie loudly)
>   Bonnie, you have to take your medicine. We
>   want you to get better.

Bonnie takes her last breath and spits in the doctor's face.
He wipes his glasses and turns to the nurse.

>   **PSYCHIATRIST (cont'd)**
>   Alright then, let's keep her sedated and
>   confined to the quiet room till this episode
>   subsides. Up her dosage until she is back
>   to a manageable level. Short of that ...

He looks back at her as they carry her off.

>   **PSYCHIATRIST (cont'd)**
>   ... I don't know what else to do.

>   **NURSE**
>   Yes doctor.

As Bonnie is being pulled down the long hallway, her sedative begins to take effect.
She makes a few last mumbles, not distinct enough to be called words.
As her vision goes blurry, the last thing she sees is a janitor pushing a cleaning
cart.
They pass the janitor, he turns, looks up, tilts his head and smiles at us. He has
a striking resemblance to DUNCAN, and you can't help but notice the "DABBIT" hat he
is wearing and the bandage on his ear.
He pulls out his trusty "TIN SANDWICH" and begins to play. As he LIMPS down the hall
the sound of HARMONICA MUSIC fills the corridor.

FADE TO BLACK

STOP

Noise Control

Noise Control is an 8-minute film written by Terence Doyle, directed by Alexis Bicât, and produced by Danielle Anneman and Terence Doyle. The full script appears at the end of this chapter.

Movies are magic. But to make the magic work, the coincidence of opportunity needs the backing of preparation.

That was the experience of writer Terence Doyle.[1]

He was lamenting the state of his various feature projects in a pub one night when TV director Peter Chapman mentioned that he could get hold of a jet plane—for free. By the time his glass was empty, Terence had made two promises: to write a feature with "the pace of *Top Gun*, the poignancy of *Local Hero* and the humor of *Withnail and I*," and to get the project rolling with a short.

49 Nick Moran

■ ▶▶ P.185

Such are pledges *in vino veritas*. But he knuckled down, wrote the short version of *Noise Control* over the coming weeks and at the Cannes Film Festival showed it to *Lock Stock and Two Smoking Barrels* star Nick Moran. The short, to quote the synopsis, is an action comedy about "a TV crew, doing a story on the problems from low-flying jets in the Welsh valleys, meeting its match in the shape of a single-parent family on the ground and a heroic fighter pilot in the air."

Nick Moran just happened to be learning to fly single-engine Cessnas in his spare time. Would he take the role of the pilot in the short?

50 On location

■ ▶▶ P.185

"Just try and stop me," he replied.

That's movie magic.

Terence, the editor of *BritishFilm* magazine, had joined the London Filmwriters' Workshop five years before to learn screenwriting. He had written several features, and sold options on some of them, but believes he truly got to grips with the writer's craft by working on the short.

www.britishfilmmagazine.com

51 Framing the shot

■ ▶▶ P.185

"You come to understand the complexity of the film-writing process by seeing what actually works and what doesn't. There are things on the page that seem funny—that are funny—but they're just not funny on the screen. On the other hand, we found humor where it had not been planned on the page but it appeared out of thin air on set," he says. "So much goes into setting up each scene and you take this knowledge with you into future projects. I now look at all my past scripts in a different light and, of course, the feature based on the short embodies everything that I've learned."

Terence Doyle's initiation into screenwriting coincided with the buzz created by the new cash injected into the lottery franchises in the UK and he has seen the opportunities for filmmakers increasing ever since. There are more production companies and, even if the number of features being made has remained static at around 100 a year in the UK, the growth in outlets for short films has been exponential.

Most commercial shorts are self-funded, and Terence Doyle had deliberately set out to write something that was commercial: "When people go to the movies they want to be entertained; they want to see something humorous, colorful, light in tone. That's what we were striving for in the short, because we wanted to keep the cast on board when we set out to fund the feature."

Top actors make short films because they like the exposure. Everyone wants to get out and work and, if it's an interesting script, they would rather be working for nothing than not working at all. "I imagine," says Terence, "the time will come when you will need a big name just to get your short film shown."

Not only actors, but technicians who work on features as the assistant to the assistant come into a short as the head of a department and finally get the chance to put their hard-earned skills into practice. Standards are constantly improving. More shorts are being shot on film stock with full lighting kit and high-quality sound equipment. "You can learn a lot at film school, but there's nothing quite like being out there and actually doing it."

52 Alex Bicât & Nick Moran
◼ ▶▶ P.185

By the time *Noise Control* was ready to roll, Peter Chapman, the man with the spare fighter jet at his disposal, was working on a new project; such is the film world. Alexis Bicât switched hats from co-producing to directing and Danielle Anneman came on board as producer. At just twenty-one, the Texan ex-model already had seven years' experience working on film sets in Los Angeles and London and showed, according to Doyle, the organizational genius required for the tight budget.

With Nick Moran already at the party, Danielle went through her contacts at the casting agents and signed up Gail Downey, Nigel Hastings, Sarah McNicholas, Thomas Myles, Daniel Macnabb, and Søren Munk. A crew of twenty-three was assembled and moved en masse to the countryside for four days on location.

53 Alex Bicât directs
◼ ▶▶ P.186

"Everyone's heart sank—including mine—when we rolled up at the youth hostel," says Danielle. "When actors and crew agree to work on a low-budget film they know what they are letting themselves in for, but it was pretty bleak and, if we'd had more money, I would have put it into decent accommodation."

Doyle continues: "The first day was the brightest April day I had ever seen. It was a miracle. Then, when we set out to drive to the airport at Kemble, the road vanished as we were consumed by fog. We weren't shooting a movie. We were in a movie. It was so bad," he recalls, "they had to send out a rescue team to bring us in. We stood around in the hangar until about two o'clock in the afternoon, when the fog finally lifted and we started our day."

54 Bicât directs on set
◼ ▶▶ P.186

After the ill-starred beginning, the rest of the shoot went according to schedule and "we began the nightmare of post." Unlike a feature, as Terence

55 Nigel Hastings

▶▶ P.186

Doyle was to learn, about half the budget on a short is required for post-production. The blow-up from 16mm to 35mm (essential for cinema exhibition) is expensive, as are digital effects and the use of blue screen. *Blue screen?*

Terence Doyle explains: "The blue screen is literally that. You shoot against a blank screen, onto which you can later project images as background. For example, you may have a couple talking in a car. You shoot that in the studio with a blue screen, then superimpose the landscape."

There were problems with the digital effects, which caused a knock-on effect in post-production. The company making the blow-up from 16mm failed to print the edge code numbers aligned to each frame (when this is done properly, it means that when you add the digital effects, you can just refer to the number). Since that had not been done on the 35mm print, the special effects technician had to do it by eye. This required him to look at every frame individually—and at 24 frames a second, that's a long and complicated business. Terence and Alexis were fortunate to secure downtime in an editing suite at Remote Films in Battersea, and editor Brad Watson patiently cut the film together during spare weekends over many months.

Just as the budget for Martin Scorsese's *Gangs of New York* doubled from $50m to $100m, the cost of making *Noise Control* went up by the same proportion—from £5,000 to £10,000. There are always hidden costs, according to Terence; even short films need end credits, and then there's the cost of making videos for festivals, the press kits and postage. When you think it's all over, there are yet more unforeseen costs: in the United States, for example, they charge around $30 as an entry fee to festivals, whether the film is shown or not.

Was it all worthwhile?

There was a reflective pause, and the sound of Doyle's fingers scratching his chin. Then his Irish eyes lit up. "Absolutely. It's worth it to see your characters transforming into people; hearing them speaking your lines. Seeing the story you wrote come to life is an enormous thrill; it's an education and, for me, many of the scenes look better than I had ever hoped."

What Terence took away as a final lesson from *Noise Control* is that the writer and director have to work closely together and understand exactly what they are trying to achieve, what each thing means, the subtext, the humor, and the pathos. The writer and director must have the same vision and a good producer will make sure they are looking through the right end of the telescope—and at the same time.

www.parent.co.uk/noisecontrol

▶

TITLE

Noise Control

A Bicât / Doyle film
Directed by Alexis Bicât
Screenplay by Terence Doyle

1. EXT – FOREST – DAY

FADE IN:

A three-man TV crew - INTERVIEWER, CAMERAMAN and SOUND MAN (nickname BIG EARS) - is rushing through a dense forest. They can't be seen clearly. Close-ups only of the branches ahead and their pounding feet as they run puffing and panting and swearing. Suddenly the Interviewer breaks out into open sunshine. He struggles to make himself stop — there is obviously some kind of drop.

> INTERVIEWER
> Whooaa.
> (He turns)
> Careful ... There's a cliiii ...

The cameraman thunders up behind the Interviewer and doesn't manage to stop in time. He bumps into the Interviewer. The Interviewer falls off screen with a yelp. The crew stop at the top of a precipice and look up, wondering where the Interviewer is. The cameraman admires the sheer drop; he holds the camera over the edge, then moves it back and forth, admiring the stomach-churning effect. No sign of the Interviewer yet.

> CAMERAMAN (O.S.)
> Nigel??? ... Nigel??? ... Nigel????

> INTERVIEWER (O.S.)
> (Ruffled)
> Will someone give me a hand?! ...

The camera whip-pans right to reveal the Interviewer pulling himself back to safety. The Cameraman hurriedly puts his camera down, facing in the opposite direction into the woods. We see a beautiful "Chinese Angle" view of nature. Dappled sunlight streams through the forest canopy and the delicate chirping of birds is set against the gentle movement of the trees. Off screen we hear the crew helping the interviewer up.

> INTERVIEWER (O.S.)
> Alright. Alright. Get off. Get off.
> (Panting)
> (Beat)

       Okay, this is good. We'll set up here ...
          (Breaks off, with a chunky, throaty,
          smoker's cough)
       ... I've got to give up these sodding
       nature gigs ...
          (More coughing)

The Cameraman has started to fiddle with the camera, which affects our beautiful view of the forest. He straightens up the shot, zooms slightly, focuses and perhaps tries a different filter.

               BIG EARS (O.S.)
       Gotta give up the fags first.

              INTERVIEWER (O.S.)
       Alright genius.
          (Pause for cough)
          (Calls to Cameraman)
       Fred.
          (Beat)
       Hey, Fellini. (sarc.)

Finally the camera jerks around from the forest to focus on a full body shot of the Interviewer, an ageing media "still-trying-to-be-star" looking ridiculous in the latest tracksuit.

              CAMERAMAN (O.S.)
          (Faking Italian accent)
       Pleasea, you cana calla me Fedrico.

The camera crash-zooms in on Interviewer's face to focus and crash-zooms out to frame him in a very media-friendly and convincing manner.

              INTERVIEWER
       Sure ...
          (fake Italian accent)
       ... when you starta bringa me zee women ...
          (Beat, normal voice)
       ... Ready, Ears. Soundcheck ...
          (Beat, exaggerated "presenter" voice)
       ... Good morning, this is ...
          (Clears his throat, tries again)
       ... Good morning, this is ...
          (Another pause, more coughing, really
          throaty)
       ... Good morning, this ...
       Okay, that's good.
          (He snaps into presenter mode)
       We have come to this pristine North Wales
       valley to report on one of the great
       evils of our time. Listen for a moment to
       the incredible silence around me ...

He pauses to allow his audience to hear, and for a moment, there is absolute silence.

> **INTERVIEWER (CONT'D)**
> (To the crew)
> Scary, isn't it, lads?

Then there is a shrieking sound in the distance.

> **INTERVIEWER (CONT'D)**
> What the? ...

He breaks off as a low-flying jet rips past, its engines shaking the microphone.

2. EXT - COCKPIT VIEW OF THE VALLEY SWEEPING PAST - DAY

> **PILOT (O.S.)**
> There is an adrenaline rush.
> (Beat)
> That's not why I fly ... the buzz, the
> thrill, whatever ... It's there but ...
> this is serious business.

Simulated Attack Profile.

3. EXT - BACK GARDEN, FAMILY HOME - DAY

Laundry on a line — white in the wind. The sound of a BOY and a GIRL, eight and ten, playing idyllically with simple toys while their MOTHER sorts clothes. The TV crew arrives and dodges through the laundry.

> **INTERVIEWER**
> Excuse me ... Hello, good morning ... Yes,
> hello.

The camera shocks the woman. She backs away and fusses with her hair.

> **INTERVIEWER (CONT'D)**
> Don't be embarrassed. You look ...
> you look...
> (Beat)
> We're doing a program on the effects of
> low-flying jets on the valley. I wonder if
> you would tell us about their effect on
> your life?

The woman looks around, confused. The kids begin to chatter in the background.

> **WOMAN**
> The jets?

> **INTERVIEWER**
> The low-flying jets. Listen, right now it
> is blissfully quiet here.

He pauses to take in the silence ... and the air is filled with shrieks as the kids suddenly start yelling.

> **LITTLE GIRL (O.S.)**
> No he's not.

> **LITTLE BOY (O.S.)**
> Yes he is.

> **LITTLE GIRL (O.S.)**
> Shut up, you're a little prat.

> **INTERVIEWER**
> Hey, can you keep it down for a minute?
> (Beat)
> Hey ...
> Can somebody get those kids? ...

The kids are suddenly quiet, smothered by the crew.

> **INTERVIEWER (CONT'D)**
> (Sigh)
> That's better. Now ...

It is beautiful again, the laundry flapping in the breeze.

> **INTERVIEWER (CONT'D)**
> (Mock enthusiastic)
> It's wonderful, isn't it?

> **WOMAN**
> What?

> **INTERVIEWER**
> (Impatiently stressing)
> The peace. The quiet. The tranquillity.

> **WOMAN**
> Are you from a television station?

> **INTERVIEWER**
> (Laboriously explaining)
> That's right. We're doing a piece on the
> impact of modern life in the valley.

The woman starts primping again.

> **INTERVIEWER (CONT'D)**
> You look er ... You look...
> (Beat)
> Now can you please tell me about the
> negative effects of these jets on your
> simple lifestyle?

The woman looks at him for a long time as if she has no idea what he means, then ...

> WOMAN
> The jets?

> INTERVIEWER
> That's right.

Another long moment of waiting.

> WOMAN
> (Finally)
> You're right, of course. There are jets ...

Again there is the hornet's shriek of a jet in the distance, growing rapidly louder.

> WOMAN (CONT'D)
> There are ...
> (her words are drowned out)

> INTERVIEWER
> (Overlapping, screaming)
> Ohhh. Not now! ...
> (Even he is drowned out)

Then the plane is past and there is silence again.

> INTERVIEWER (CONT'D)
> Ears, did we get any of that? Ears? ...

Ears shakes his head solemnly.

> INTERVIEWER (CONT'D)
> Bloody hell ...
> (To woman)
> Could you say that again, please?

> WOMAN
> I said: There are planes but you get
> used to them. They become part of the
> background. They don't bother us.

4. EXT - VIEW FROM THE COCKPIT AGAIN - DAY

More scenery sweeps rapidly past.

> PILOT (O.S.)
> I know some people aren't happy. But when
> you're doing Mach 2 at a hundred and fifty
> feet you don't start worrying about peace
> in the valley.

5. EXT - BACK GARDEN, WELSH FARMHOUSE - DAY

Close-up on the beautiful little girl in a pink dress, smiling.

> INTERVIEWER
> Can you tell me about the effects of
> these low-flying jets on the valley?

The Girl smiles beguilingly. Suddenly we hear the Sound Man make an impression of an approaching jet.

> INTERVIEWER (CONT'D)
> (Believing the sound to be real)
> No.

The Interviewer realises it is Big Ears playing a prank. He leans into shot and looks off screen left. We see his face clearly.

> INTERVIEWER (CONT'D)
> (Frustrated)
> You think that's funny?

The Interviewer walks across the shot and exits frame left; we hear a thump and the boom falls through the shot, crashing to the ground in front of the Girl, completely unfazed. The Interviewer walks back to his first position.

> INTERVIEWER (CONT'D)
> (To Girl)
> I'm so sorry about that.
> (To Ears)
> Ears. Come on. Come on. Pick it up.

The boom slowly rises up through the shot, shaking as it goes. The Girl smiles sweetly all the time.

> INTERVIEWER (CONT'D)
> Right. Going again.
> (To little girl)
> Would you say that the jets are a
> negative influence on the quality of your
> idyllic life?

The Girl has been waiting for this interview all her life and she knows how to use a camera.

> GIRL
> I want to be a supermodel. And I want to
> live in a big house in the city.

Interviewer laughs artificially.

> INTERVIEWER
> How sweet ...
> (Aside)
> Give me a call when you get there ...
> (Beat)
> But can we talk about the jets for a
> moment?

The girl pauses; smiles beguilingly.

> **GIRL**
> I want to make a lot of money and travel
> around the world and have men at my feet.

Interviewer chuckles again. Then lets out a sigh.

> **INTERVIEWER**
> But the jets ... Can we please...

There is the hornet's shriek of a jet quickly approaching.

> **INTERVIEWER (CONT'D)**
> (Continues, looking skyward)
> Oh ... for Christ's sake ...

The jet drowns him out. And he walks off screen fed up.

6. EXT - TARMAC, JET AIRPORT - DAY

The pilot approaches his jet and about-faces to speak to camera. His helmet is off, held under his arm. He is a handsome twenty-something; smiling and ingenuous.

> **PILOT**
> There's no permanent damage. We come. We
> go. A couple of seconds. Ba-Boom. We're
> gone in a flash. Who can complain about
> that?

7. EXT - BACK GARDEN, WELSH FARMHOUSE - DAY

Close-up on the second child, an impish little boy with red hair and freckles.

> **INTERVIEWER (O.S.)**
> (Tiring now)
> Can you tell us about the effects of
> these low-flying jets on your life?

A long hold on the little boy's face, as if he is never going to speak.

> **INTERVIEWER (O.S.) (CONT'D)**
> (Continues, an edge to his voice)
> Go on. Say whatever you like.

The boy pauses, as if forever.

> **INTERVIEWER (O.S.) (CONT'D)**
> Well yes, well? ...

The boy hesitates, then finally ...

> **BOY**
> I can say whatever? Really?

> **INTERVIEWER (O.S.)**
> Yes.
> (Beat, irritated)
> ... Just get on with it.

His silent face again. Again we hear the screech of an approaching jet. The interviewer gives up.

> **INTERVIEWER (O.S.) (CONT'D)**
> Right that's it. I've ...
> (Breaks off)

The jet gets louder.

> **BOY**
> (Screaming, excited by the sound)
> I want to be a pilot. I want fly a jet
> plane. And touch the stars...

The jet roars by overhead, drowning him out.

8. EXT - VIEW FROM COCKPIT AS PLANE FLIPS UPSIDE DOWN - DAY

The plane flips upside down. The landscape is inverted.

> **PILOT (O.S.)**
> You want to know what I really think?

> **INTERVIEWER (O.S.)**
> (Strained by being upside down)
> Yes. Yes. Please.

> **PILOT (O.S.)**
> You want to know where I really stand?

> **INTERVIEWER (O.S.)**
> (About to puke)
> Please tell me. Please. Quick.

> **PILOT (O.S.)**
> I'll tell you ... Up here it's you and the
> machine. In combat ...

Suddenly there is an ominous rattling sound.

> **PILOT (O.S.) (CONT'D)**
> What the?...

> **INTERVIEWER (O.S.)**
> What was that?

The plane rights itself.

PILOT (O.S.)
Pan, pan, pan. This is Blackjack Five.
I've got a problem. Engine down.

INTERVIEWER (O.S.)
Is that a bad thing?

PILOT (O.S.)
Requesting "Nearest Suitable"; over.

The landscape flashes by, but in an oblique, jerking manner now.

CONTROL (O.S.)
Blackjack Five. This is London Control.
"Nearest Suitable" Five four two seven
North. Zero six three four East.

PILOT (O.S.)
Copy that.

The Pilot looks at the cockpit indicators to see them all turn red one by one.

PILOT (CONT'D) (O.S.)
This is very bad
    (Beat)
Mayday, mayday, mayday. Blackjack Five
preparing to eject.

INTERVIEWER (O.S.)
I don't want to eject.

PILOT (O.S.)
Blackjack Five going down right now.
Altitude 500 feet and falling. 400. 300.
    (To Interviewer)
...We're gonna eject mate. Just like the
drill ... Are you ready?
    (Beat)
Ready.
    (Beat)
Now!

PILOT
Eject! Eject! Eject!

INTERVIEWER (O.S.)
Eject! Eject! Eject!

The canopy blows off and there is a sudden swoosh ... but something is wrong ...
the Pilot has ejected but the Interviewer is still in the cockpit. He holds his
broken ejection cord.

INTERVIEWER
    (Frantically)
Eject! Eject! Eject!

The Interviewer looks incredulously at the broken cord from his ejection device, which has come away in his hands leaving him stranded.

> **INTERVIEWER (CONT'D)**
> Hey!
> (Looks up)
> Come back here. My seat is stuck. Hey!

9. EXT - BACK GARDEN, WELSH VALLEY - DAY

The little boy is standing in the garden, looking skywards, frozen in horror as the jet falls toward him. MS contra-zoom of the little boy.

> **LITTLE BOY**
> Oh Muuuuuuuu...!

10. INT - COCKPIT

ECU of Interviewer's face, shaking violently with the jet. He sees the little boy through the windscreen. He utters his last words.

> **INTERVIEWER**
> Oh no, it's that family again!
> (He screams)
> Nooooooo! ...

CUT TO BLACK ... A SINGLE BIRD CHIRPING ... MAIN END CREDITS ... THEN

11. EXT - SOMEWHERE NEAR BACK GARDEN - DAY

The little boy (blackened by the explosion) staggers into a shot from a camera positioned in a tree. There is some smoldering wreckage.

> **LITTLE BOY**
> (Yelling excitedly)
> Hey ... Mum, Sis. Over here! Come on.
> Quick. The pilot's stuck in a tree ...

The little boy looks up admiringly into the tree.

> **LITTLE BOY**
> Can I have your autograph?

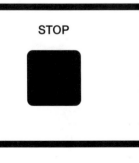
STOP

49 Nick Moran. Photo by Cleo Bicât

50 The cast and crew of *Noise Control* fake Wales in a Gloucestershire garden. Photo by Cleo Bicât

51 Director of photography Simon Dinsel (left) frames the shot with director Alexis Bicât. Photo by Cleo Bicât

52 Alexis Bicât and Nick Moran. Photo by Cleo Bicât

53 Bicât (standing) readies his stars for the next take. Photo by Cleo Bicât

54 The cast and crew look on as Bicât (far left) directs the action on the set of *Noise Control*. Photo by Cleo Bicât

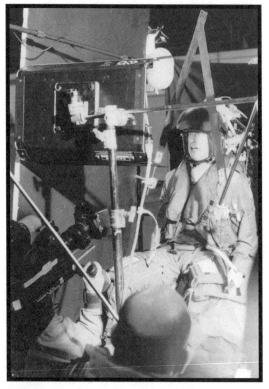

55 Leading man Nigel Hastings (center) readies himself for his final cinematic moment. Photo by Cleo Bicât

G.M.

G.M. is an 8½-minute film written and directed by Martin Pickles, and produced by Kate Fletcher.

This surrealist film, in which an Edwardian gentleman is tormented by spirits who appear through holes in his sitting-room wallpaper, was inspired by the work of Georges Méliès and was timed to coincide with the hundredth anniversary of the film pioneer's first screening of *Le Voyage Dans La Lune* (A Trip to the Moon).

Though a period drama, it makes use of the latest digital post-production techniques to create "a modern silent horror film about birth, sex, and death,"[1] and bridges time from the artisan magic of Méliès's short films to the digital magic of today. *G.M.* was made with a £15,000 grant from the London Production Fund, Martin Pickles's first film to receive formal industry backing.

It took a long time for Martin to get funding because his wonderfully eccentric films are neither dramas in the conventional sense, nor work suitable as gallery installations. Pigeonholing projects is clearly more of an obsession in the UK and, up until the time when *G.M.* started to get noticed, his shorts found better response elsewhere in Europe.

Martin came to filmmaking after studying classics and, following a childhood enthusiasm for drawing cartoon strips, he went from Oxford to art school to study fine art. In his mid-twenties he was still not qualified to do very much at all—he comes, he says, from a long line of late starters—and finally did something practical: a course in computer art which led to a job as a designer. By then, he had started experimenting with a Super 8 camera and discovered his passion for film.

With a borrowed camcorder, he made the 5-minute *Shaving*. Inspired by surrealist painter René Magritte, it shows a man getting up in the morning, putting on shaving foam and carefully shaving off his face. He sprays on a suit with an aerosol, places a bowler hat on his head, and goes faceless through his day. In order to achieve this effect, Martin and graphic designer Jonathan Mercer had to repaint the film frame by frame on computer, using the PhotoShop program, a task performed in their spare time and which took nine laborious months to complete.

Shaving cost £500 (as an artist, Martin Pickles didn't factor time in the budget); the film won a prize at the Ars Digitalis Festival in Berlin, was screened

56 *G.M.* director Martin Pickles

P.191

on Channel 4, on ITV, and at various festivals, and was acquired by Canal Plus in France for £1,600, putting the project suddenly into profit. A shortened version was taken by the Berlin metro to amuse passengers between stations in a scheme launched in 2003, giving the film an unexpected new life and commuters the chance to save their daily papers for the coffee break.

After *Shaving*, Martin stayed his course with experimental films. He shot a pair of short, commercial comedies, but climbed straight out of the mainstream, dried himself off and concluded that, for him, it was more important to make the sort of films he wanted to make: surreal, eclectic, and without compromise. He also came to realize that, paradoxically, by keeping the day job and self-funding his films, he had been taking the easy option and validation of his work, particularly at home—often the hardest market—would require proper funding, a professional shoot, trained crew and actors, and a more businesslike approach.

THE DREAM

While thinking through this conundrum, Martin happened to be reading a book about the working methods of Georges Méliès. He dreamed that night that he was at a film festival and saw snatches of a short silent film. He woke up feeling annoyed that he had not seen it all and, as if guided by the hand of Freud, jotted down what he remembered. The next day, he wrote the first draft of *G.M.* "I don't want people to think I'm completely mad, but it really happened like that, in a dream, and I knew it was the one."[2]

Martin had already discussed his ideas with Angie Daniell and Kate Fletcher at the pop-promo production company Momentum Video. They had advised him to research what funding schemes were available, locally and nationally, and to make a habit of applying to them regularly. He still doubted that a funder would back this off-the-wall project but, remembering Kate and Angie's advice, started sending out proposals anyway. One important thing he discovered was that when you have to justify why your film is good enough to deserve public money, the discipline crystallizes the concept, you start to see it from the audience point of view and, if there are holes in the script, you're more likely to find them.

G.M. is in fact full of holes—characters and objects appearing and disappearing through holes, characters seeing themselves through holes—but the point is clear. Martin knew he wasn't nursing a slick, commercial idea and put as much effort into writing the proposal and drawing the storyboards as he had previously put into the entire productions of his guerrilla films. His former modus operandi had been to get out and start shooting from the hip, but when the award finally came through from the London Production Fund, a scheme run by the LFVDA, now Film London, he controlled that urge and asked Kate Fletcher, who'd liked the idea from the outset, to nurture the project (read: Martin P.) as his producer.

While Kate began to organize the crew, cast, equipment, studio hire "and the entire universe of logistical issues," Maggie Ellis at the LFVDA worked with Martin to further develop and refine the script. "Even if the whole thing is in your head, the rewrites and discussions clarify the concept and make it easier when you get on set."

57 Neil Edmond

◼ ▶▶ P.**192**

58 Isabel Rocamora in *G.M.*

◼ ▶▶ P.**192**

59 *G.M.* set

◼ ▶▶ P.**193**

60 Tracking shot

◼ ▶▶ P.**193**

THE SHOOT

They had enough money for a three-day shoot at the Bow Road Studios. Paul Nash was brought in as director of photography, John Pattison wrote the music score, and actors Neil Edmond, Leslie Cummins, and Isabel Rocamora filled the three roles. Martin was free for the first time to concentrate on his work directing and came to realize that when you move away from low-budget productions, the specialized skill of a producer is not just advisable, but essential.

The film required a number of trick shots, including the lead actor playing two characters at the same time. With only three days to shoot, they got behind on the first two days and Martin had to work out what shots he could afford to sacrifice on the third day in order to wrap with the film complete. "Even if my film is not to everyone's taste, it has the production values I wanted and it is at least the best possible film I could have made."

G.M. was shot on DigiBeta, the tape format used in most TV production, and was transferred to VHS for the rushes. The VHS copy was burnt with the timecode reference from the master tape visible on screen, allowing Martin to select the takes and make a preliminary edit on paper with the timecode references. Editor Brian Marshall digitized the rushes using the computer editing system Discreet Edit, and made an assembly edit based on Martin's paper edit. Martin used After Effects, another useful program, for the special effects and to retint the frames.

In the editing process, they used similar effects and stylization to those pioneered by Méliès, albeit in a different form. Méliès would have had teams of people hand-painting his film. Martin painstakingly tinted his film digitally in order to get a feeling of being removed from the real world, without merely creating a pastiche.

The film, after months of slow, intricate work in post-production, was completed in summer 2001. Kate Fletcher and Maggie Ellis then had to persuade Martin to take a minute out of the center of the film to give it more pace. "I would probably not have seen the need to do this myself, but they were right, and I did it."

It required another grant to get the film blown up on to 35mm—essential, according to Martin, to give a "seal of legitimacy." Only on 35mm can a film go into cinemas and many of the festivals, which is where *G.M.* began its journey, first at the London Calling screenings at the London Film Festival in November 2001. The British Film Institute added *G.M.* to its listings as sales agent and took it to the festival at Clermont-Ferrand; it was shown at the Dalí Universe, in the old County Hall on the South Bank in London, and several more festivals across Europe. Cut to 8½ minutes, the film is the perfect fit for festival and TV schedules.

A FILMMAKER'S VISION

Drawing on inspiration from Méliès, Buñuel and the painters Magritte, de Chirico and Dalí, Martin Pickles has stuck to his own vision. He has come to see filmmaking as a multiskilled pursuit and, if you haven't been to film school, it is useful for filmmakers to bring other life experiences to their work. In

Martin's case, reading classics, studying art, drawing cartoons, and mastering computer techniques combined in a surreal way with his Méliès dream for him to find a story that Joseph Cambell would have said was always there, waiting to be found.

If you track Martin's course through the firmament, as an astronomer may track the orbit of a new star, it is his single-pointedness and a belief in his own vision that has got him noticed. When the UK TV production company TalkBack was making a series of sketches in a Victorian style, Martin got his first industry commission as a director.

He is still, however, creating shorts, animation, and new media work. He sees the short film as an art form in its own right and his style of filmmaking suits the genre.

He declares: "Short films can pursue one topic, be single minded; they can be experimental, which is hard to sustain over ninety minutes."

I caught all the enthusiasm of the perennial university student in his tone and guessed that a feature was now on the agenda.

"It's the inevitable next step. I am working on a comedy with another writer," he explains. "I have always made films to please myself and could not work on a film that I didn't completely believe in. All my sensibilities are contained in the feature, but it is my co-writer who brings me back into the real world."
www.gmfilm.co.uk/GM

56 *G.M.* director Martin Pickles. Photo by Kalpesh Lathigra

57 Neil Edmond takes to the streets. Photo by Kalpesh Lathigra

58 Isabel Rocamora in *G.M.* Photo by Kalpesh Lathigra

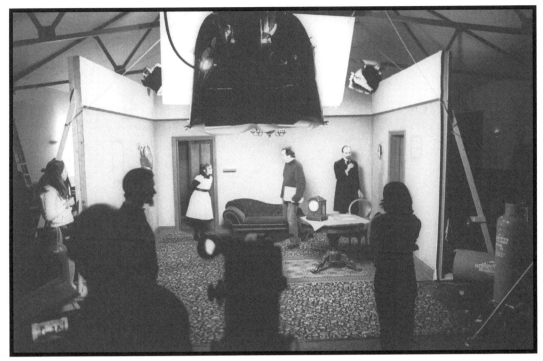

59 *G.M.* set. Photo by Kalpesh Lathigra

60 Tracking shot. Photo by Kalpesh Lathigra

TITLE

G.M.

Script / summary by Martin Pickles
Storyboards drawn by Martin Pickles

Please note: the film has no dialogue so this is merely a list of stage directions

INT. EDWARDIAN SITTING ROOM. DAY.

A man ("G.M.") sits at a table reading his correspondence. The remains of a light lunch sit in front of him.

His HOUSEKEEPER enters the room and walks over to pick up his breakfast tray. They exchange pleasantries, after which she leaves the room.

G.M. gets up for a pace around. The clock on the back wall stops ticking with a clunk. G.M. compares the time on the clock — two minutes to twelve — with his pocket watch, which reads ten past one.

He goes over to the clock, takes it down off the wall very carefully, and puts it on the table. He turns back to the wall to get the clock's key and finds, where the clock was hanging, a hole in the wallpaper (hole 1) through which a human eye is looking out. G.M. does a shocked double take and then turns back to the wall: the eye has gone and the hole is empty.

G.M. looks into the hole.

G.M. sticks his fingers in the hole: it moves slightly along the wall. He continues and pushes it right the way across the wall and eventually it passes the face of a GIRL inside the wall. She has a serene expression with both eyes closed.

G.M. looks on in amazement. The GIRL's face disappears as a shadow covers her.

G.M. tears at the hole (hole 2) until it becomes large and tattered. Inside the wall is an array of figures draped across each other, wearing the clothes of decades earlier. They all have their eyes closed and move only slightly, like figures in their sleep. The sides of the hole grow back slowly until the hole is as small as it was to begin with.

G.M. turns away in shock and flops onto the chaise longue. He thinks for a moment and notices the mirror on the right-hand wall. He looks from the mirror to hole 2 on the back wall and gets up, walks over to the mirror and takes it off the wall.

G.M. takes the mirror off the right-hand wall and reveals a much larger hole (hole 3) through which an evil version of his own face ("M.G.") stares back at him. The surprise makes G.M. drop the mirror, which lands at his feet and breaks. He looks down at the mirror, which nearly hit his toes, and as he does so, M.G. shoots out of hole 3. By the time G.M. looks back at the hole, it is empty. G.M. sticks his head into the hole. Unknown to him, M.G. is hiding behind the table behind him.

As G.M. stares into hole 3, the GIRL appears out of hole 2. She skips around the room, unconcerned by her surroundings and then exits via the left-hand door.

M.G. rushes G.M. from behind and pushes him into hole 3. He grins triumphantly at the imprisoned G.M. and places the mirror back over the hole.

M.G. prances across the room to the left-hand wall and takes down a small ornamental sword. He tests its strength and shoots a grin at the camera. He walks back to the right-hand wall where G.M. is trapped, brandishing the sword as he goes. He carefully pushes the sword into the wall just under the mirror.

As he does so, the GIRL reenters the room via the left-hand door. The sight of M.G. stabbing the wall brings her out of her thoughts and she stares at him in terror before turning on her heel and running out of the room. M.G. chases after her through the left-hand door. A moment later he reappears through the right-hand door. The GIRL is nowhere to be seen.

M.G. thinks for a minute. He looks over at hole 2 and grins at the camera.

Some time later: the GIRL reenters the room through the left-hand door. She finds the room empty but looks around cautiously. She goes over to the left-hand wall and takes down the remaining ornamental sword, which she secretes in her dress. She runs toward hole 2 in the back wall and jumps into it.

As she does so, inside the wall M.G.'s jaws slam shut, devouring her. He wipes his mouth gleefully.

Outside the room is quiet once more. The sword, which is still stuck in the wall under the mirror, is slowly pushed out and drops out onto the floor. G.M.'s eye appears at the hole. Inside the wall we see him alive but in considerable distress.

Hearing the sound of the sword, the HOUSEKEEPER reenters the room calling for G.M. Surprised that the room is empty, she looks around and sits for a moment on the chaise longue. She gets up to go out, notices the clock on the table as she passes it, and puts it back on the wall. She exits.

Inside the wall G.M. sees her so near to him, yet oblivious to his cries. As she leaves he sinks into despair. The room is empty once more.

The clock on the back wall starts to tick again. The paper on the back wall becomes stained with blood.

Over on the right-hand wall we can see the hole and G.M.'s downcast eye. A shadow falls across the wall. A blade starts to cut upward through the paper below the mirror. G.M. is revealed through the expanding gash in the wallpaper. He looks up at his savior: it is the GIRL, holding an ornamental sword.

She holds out her hand and helps him to his feet. Serenely he follows her into the room. He looks around at the back wall: it has a huge bloody gash in it and the deflated remains of M.G. lie in a pool of blood on the floor. The GIRL smiles at G.M., who smiles back, unconcerned, even amused, by the gory scene.

The clock strikes twelve. G.M. and the GIRL look at the clock and each other and laugh. They kiss.

STOP

61 *G.M.* storyboards by Martin Pickles

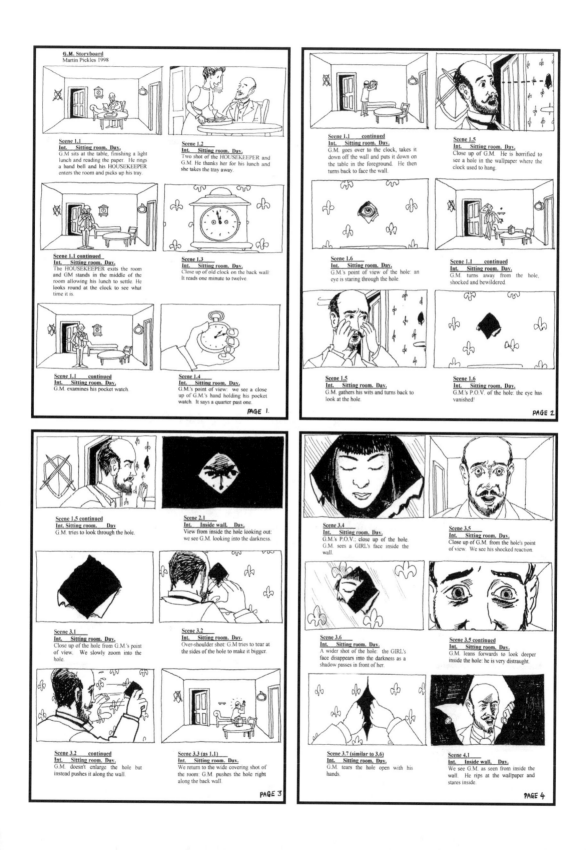

G.M. Storyboard
Martin Pickles 1998

Scene 1.1
Int.   Sitting room. Day.
G.M sits at the table, finishing a light lunch and reading the paper. He rings a hand bell and his HOUSEKEEPER enters the room and picks up his tray.

Scene 1.2
Int.   Sitting room. Day.
Two shot of the HOUSEKEEPER and G.M. He thanks her for his lunch and she takes the tray away.

Scene 1.1 continued
Int.   Sitting room. Day.
The HOUSEKEEPER exits the room and GM stands in the middle of the room allowing his lunch to settle. He looks round at the clock to see what time it is.

Scene 1.3
Int.   Sitting room. Day.
Close up of old clock on the back wall. It reads one minute to twelve.

Scene 1.1   continued
Int.   Sitting room. Day.
G.M. examines his pocket watch.

Scene 1.4
Int.   Sitting room. Day.
G.M.'s point of view: we see a close up of G.M.'s hand holding his pocket watch. It says a quarter past one.
PAGE 1.

Scene 1.1   continued
Int.   Sitting room. Day.
G.M. goes over to the clock, takes it down off the wall and puts it down on the table in the foreground. He then turns back to face the wall.

Scene 1.5
Int.   Sitting room. Day.
Close up of G.M. He is horrified to see a hole in the wallpaper where the clock used to hang.

Scene 1.6
Int.   Sitting room. Day.
G.M.'s point of view of the hole: an eye is staring through the hole.

Scene 1.1   continued
Int.   Sitting room. Day.
G.M. turns away from the hole, shocked and bewildered.

Scene 1.5
Int.   Sitting room. Day.
G.M. gathers his wits and turns back to look at the hole.

Scene 1.6
Int.   Sitting room. Day.
G.M.'s P.O.V. of the hole: the eye has vanished!
PAGE 2.

Scene 1.5 continued
Int. Sitting room.   Day
G.M. tries to look through the hole.

Scene 2.1
Int.   Inside wall. Day.
View from inside the hole looking out: we see G.M. looking into the darkness.

Scene 3.1
Int.   Sitting room. Day.
Close up of the hole from G.M.'s point of view. We slowly zoom into the hole.

Scene 3.2
Int.   Sitting room. Day.
Over-shoulder shot: G.M tries to tear at the sides of the hole to make it bigger.

Scene 3.2   continued
Int.   Sitting room. Day.
G.M. doesn't enlarge the hole but instead pushes it along the wall.

Scene 3.3 (as 1.1)
Int.   Sitting room. Day.
We return to the wide covering shot of the room. G.M. pushes the hole right along the back wall.
PAGE 3

Scene 3.4
Int.   Sitting room. Day.
G.M.'s P.O.V.: close up of the hole. G.M. sees a GIRL's face inside the wall.

Scene 3.5
Int.   Sitting room. Day.
Close up of G.M. from the hole's point of view. We see his shocked reaction.

Scene 3.6
Int.   Sitting room. Day.
A wider shot of the hole: the GIRL's face disappears into the darkness as a shadow passes in front of her.

Scene 3.5 continued
Int.   Sitting room. Day.
G.M. leans forwards to look deeper inside the hole: he is very distraught.

Scene 3.7 (similar to 3.6)
Int.   Sitting room. Day.
G.M. tears the hole open with his hands.

Scene 4.1
Int.   Inside wall. Day.
We see G.M. as seen from inside the wall. He rips at the wallpaper and stares inside.
PAGE 4

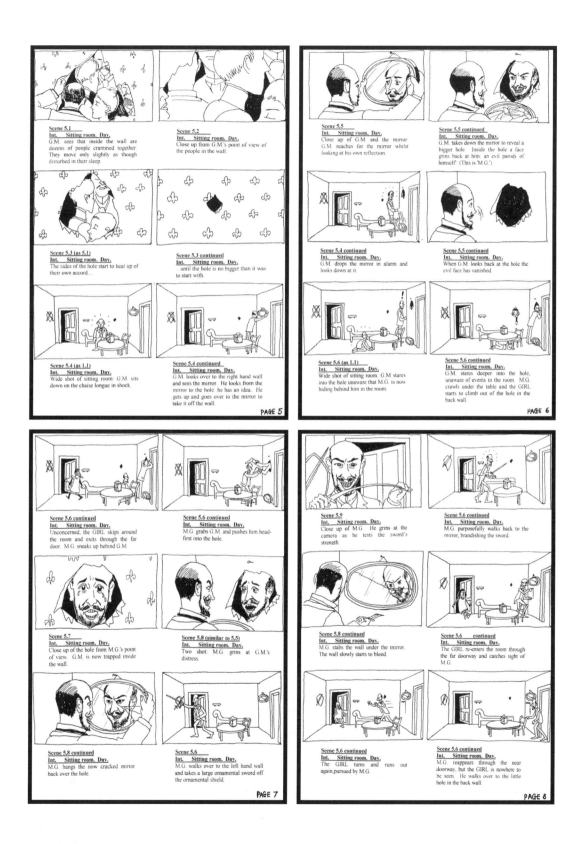

Scene 5.1
Int.   Sitting room. Day.
G.M. sees that inside the wall are dozens of people crammed together. They move only slightly as though disturbed in their sleep.

Scene 5.2
Int.   Sitting room. Day.
Close up from G.M.'s point of view of the people in the wall.

Scene 5.3 (as 5.1)
Int.   Sitting room. Day.
The sides of the hole start to heal up of their own accord...

Scene 5.3 continued
Int.   Sitting room. Day.
... until the hole is no bigger than it was to start with.

Scene 5.4 (as 1.1)
Int.   Sitting room. Day.
Wide shot of sitting room: G.M. sits down on the chaise longue in shock.

Scene 5.4 continued
Int.   Sitting room. Day.
G.M. looks over to the right hand wall and sees the mirror. He looks from the mirror to the hole: he has an idea. He gets up and goes over to the mirror to take it off the wall.

PAGE 5

Scene 5.5
Int.   Sitting room. Day.
Close up of G.M. and the mirror: G.M. reaches for the mirror whilst looking at his own reflection.

Scene 5.5 continued
Int.   Sitting room. Day.
G.M. takes down the mirror to reveal a bigger hole. Inside the hole a face grins back at him: an evil parody of himself. (This is 'M.G.')

Scene 5.4 continued
Int.   Sitting room. Day.
G.M. drops the mirror in alarm and looks down at it.

Scene 5.5 continued
Int.   Sitting room. Day.
When G.M. looks back at the hole the evil face has vanished.

Scene 5.6 (as 1.1)
Int.   Sitting room. Day.
Wide shot of sitting room: G.M. stares into the hole unaware that M.G. is now hiding behind him in the room.

Scene 5.6 continued
Int.   Sitting room. Day.
G.M. stares deeper into the hole, unaware of events in the room. M.G. crawls under the table and the GIRL starts to climb out of the hole in the back wall.

PAGE 6

Scene 5.6 continued
Int.   Sitting room. Day.
Unconcerned, the GIRL skips around the room and exits through the far door. M.G. sneaks up behind G.M.

Scene 5.6 continued
Int.   Sitting room. Day.
M.G. grabs G.M. and pushes him head-first into the hole.

Scene 5.7
Int.   Sitting room. Day.
Close up of the hole from M.G.'s point of view. G.M. is now trapped inside the wall.

Scene 5.8 (similar to 5.5)
Int.   Sitting room. Day.
Two shot: M.G. grins at G.M.'s distress.

Scene 5.8 continued
Int.   Sitting room. Day.
M.G. hangs the now cracked mirror back over the hole.

Scene 5.6
Int.   Sitting room. Day.
M.G. walks over to the left hand wall and takes a large ornamental sword off the ornamental shield.

PAGE 7

Scene 5.9
Int.   Sitting room. Day.
Close up of M.G. He grins at the camera as he tests the sword's strength.

Scene 5.6 continued
Int.   Sitting room. Day.
M.G. purposefully walks back to the mirror, brandishing the sword.

Scene 5.8 continued
Int.   Sitting room. Day.
M.G. stabs the wall under the mirror. The wall slowly starts to bleed.

Scene 5.6   continued
Int.   Sitting room. Day.
The GIRL re-enters the room through the far doorway and catches sight of M.G.

Scene 5.6 continued
Int.   Sitting room. Day.
The GIRL turns and runs out again,pursued by M.G.

Scene 5.6 continued
Int.   Sitting room. Day.
M.G. reappears through the near doorway, but the GIRL is nowhere to be seen. He walks over to the little hole in the back wall.

PAGE 8

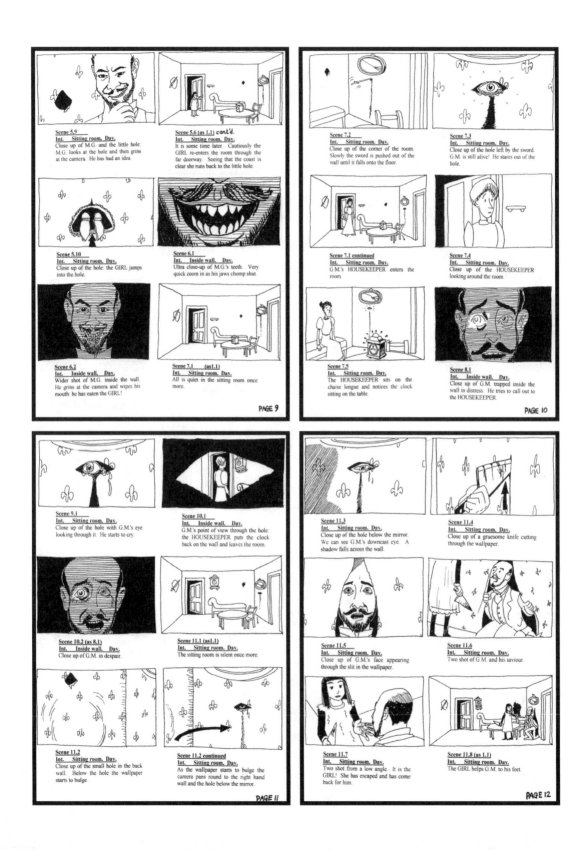

Scene 5.9
Int. Sitting room. Day.
Close up of M.G. and the little hole:
M.G. looks at the hole and then grins
at the camera. He has had an idea.

Scene 5.6 (as 1.1) cont'd.
Int. Sitting room. Day.
It is some time later. Cautiously the
GIRL re-enters the room through the
far doorway. Seeing that the coast is
clear she runs back to the little hole.

Scene 5.10
Int. Sitting room. Day.
Close up of the hole: the GIRL jumps
into the hole.

Scene 6.1
Int. Inside wall. Day.
Ultra close-up of M.G.'s teeth. Very
quick zoom in as his jaws chomp shut.

Scene 6.2
Int. Inside wall. Day.
Wider shot of M.G. inside the wall.
He grins at the camera and wipes his
mouth: he has eaten the GIRL!

Scene 7.1 (as1.1)
Int. Sitting room. Day.
All is quiet in the sitting room once
more.

PAGE 9

Scene 7.2
Int. Sitting room. Day.
Close up of the corner of the room.
Slowly the sword is pushed out of the
wall until it falls onto the floor.

Scene 7.3
Int. Sitting room. Day.
Close up of the hole left by the sword.
G.M. is still alive! He stares out of the
hole.

Scene 7.1 continued
Int. Sitting room. Day.
G.M.'s HOUSEKEEPER enters the
room.

Scene 7.4
Int. Sitting room. Day.
Close up of the HOUSEKEEPER
looking around the room.

Scene 7.5
Int. Sitting room. Day.
The HOUSEKEEPER sits on the
chaise longue and notices the clock
sitting on the table.

Scene 8.1
Int. Inside wall. Day.
Close up of G.M. trapped inside the
wall in distress. He tries to call out to
the HOUSEKEEPER.

PAGE 10

Scene 9.1
Int. Sitting room. Day.
Close up of the hole with G.M.'s eye
looking through it. He starts to cry.

Scene 10.1
Int. Inside wall. Day.
G.M.'s point of view through the hole:
the HOUSEKEEPER puts the clock
back on the wall and leaves the room.

Scene 10.2 (as 8.1)
Int. Inside wall. Day.
Close up of G.M. in despair.

Scene 11.1 (as1.1)
Int. Sitting room. Day.
The sitting room is silent once more.

Scene 11.2
Int. Sitting room. Day.
Close up of the small hole in the back
wall. Below the hole the wallpaper
starts to bulge.

Scene 11.2 continued
Int. Sitting room. Day.
As the wallpaper starts to bulge the
camera pans round to the right hand
wall and the hole below the mirror.

PAGE 11

Scene 11.3
Int. Sitting room. Day.
Close up of the hole below the mirror.
We can see G.M.'s downcast eye. A
shadow falls across the wall.

Scene 11.4
Int. Sitting room. Day.
Close up of a gruesome knife cutting
through the wallpaper.

Scene 11.5
Int. Sitting room. Day.
Close up of G.M.'s face appearing
through the slit in the wallpaper.

Scene 11.6
Int. Sitting room. Day.
Two shot of G.M. and his saviour.

Scene 11.7
Int. Sitting room. Day.
Two shot from a low angle. It is the
GIRL! She has escaped and has come
back for him.

Scene 11.8 (as 1.1)
Int. Sitting room. Day.
The GIRL helps G.M. to his feet.

PAGE 12

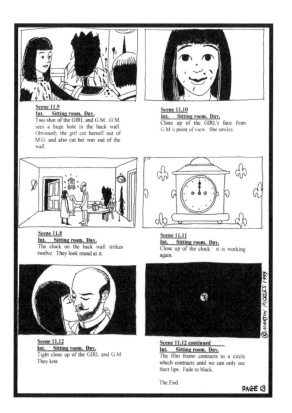

Scene 11.9
<u>Int.</u>   <u>Sitting room. Day.</u>
Two shot of the GIRL and G.M.. G.M.
sees a huge hole in the back wall.
Obviously the girl cut herself out of
M.G. and also cut her way out of the
wall.

Scene 11.10
<u>Int.</u>   <u>Sitting room. Day.</u>
Close up of the GIRL's face from
G.M.'s point of view. She smiles.

Scene 11.8
<u>Int.</u>   <u>Sitting room. Day.</u>
The clock on the back wall strikes
twelve. They look round at it.

Scene 11.11
<u>Int.</u>   <u>Sitting room. Day.</u>
Close up of the clock: it is working
again.

Scene 11.12
<u>Int.</u>   <u>Sitting room. Day.</u>
Tight close up of the GIRL and G.M.
They kiss

Scene 11.12 continued
<u>Int.</u>   <u>Sitting room. Day.</u>
The film frame contracts to a circle
which contracts until we can only see
their lips. Fade to black.

The End.

PAGE 13

CHAPTER 20

Room Eleven

Room Eleven is a 15-minute film written by Eoin O'Callaghan, directed by Clive Brill, and produced by Tom Treadwell and Maureen Murray. The full script appears at the end of this chapter.

Room Eleven is a horror pastiche where the slaughter of an innocent child may or may not have occurred and a Hitchcockian twist provides the essential intake of breath that comes with the unsettling ending. Here the dead return, not as zombies revived by radiation, as in George Romero's low-budget *Night of the Living Dead*, but as an obsessive memory that moves as if by osmosis between the minds of the principal characters.

At fifteen minutes, the film breaks the ten-and-under barrier that is self-imposed by producers faced with the usual twins of evil: cash constraints and an eye for the bite-sized time slots in typical festival and broadcasting schedules.

These considerations were secondary in green-lighting *Room Eleven*. Pacificus Productions was in the process of developing a horror script with Clive Brill attached to direct, and needed to show potential backers that their established radio, TV, and theater director could leap the gap to a feature.

The production company dropped £30,000 into the kitty and engaged Maureen Murray to make it happen. After ten years of working with *enfant terrible* Ken Russell and another ten as an independent producer, Maureen had the web of friends and favors needed to bring in a crew of experienced technicians, hire the equipment, catering, makeup and wardrobe, and shoot in five days a short film with the feeling and style of a feature. Impossible?

Maureen's answer: "It's like skiing blindfold. I wouldn't recommend it, but yes, it's possible."[1]

Maureen began where the process always begins: with the script. Working closely with writer Eoin O'Callaghan, she helped trim off the fat and encouraged the writer to ensure that every word and gesture carried its weight. She explains: "Writers often resist this—their darlings cast into the abyss—but when the job's done and you read through the new draft, it always reads better."

With the script more sharply in focus, director Clive Brill had to be convinced that the very scene he cherished most, where one of the characters throws herself out of a window, needed a hard cut from her climbing up on the sill to the body lying spread-eagled on the ground below: just as dramatic, if less spectacular, and a whole lot of saving in terms of time—the most expensive commodity on set. On a feature, it is normal to get about 2½ minutes of cut and finished film a day. On *Room Eleven*, they were aiming to get at least 3 minutes a day and still maintain feature quality.

Another crucial decision was to hire Roger Tooley and his Steadicam for a day. This 80lb piece of equipment, which straps onto a body harness, and looks a lot like a military flamethrower, can chase through gardens and upstairs, as ghosts are wont to do, and prevents the director of photography from having to roll over miles of track on a dolly. Garrett Brown had developed this gyro-stabilized camera for the film industry and when Stanley Kubrick tried it out in 1977, he discovered that the operator could "walk, run, and climb stairs while retaining a rock-steady image."[2]

Kubrick had just purchased Childwick Bury, a remote manor house in rural Hertfordshire, and tested both the camera and its inventor to their limits on *The Shining*: the story of a man coping with writer's block. Kubrick wanted the Steadicam to do things it had never done before and Brown was employed to make it possible. "I realized by the afternoon of the first day's work," Brown was to observe phlegmatically, "that here was a whole new ball game, and that the word 'reasonable' was not in Kubrick's lexicon."[3] It is probably why Kubrick's films remain memorable and why the camera movements envisaged for *Room Eleven* were inspired by *The Shining*.

Like all good ghost stories, the script required a gothic mansion with turrets, towers, and macabre gargoyles for intermittent close-ups and reaction shots: not clichés but de rigueur for the genre. First assistant director (first AD) Simon Hinkley had become attached to the project and he recalled just the place: Chenies Manor House, a Tudor pile that began life as a settlement mentioned in the Domesday survey of 1086 and where "the sepulchral footsteps of a lame man are occasionally heard on the staircase." The lame man is said to be Henry VIII, who visited the house with Katherine Howard, the fifth queen; she was having an affair with royal aide Thomas Culpepper at the time, so haunting footsteps are hardly surprising.

Chenies is open to the public from spring until fall and the present owner, Elizabeth MacLeod Matthews, agreed to allow the house to be used for the shoot with a generosity that extended to her taking part as an extra in the dining scene. I do not know who suggested this, but can safely assume it was Maureen Murray, who knew I was writing this book and called to suggest that I fill another of the vacant seats at the table.

With the cast, extras, and crew in place, Maureen began calling hire facilities for equipment and film stock. There had been a surge of projects green-lit at the same time, but having brought in the bucks on numerous features, Maureen used her long-standing contacts to acquire everything needed for the five-day shoot at about a quarter of book price. "You always have to bargain with the hire companies. No one pays list price and, with a short film, they tend to be generous," she adds. "There was the usual Friday frenzy and everything finally arrived at the last minute."

I was able to observe how the budget is stretched from my point of view as an extra, and discovered that the crew were working that week for nothing, or next to nothing, for many diverse and complicated reasons: a gaffer wanted to partner with a particular director of photography; a third assistant director got the chance to be a second assistant director; assistants in set design, wardrobe, and makeup graduated to heads of department; camera loaders and focus pullers exchanged jobs, and assisted the sound man by holding the boom, or the props department by sticking something onto something. The film set is hierarchical, the master in each department taking on acolytes— much like teachers in Eastern philosophy—and training them to one day replace him.

On a short film, everyone pitches in, scurrying around with determined expressions and silver wheels of gaffer tape hanging from their belts. There are two things that hold the film industry together: gaffer tape and networking— who you know (as in most fields) as important as what you know, the result being an odd blend of the egalitarian and nepotistic. When we broke for lunch on *Room Eleven*, Tom Treadwell queued up in the biting cold for his chicken green curry and rice, the same as everyone else.

Another reason for taking on a short film is that top technicians use the opportunity to experiment. "It's like going back to film school and being tested," says director of photography (DOP) Philip Robertson. "You don't have this lens or that piece of equipment—so what are you going to do about it? And what you do is make do. It's good not to become too spoilt. On a short film resources are scarce so you have to stretch yourself and make things work."

The DOP has an assistant, camera loader, and operator, each with his own vital functions and serving the long apprenticeship that leads to becoming a director of photography. The DOP will often be asked to choose the gaffer and grips because the producer knows that when people have worked together before, they have, like formation dancers, learned how to move in harmony.

A producer or director will often contact a DOP because they admire the lighting and camera work on a particular film. It should not be forgotten that, experimentation aside, with *Room Eleven* being shot with high production values, the crew and cast would have, at the end of that week, a further credit, a valuable showreel, and an extended loop on their web of industry contacts.

Philip Robertson learned long ago that some directors want you "to light up and shut up." Others, he adds, want a little bit more, and his calm presence on set was ideal for Brill's debut. They discussed shots and tried alternatives, listened to suggestions from first AD Hinkley, and bowed always to Brill's final decision. Glenda Jackson once told a *Guardian* interview at the National Film Theatre on London's South Bank that a good director listens to everyone— "unlike a politician." It's an unwritten law: the director's always right, even when he's wrong.

Roger Tooley puts it another way. "With inexperienced directors, you are walking a tightrope. Some are arrogant, but most ask what you think, and when they do, you can insert your own artistic vision, which is what it's all about." He adds: "As a cameraman, you have to extract the shot the director wants and, if they are new to the game, you have to understand what it is they are trying to achieve when they don't actually know how to achieve it."

It is the independence of operating his own Steadicam that attracts Tooley, but the real world for a cinematographer he sees is in "the green eye of an Arri 35mm camera," and that's the work he prefers. He describes the film business as an addiction worse than any drug. Once you start, you can't stop. He spent two months working on a French film set in the desert. There were sand storms on a daily basis, the hours were long, he hated every minute he was there—and looked back with nostalgia the moment the plane touched down back at London's Heathrow Airport.

"You would think that a big-budget film would be more organized, but that's not the case," says Tooley. "On a short film you have to be organized, and after the intensity of working on a feature, there's nothing like the close atmosphere and the sense of working as a team you get on a short."

COSTUME

I had joined the team a few days before on a bleak, rainy Wednesday when Maedhbh McMahon arrived like a glimpse of sunshine with sparkling eyes, a shooting script under her arm, and a camera in her bag. A quick kiss on the cheek and she was bounding upstairs to poke around in my wardrobe. She pulled out various shirts and decided on pale blue, some fawn cargo pants, brown docksiders and a light jacket with a faint check. She ummed and aahed over the jacket and took some photo stills to show the director. My big scene was being shot in a room rich in patterns, so the cast was being dressed in solid colors.

As the costume designer, Maedhbh (pronounced Maeve) had been poking into quite a few wardrobes during the hectic days prior to shooting. She had worn her heels flat walking around Camden Market and had popped into the National Theatre's warehouse in Brixton in search of a 1960s outfit to be used in the flashback sequence. Renting from hire houses isn't cheap—anything from £60 per week per costume—but the National does special deals for budget filmmakers.

Maedhbh starts out by breaking down the script in order to relate the costumes to the characters and figures out which costumes are going to be needed for each day's shooting. As films are not shot chronologically, all the costumes have to be ready in case the shooting schedule changes. Sometimes the director may decide a character doesn't look right in a certain color; it throws out the entire design "and everyone," says Maedhbh, "ends up running around like headless chickens."

When the budget permits, the costume designer will need at least two sets of clothes for each character, but even that is rarely sufficient. If a scene is shot in pouring rain, a dry jacket becomes wet, and while the actor wears the spare costume for the second take, the wardrobe department is anxiously drying everything with a hairdryer ready for the third. If a scene requires characters to wade through mud, the problem is easy to imagine—more "headless chickens."

And then there's the nightmare of squibbing—the bloody patches that explode when characters are shot and, of course, it looks far better on a nice crisp white shirt. In gangster movies and war films, the costume department spends all night in the laundry like a cleanup party for the mafia.

Are there any tricks to the trade?

Maedhbh McMahon would only give away two: new clothes are soaked in cold tea to take out the stiffness and age them; and that by the end of a film, costumes are held together by safety pins and gaffer tape. "What the eye can't see, the director's not going to worry about."

Maedhbh began her career after studying art history and spent five years working as a milliner. She helped make props as an assistant on *Captain Corelli's Mandolin*, the big-budget Nick Cage/Penelope Cruz feature shot in Greece, and moved straight on to making hats for the extras in the *Harry Potter* films. "To become a costume designer it is important to make contacts," she says. "I was lucky because there were seven different designers working on *Captain Corelli*. When I returned to London, they were all preparing different films and I was offered work straight away."

Even though she now has wide experience on features and TV drama, Maedhbh enjoys the intimacy of short films. "The atmosphere is always very friendly," she says, echoing Roger Tooley, "and you get this nice feeling that you are working as a team."

THE SHOOT

The following day I received a four-page fax from production manager Sam Holt with directions to Chenies, a map, and final instructions: wear warm clothes. I understood why as we approached the house. Horses were galloping through the low-lying mist clinging to the fields and the brick chimneys and towers had the look of enormous props below the leaded vault of the sky. It only needed a flash of lightning and we would have been in a Dracula movie. I was brought down to earth by the piquant, early-hour smell of frying bacon.

It had just gone seven and the caterers were serving robust portions of egg, bacon, sausages, hash brown potatoes, and beans. "Heart attack on a plate," said the first AD, leading me and my laden dish from the cold courtyard and into the dining room where there were urns of coffee, boxes of cereal, and plates of Danish pastries. It was Tuesday. The crew had worked a solid twelve hours the previous day and everyone was stoking up for the day ahead. Like an army going into battle, a film crew marches on its stomach. In fact, as Simon Hinkley pointed out, when the film business was reviving after the Second World War, a large number of sergeants major joined the profession as first assistant directors.

It was easy to see why as Hinkley managed the schedule, barking out orders to the crew, and protecting his officers (the director and DOP) while they considered performance and the visual realization of Eoin O'Callaghan's script.

THE FIRST ASSISTANT DIRECTOR

The first AD's role is to ensure that the director's vision is accomplished with the minimum of fuss or delay. He will make sure the extras are ready when they are needed; he'll tell makeup to bring a shawl for the scantily clad actress to keep warm between takes. If a horse is going to be sent galloping across the misty fields, he'll be behind the groom making sure the beast is saddled and biting at the bit. A good first AD—and that's why Simon Hinkley was brought into *Room Eleven*—will see problems before they happen, and stop them happening. It is up to him, finally, to see that the director gets through his day's schedule and is prepared for the next day. In this respect, the assistant director also has one eye on the money; if a film does fall behind, he's likely to get the blame.

After the first AD has ensured that everyone is ready for a take, on set he directs the extras and controls crowd scenes. While the director is concentrating on his leading players, the first AD must capture the same vision from the rest of the cast and, in this way, he is in training for that day when (and if) he wants to move up the greasy pole. The first AD is assisted by a second AD, who runs around on the first AD's instructions and fills out the production reports with the aid of the script supervisor's notes. The first AD needs eyes in the back of his head: the second AD is that pair of eyes.

After breakfast, I watched Roger Tooley, strapped into his Steadicam, running through the drifting mist among the pruned rose bushes in the garden, capturing the movements of the unseen poltergeist. Andrew Ellis, another extra, had turned up with a camera and was quietly wandering around the set taking photo stills. Sisters Helena and Lottie Rice, two more extras, had skived off school and were wisely using the day to do some exam revision. An extra's day is long and, if directing is death by a thousand questions, for bit-part players it's death from waiting.

MY SCENE

It was almost noon when Simon Hinkley finally rounded us up, rushed us through makeup and readied Andrew Ellis, Helena, Lottie, and myself for the dining scene. The skyscraper-tall American producer Tom Treadwell sat at the head of the table and Elizabeth MacLeod Matthews appeared from the warren of rooms at Chenies to join us.

We sat sipping apple juice from crystal glasses and imagined—with little success on my part—that it was Chardonnay, and invented *polite* conversation as we waited for Avril King, our host. We turned *with courteous interest* on hearing her voice, but the moment she entered, she was hurrying out again, distressed by the vision she saw, though it was not we extras. We now looked suitably astonished—so astonished, in fact, that Clive Brill called a quick cut and we did it all again, with slightly less awe.

The scene was repeated several times until Clive and DOP Philip Robertson both nodded judiciously, a quiet understanding reached between them, and the process was repeated with Celia Barry floating through the dining room, a ghostly presence all in white, unseen by us, but terrifying for Avril King.

We controlled our gasps, looked surprised rather than shocked, and in little more than an hour the two twenty-second scenes were in the can. While the grips started dismantling the kit, we followed the smell of curry out to the parking lot and stamped our feet as we queued before the catering van. It was lunchtime. I was starving—a big breakfast always does that—and I sat down with Maureen Murray, curious as to why she was producing a short film, her first, after being involved in various capacities with more than twenty features. "I wanted to work with the writer and director," she answered without hesitation. "Eoin O'Callaghan and Clive Brill have a strong synergy between them and this was an opportunity to see them in action. Often you are invited to work on a project that has already started; it's like a moving train. This one was waiting at the station." She continued, warming to the metaphor: "Often, the rails have already been laid and you know the train's going to derail before it gets to the next station. On *Room Eleven* I had the chance to get in at the beginning and set the film up properly. Keep it on track."

For Maureen, the most important aspect of a short film is preparation. The producer must ask two key questions at the outset: "Why are we making this film?" and "What is the market for it?" If both questions can be answered positively, it is then essential not to compromise when it comes to finding crew, hiring equipment, and casting experienced players, in this case the well-known actors Anton Lesser, who plays the psychiatrist, Susan Brown, as Avril King, and Poppy Miller in the dual roles of Sophie Calder and Celia Barry.

Maureen states: "Making a short film shouldn't be really that different from making a feature. You need to keep everyone involved, from the runner to the star, and set up a thoroughly professional level of production."

THE DIRECTOR

A sympathetic and flexible editor was needed to allow director Clive Brill to immerse himself in the editing experience. Maureen signed up Xavier Russell, who has both the quick-turnaround flair fundamental to television, and the more measured proficiency brought into 35mm features. Even from rough cut to fine cut, a few nips and tucks were required and Xavier, she knew, had the artistic and technical skills, as well as the understanding of how to achieve the pace and character development visualized by the director.

Clive was completing the process when I called to ask him about his experience of directing *Room Eleven*. This was his response:

The first thing that hits a new director is the sheer number of aspects of the film he has to take responsibility for while simultaneously respecting the art of those he has chosen to work with. Actors will give you a whole range of performances you hadn't necessarily thought of; learning how to shape, accept and sometimes reject what they have to offer is key. But from the script up, everyone and everything is offering you an almost bewildering range of choices. The budgets on short films are tight, so you simply don't have the luxury (as in, say, theater or radio) of trying out quite a few things before committing to a decision. It suddenly hits home that decision-making—from placement of props to choice of wigs, placement of camera, and interpretation of lines—requires a rapid and committed response.

Looking at the rushes, I can see all the places where I allowed my judgment to be slightly compromised by being focused on something else I thought more important. Watching a scene unfold on a monitor requires a hundred eyes. How's the frame? How was the move? Does the color of the picture behind draw the eye away from the actor? Is the camera moving in a way that organically complements the scene? Above all—are you telling the story, and making the audience understand the way you want them to?

It is impossible to say how closely the finished product resembles the initial picture in your mind. The dreams I had before I started shooting were a mixture of

interpretation of script—other film moments I had seen—and knowledge of what I thought the actors and key crew might bring to the set. But inevitably nothing is quite as envisioned. A new, fresh, sometimes alarming perspective is flickering before me.

The editing process is like a new buzz of electricity after the film is exposed. All this mass of material sometimes appears limiting. But the joy of working with a new pair of eyes—and amazing Avid technology—suddenly gives you myriad choices you hardly dared suspect were there. More choices equals more decision-making. Of course ...

I had always known, right from the beginning of my career in radio, that sound played a hugely significant role in filmmaking. (I mean the combination of FX, speech, and music.) A few days before the final dub we have a locked-off picture; with luck it has the best performances and the most imaginatively edited version of the material we shot. And yet—the music's not on, the well-placed shut door is unheard—even the speech is woolly. I won't know if the film's any good until the final sound effects are added. And I feel instinctively that, without sound, the pictures will never completely work. I think like all directors I wish I'd had four times the shooting time I was given. To me, every scene shouts a missed camera angle, a lost CU, a slight mis-emphasis, a head turned a fraction too far. I pray the audience doesn't notice.

The whole experience has confirmed to me what I always suspected. With all the frustration of never being completely in control of everything—of always feeling that the picture might slip away from one's grasp—of hoping that the art at the end will justify the process of getting there—it's the most exhilarating job on the planet.

START

▶

TITLE

Room Eleven

Screenplay by Eoin O'Callaghan
Directed by Clive Brill
Produced by Tom Treadwell and Maureen Murray

Immense pillars topped with stone cherubs support a distinctive wrought-iron gate, leading onto A GRAVEL DRIVEWAY. We follow the driveway around to the right.
CU Of cherub.

EXT. MAYFIELD HOUSE, ENTRANCE AND GRAVEL PATHWAY. EVE

A GATE leading onto the garden. Through this we discover a second GATE — which leads us past the nursery garden and which sweeps up to a gloomy TUDOR PILE with hooded eaves and heavy with ivy. It is forbidding and uninviting - a Mervyn Peake drawing.
The front door creaks open and yields to black. O/S we hear a baby's insistent CRYING.
CU Of cherub.

INT. MAYFIELD HOUSE. EVE

We travel along a corridor and into the main Reception area. This in turn leads onto an anteroom and then a dining room. Five GUESTS are seated for dinner. We pass them and swing hard right into a corridor, past a sitting room with another guest, and up a spiral staircase. Establish: photos of boy and girl and yellow cross on window of the stairwell.
Now on to the upper floors. Paneled corridors lead left and right. We head to the left past the tapestry room. The crying MORE SHRILL now. Straight ahead is ROOM 11 — an ornate bedroom. We enter. In the corner of the room a small wooden door stands ajar.
CU Of cherub.

INT. ANTEROOM & ARMORY. EVE

We follow the source of the crying up some stairs.
Through a small anteroom to a long wooden corridor: the armory. Through the gloom at the end we pick up SOPHIE CALDER, 30s, by a window — her face bleak and tear-strewn. A bottle of TRANQUILIZERS lies half spilled on the table at which she is seated. In another corner is a CRIB.
The baby's crying is now unbearable.
ANGLE ON the anguished face of SOPHIE as she hauls herself to her feet. She almost

sleepwalks to the crib.
She takes THE PILLOW from the cot and without emotion places it over the baby's mewling mouth.
HEART-THUMPING exertion fills SOPHIE'S face as she presses downward.
At last THE NOISE CEASES. There is a moment of absolute calm.
SOPHIE walks to the window and presses her hands against it.

EXT. MAYFIELD HOUSE. EVE

PU shot from EXT below.
Sophie pressing against the window. Is she going to jump?

INT. ARMORY. EVE

ANGLE ON Sophie as she turns back to face the room and catches sight of herself in the mirror beside the crib.
The mirror smashes in a tremendous explosion of sound.

INT. ARMORY. EVE

POV from the window.
Sophie's broken body on the gravel below.

EXT. HOUSE. EVE

POV the ground.
Sophie's broken body.

INT. HARLEY ST. OFFICE OF THERAPIST PAUL LAVELLE, 47. DAY

SOPHIE sits opposite LAVELLE in a leather chair. She looks stricken.
LAVELLE is lean and intellectual, a man born to listen.

> **LAVELLE**
> (Gently prompting)
> And?

> **SOPHIE**
> (Nonplussed)
> That's it. That's all there is.

> **LAVELLE**
> Do you think you killed the baby?

> **SOPHIE**
> Yes. Of course.

> **LAVELLE**
> (Pressing her)
> And why do you think you did that?

Silence.

> **LAVELLE (CONT'D)**
> Might it have something to do with the termination?

> **SOPHIE**
> (Losing patience)
> Look,I know *why* I keep having this dream. I just want it to stop.

LAVELLE picks up SOPHIE's file.

> **LAVELLE**
> When did you last have a holiday - I mean a complete break from work?

> **SOPHIE**
> I haven't the time.

> **LAVELLE**
> Don't you and ... er ... Danny get out of London occasionally?

> **SOPHIE**
> Danny's not around any more ...

Silence.

> **LAVELLE**
> If I were to recommend a quiet country house, where you could take time alone, read a few books, walk in the fields, what would you say?

> **SOPHIE**
> I'd be bored out of my brain.

LAVELLE sighs.

> **LAVELLE**
> Let some air at the wound, Sophie. Make some space. Will you at least think about it?

He hands her a card with the legend:

MAYFIELD HOUSE — COUNTRY HOUSE RETREAT. PROP: AVRIL KING.

> **SOPHIE**
> Is this one of those Harley Street scams where the analysts get a percentage on referrals?

> LAVELLE
> You've been working in the media too
> long.

He rises and she takes the card.

> SOPHIE
> I'll think about it.

As the door closes behind her, LAVELLE experiences a flash image of SOPHIE SMOTHERING A CHILD.

RESUME SCENE 2.

Shocked at the vividness of this image, he puts his head back in his chair and shuts his eyes.

FADE OUT.

EXT. THE A1. SOPHIE'S CAR. DAY.

Up and past.
She passes a sign for the North.

INT. SOPHIE'S CAR. DAY

Angle on SOPHIE driving intently. The rain beats down on the windscreen.
She punches out LAVELLE's number on her hands-free mobile.

INT. LAVELLE'S OFFICE. DAY

Lavelle's phone buzzes and he picks it up.

> LAVELLE
> Hello. Paul Lavelle.

INT. SOPHIE'S CAR / LAVELLE'S OFFICE. DAY

We cut between the two:

> SOPHIE
> (Jokily)
> Hi. I wanted you to know I'm on my way to
> your "country house retreat."

> LAVELLE (O.S.)
> Hey. Good for you.

> SOPHIE
> It's not a health farm, is it?

> LAVELLE
> God, no. Guaranteed heart attack on a plate.

> SOPHIE
> Great; soon I'll be clinically depressed *and* overweight.

> LAVELLE (O.S.)
> You are not clinically depressed.

> SOPHIE
> (Sarcastic)
> Right, I forgot. I'm just having bad dreams ...

> LAVELLE
> Sophie. Stop it. Relax.
> I'll talk to you next week.

She ends the call and drives on through the lashing rain.

FLASHBACK TO SC. 1:

As the windscreen wipers deal with the rain, each wipe presents SOPHIE with a quick succession of flashbacks to her dream:
ROOM 11, THE BABY, THE PILLOW pressing down.

RESUME SC. 5: SHE SHUTS HER EYES ON THESE IMAGES.

The blast of an air horn makes SOPHIE suddenly open her eyes.
Rear View as Sophie veers dangerously.
Close up as she regains control of the car and herself.
The air horn crosses to:

INT. LAVELLE'S OFFICE. DAY

LAVELLE's eyes open suddenly. Disconcerted, he gathers his notes on Sophie Calder and puts them in a drawer.

INT. SOPHIE'S CAR. EVE

SOPHIE as she spots the stone cherubs atop the immense gateposts. The house's familiarity begins to register.
The rain has abated. The sun shimmers off the wet tarmac. Mayfield House looms imposingly.

INT. MAYFIELD HOUSE. EVE. POV FROM WINDOW

Sophie's car is seen entering the driveway; the car makes its way round to the right of the house and toward the rear.

<u>**EXT. MAYFIELD HOUSE. EVE**</u>

SOPHIE now on foot. A wooden door leads onto the garden. Through this we discover a second door, which leads past the nursery garden and which sweeps up to the great house.
By the time she reaches the front door it has dawned on SOPHIE that Mayfield House is, indeed, the house in her nightmare.
Her first instinct is to ring LAVELLE again, but her cell phone has "no service." A moment of apprehension. Then a decision to press on.

<u>**INT. MAYFIELD HOUSE. RECEPTION. EVE**</u>

SOPHIE enters cautiously. She rings a BELL and studies the somehow familiar surroundings. She tries the bell again. She calls out.

> **SOPHIE**
> Mrs King.

There is movement in the office behind reception.

> **SOPHIE (CONT'D)**
> Sophie Calder. We spoke on the phone.

The proprietor, AVRIL KING, emerges cheerily from an office.

> **AVRIL**
> You made good time.

> **SOPHIE**
> Yes, struck it lucky on the motorway.

AVRIL stops short—stunned when she sees SOPHIE's face.
An awkward silence. The color drains from AVRIL's face.

> **SOPHIE (CONT'D)**
> Mrs King. You alright?

AVRIL steadies herself without answering.

> **SOPHIE (CONT'D)**
> (Pleasantly)
> Room 11? Isn't it?

AVRIL struggles to regain her composure. She reaches for a room key.

> **AVRIL**
> Yes, that's right. Room 11.

> **SOPHIE**
> Second floor.

How can she have known that? AVRIL regards her with fear.

> AVRIL
> (Abruptly)
> Dinner's at 8.30.

> SOPHIE
> (Taken aback)
> Thank you.

SOPHIE lifts her case and heads for the stairs. She drinks in the details of the house.
AVRIL watches her. SOPHIE appears to know exactly where she is going.

INT. MAYFIELD HOUSE. CORNER OF RECEPTION. EVE

AVRIL shakily pours a long stiff drink. She is extremely agitated.

INT. MAYFIELD HOUSE. EVE

As if by instinct, SOPHIE heads for ROOM 11 through the empty dining room.

INT. MAYFIELD HOUSE. STAIRWELL AND SECOND FLOOR CORRIDOR. EVE

SOPHIE climbs the stairwell, passes though the tapestry room and reaches THE DOOR OF ROOM 11.
She notices her hand is trembling. The door opens to reveal the room exactly as she had seen it in her dream. She goes rigid as if a blast of ice-cold air has taken her breath away. She proceeds cautiously into the room.

INT. MAYFIELD HOUSE. CORNER OF RECEPTION. EVE

AVRIL draws hard on her cigarette. She catches sight of herself in a mirror in the corner of the reception. She is not pleased at her appearance.
Now, suddenly, beside her face in the mirror there appears the face of SOPHIE — or rather, someone very like SOPHIE. It is CELIA BARRY (as we will discover), the previous owner of Mayfield House — now dead.
CELIA — bleached hair and 1960s dress — produces a lipstick and touches up her heavy carmine makeup. She dabs her lips then gazes resentfully at AVRIL.
The image disappears. AVRIL shudders, drains her drink in one and lifts the phone.

INT. LAVELLE'S OFFICE. EVE

LAVELLE sits quietly at his desk. The answering machine clicks on.

> AVRIL (O/S)
> (Sotto and full of anxiety)
> Dr Lavelle. That woman you sent to me,
> Sophie Calder...

INT. RECEPTION MAYFIELD HOUSE. EVE

> AVRIL
> ... it's Celia Barry - it's her to the life
> ... Please ... please call me as soon as
> possible.

INT. LAVELLE'S OFFICE. EVE

LAVELLE regards the answering machine impassively.

EXT. SHOT OF MAYFIELD HOUSE. LIGHTS BLAZING. NIGHT

INT. MAYFIELD HOUSE. ROOM 11. NIGHT

SOPHIE sits at the dressing table. Every corner of the room is familiar to her. She turns and sees the wooden door ajar in the corner. She rises and moves toward it.

INT. MAYFIELD HOUSE. DINING ROOM. NIGHT

AVRIL, dressed for the evening with considerably more makeup, greets the dinner guests. She is suddenly distracted.
We follow AVRIL's terrified line of vision and see the ghost of CELIA BARRY seated at the table, staring at her.
AVRIL is now oblivious to the guests. Her gaze is fixed on CELIA, who heads for the second floor. AVRIL follows her.

INT. MAYFIELD HOUSE. THE ARMORY. NIGHT

SOPHIE moves along the long wooden corridor, as in her dream, toward an object she recognizes with horror:
A CRIB in the corner.
It is as though she has lost the capacity to breathe. A pain sears through her temple. She sits unsteadily on a chair by a table.
Shakily, she pulls out a bottle of tranquilizers, spilling them onto the table. She sits back in terror and despair.

INT. MAYFIELD HOUSE. STAIRWELL AND SECOND FLOOR CORRIDOR. NIGHT

AVRIL glimpses CELIA through the stairwell window and follows her.
AVRIL moves silently but briskly along the maze of corridors. It is the same journey we traveled at the very beginning of the film.
We hear a baby crying.
AVRIL momentarily freezes. But the baby's insistent crying compels her forward toward ROOM 11. The baby's crying from inside the room is now much louder.
Light spills through the half-open door of Room 11. AVRIL pushes open the door and enters ROOM 11.
CU of Stone Cherub.

INT. MAYFIELD HOUSE. THE ARMORY. NIGHT

AVRIL moves quickly through the wooden door up the final steps toward the armory.
As AVRIL enters, the crying suddenly stops.
CELIA is removing an embroidered pillow from the crib where a baby now lies
smothered. SOPHIE is nowhere to be seen.
ANGLE ON AVRIL: She looks in horror at the dead infant and screams.

> AVRIL
> Whose child is this?
> WHOSE CHILD IS THIS!

A movement attracts AVRIL's attention.
Angle on the mirror by the crib, in which AVRIL sees CELIA pressing her hands
against the windowpanes — as if attempting to force her way through the glass.
CU The mirror.
Suddenly the mirror shatters explosively.

RESUME SC. 19.

Instinctively AVRIL raises her arms to cover her head.
She whips round to look at the window. The window is intact. There is nothing
there.
AVRIL rushes to the window and looks down.

INT. MAYFIELD HOUSE. NIGHT

AVRIL's POV: CELIA lies broken on the driveway below.

EXT. MAYFIELD HOUSE. EVE

Angle on CELIA's broken body on the driveway. POV the ground.

INT. MAYFIELD HOUSE. THE ARMORY. NIGHT

AVRIL reels back from the window, shocked and appalled — but as she turns back
into the room she has the second, more awful, surprise. There is SOPHIE, sitting
by the table looking at her questioningly.
AVRIL holds her gaze. Neither is going to flinch.
As the camera pulls back we see both window and mirror intact.

INT. LAVELLE'S OFFICE. DAY

SILENCE except for a ticking clock.
AVRIL turns to look at LAVELLE's benign, all-comprehending face.

> AVRIL
> You don't believe me.

LAVELLE glances at a card for Mayfield House on the table between them.

                         AVRIL (CONT'D)
          She was there.

                         LAVELLE
          I believe Sophie was there.
          Celia Barry died in 1964.

                         AVRIL
               (Definitely)
          It was the same woman.

The clock ticks. LAVELLE makes a note.

                         LAVELLE
          Why did Celia Barry kill herself?

                         AVRIL
          She'd murdered her child. She was driven
          to distraction, I presume.

Silence.

                         LAVELLE
          Do you have many friends, Avril?

AVRIL shakes her head almost imperceptibly.

                         LAVELLE (CONT'D)
          How   much   are   you   drinking   at   the
          moment?

Silence.

She sees him glance at the clock on his desk.

                         AVRIL
          Is it time?

                         LAVELLE
          Has Celia gone?

AVRIL considers this remark, then announces simply:

                         AVRIL
          I think she has.

LAVELLE stands and ushers her to the door.

                         LAVELLE
          Then you'll call me. If you need me.

She leaves and LAVELLE shuts the door behind her.

FLASHBACK TO SC. 20 — in Lavelle's head—to the body of CELIA lying dead on the driveway of Mayfield House, exactly as AVRIL described it earlier.
The image fades.

RESUME SC. 22:

LAVELLE breathes heavily and considers.
The telephone rings. He snatches it up.

> LAVELLE (CONT'D)
> Hello.

> SOPHIE (O.S.)
> You've heard, have you?

> LAVELLE
> (Noncommittal)
> Sophie. No. How was it?

INT. SOPHIE'S CAR / LAVELLE'S OFFICE. DAY

We cut between the two:

> SOPHIE
> Avril King went berserk - burst into my room and attacked me - then had to be sedated. It was a nightmare. Has she got a drink problem?

LAVELLE considers this version of events.

> LAVELLE
> God ...

Just then LAVELLE glances into an office mirror. He sees a flash of CELIA staring straight at him.

> SOPHIE
> And, that house - Mayfield House is the house in my dream. I mean like the same in every detail. I'm dreaming about the house of one of your patients. How do you explain that?

> LAVELLE
> (Distracted)
> Lay-lines, crop circles - Psychokinetic transference ...

> SOPHIE
> (Emphatic)
> I don't know what kind of voodoo you're at - it's very, very scary - but I haven't had the dream since I went there. Bizarre, eh?

Another flash of CELIA in the mirror. Followed by:
FLASHBACK TO SC. 19A. A flash of CELIA's image shattering in the mirror.

RESUME SC. 23:

LAVELLE cries out, involuntarily.

> **SOPHIE (CONT'D)**
> Dr. Lavelle? What's happened?

Shaking and sweating, LAVELLE places his back against the wall, shuts his eyes tight.

> **SOPHIE (CONT'D)**
> Paul.

Another glance in the mirror. There is NOTHING there.
But sweat is running down LAVELLE's face.

> **SOPHIE (CONT'D)**
> PAUL. Answer me ...

> **LAVELLE**
> Yeah ... yes ... it's OK. Yes. Look, I'm
> sorry ... I can't seem to ...

> **SOPHIE (O.S.)**
> What's wrong?

LAVELLE replaces the phone. His hands are trembling. He wipes the sweat from his face with a handkerchief and breathes deeply. But:

INT. LAVELLE'S OFFICE. DAY

In the mirror LAVELLE sees images of SOPHIE CALDER then AVRIL KING, seated on his patients' couch. They stare at LAVELLE derisively from within his imagination. He breathes deeply. He begins to calm down. The images begin to fade.

INT. LAVELLE'S OFFICE. DAY

The intercom sounds. The images evaporate. LAVELLE answers. It's his receptionist.

> **LAVELLE**
> Yes?

> **MARY (O.S.)**
> You know your last patient is here. It's
> ten past now.

> **LAVELLE**
> Just two minutes.

LAVELLE goes to the mirror and peers in it. He glances back at the couch:

NOTHING.

He smoothes his hair and presses the intercom.

> **LAVELLE (CONT'D)**
> OK, Mary.

> **MARY (O.S.)**
> She's on her way.

He takes a deep breath, dabs the sweat from his face with a handkerchief. We hear the door open.

> **CELIA (O.S.)**
> Paul?

A young woman in a 1960s dress and bleached blonde hair walks in. We just see her face. LAVELLE's face freezes in terror. He is barely able to articulate her name.

> **LAVELLE**
> Celia?

> **CELIA**
> I've been having such dreadful
> nightmares.

The camera pulls back as CELIA stretches out to LAVELLE a tightly wrapped bundle - containing a child.
She smiles. Now she is his nightmare.

FADE OUT.

STOP

CHAPTER 21

Greta May—The Adaptation

Greta May is a 10-minute film adapted from a short story first published in *The Dream Zone*. Written and directed by Clifford Thurlow, it was produced by Sacha Van Spall and Maureen Murray. The complete script appears at the end of this chapter.

Francis Ford Coppola, with his three *Godfather* films, became one of the most acclaimed filmmakers of modern times. The scripts were adapted from Mario Puzo's books about the mafia, and what Coppola learned from the adaptation process was that where a writer has already labored over his narrative, the key elements of characterization and the story's major turning points are already in place. With Hollywood filmmakers in intense competition to option the latest high-profile novel, Coppola in 1998 took the original step of launching *Zoetrope: All-Story*,[1] a literary magazine that publishes innovative new fiction, and gives Coppola first rights to option a story for film. What Coppola had discovered was that in the neglected world of the short story there is a gold mine of precious material.

Short stories by their very nature contain no wasted words, and every scene is necessary; a good story has pace and rhythm, every gesture and nuance driving the narrative to a climax that is often both satisfying and unexpected: just what filmmakers are looking for. If the short story writer has done his job well, the script won't exactly write itself, but the foundations are already in place.

It is a common complaint that the film is never like the book; more frequently, not as good as the book. But the forms do not bear comparison, and each must be as good as it can be within its own medium. The scriptwriter may decide to make the climax his opening scene and let the story unfold as a long flashback. Perhaps he will see a story about twin brothers better told as twin sisters. The possibilities are limitless, but the elements are already there, like cards to be reshuffled and dealt in endless new patterns.

Greta May began life as a short story published in *The Dream Zone*, a small press magazine edited by Paul Bradshaw. When it came to adapting the story as a screenplay, I had three objectives in mind:

- To test the Eight-Point Guide to writing short scripts created for this book. (see page 38).
- To analyze the adaptation process.
- To make a worthy short film independent of the first two objectives.

A short film must stand alone as an accomplished piece of work, and that was certainly the prerogative of Sacha Van Spall when he agreed to come on board as producer. For the writer, the producer is like a strict parent, there to encourage but also to discipline. It is easy for writers, especially when directing their own screenplay, to get carried away with visions of street riots and crashing trains. The producer, with the line producer or executive producer, prepares a budget and if your crashes don't come within its confines, you'd better go back to the script.

We sat at the kitchen table with a pot of coffee most afternoons for several days and went through the incessant finessing that molds each draft of the screenplay, which comes before the final draft is ready to be presented to what we called the "3 Cs": cash, cast and crew.

Film is sometimes described as a cottage industry in the UK. It is certainly not huge and networking is invaluable. With a recommendation from screenwriter Terence Doyle, we were joined by French director of photography Jean-Philippe Gossart, who studied the script and saw the story washed in muted color.

It was his opinion that the best way to capture *Greta May* both in the darkness of a theater and the moody light of London's night-time streets was to shoot on film, not tape. Our decision to switch to Super 16mm required both a new budget and the expertise of a production manager. With twenty years in film, including a decade at the side of the iconoclastic director Ken Russell, Maureen Murray was ideally placed to shepherd us in gathering the team and would also keep an eye on the ticking meter.

62 Lighting check

▶▶ P.238

Now we were shooting on film, we had to think through every aspect of the process to see where we could streamline the production and cut corners. It is only in preparation and scheduling where money can be saved: perfecting the script, but also considering locations, rehearsing cast, having the right equipment at the right time, getting permission to film exteriors, knowing where to park vehicles, having change for meters, knowing where the toilets are. Everything must be thought through and planned for.

The chief concern of an executive producer on a big-budget film is usually putting the finances together. On a short, he is more likely to serve as a mentor: a traveler who has gone on the journey from script to screen many times and knows the pitfalls and precipices that mark the way ahead. Maureen Murray, serving in the dual role of production manager/executive producer, passed a judicious eye over our ten-page screenplay yet again; scripts are like a detective novel: every word, gesture, and shot are clues that must contribute to the final film, the audience experience. And if you try to change one word once the script is locked in place, the entire fabric, like a dropped stitch, can unravel. The importance of the script can never be overemphasized: it is the foundation upon which the entire project rests. Give a bad script to a great director and the best you can hope for is a mediocre film. Give a great script to a bad director and the quality will try and force its way through.

CASTING

63 Jess Murphy
▶▶ P.**238**

64 Emma Rand advises Greta
▶▶ P.**238**

65 Jean-Philippe Gossart lighting Philip Desmeules
▶▶ P.**239**

66 Makeup artist Jenny Spelling works the clapper
▶▶ P.**239**

After Maureen Murray had expunged a few superfluous lines, casting agent Susie Bruffin looked over the screenplay and recommended various actors' agents. We were seeking first to cast Greta May, the title character, and those agents who liked the script sent back files of CVs with glossy 10 x 8s. Jean-Philippe filmed the auditions and each actress brought a different vision, reflected in her performance, Greta May becoming posh with a plummy accent, a working-class girl struggling in the middle-class environment of the theater; a chaste virgin, and a femme fatale.

Greta May appears in every scene and it is her dilemma that is portrayed and resolved in the drama. Each of the actresses we auditioned was trained, eager, and good at her job. Each would have brought a different interpretation, and we would have had a different picture, not necessarily better or worse, just different. Imagine Gwyneth Paltrow rather than Renée Zellweger in the title role as Bridget in *Bridget Jones's Diary*. As I had based the script on my own story, Greta May had lived in my mind for a long time. I had fixed notions of her appearance and characteristics, which is not necessarily a good thing, and I wouldn't advise it, but Jess Murphy satisfied these preconceived ideas the moment she appeared at the casting. It was fortunate that she happened to be a fine actress as well.

Having found Greta May, we went through the same process to cast a suitable Rachel Gold, the mentor/friend who guides the story to its first turning point with her no-nonsense advice: *The way to get over one man is to get under another!* Emma Rand had the worldly-wise air demanded of the character and, as a blonde in contrast to brunette Jess, was perfect for the role. The girls instantly seemed like old friends and were believable as flatmates. Emma and Jess came from the same agency, Roger Carey Associates, as did Philip Desmeules, tall and gentle, the ideal Richard Bates, the new love interest in Greta's complicated life. Big Management's Thomas Snowdon, with his set jaw and steady gaze, was a shoe-in for the driven actor Oliver Morrell. (He had longish hair at the casting and showed up on set first day with his hair butchered for his part in a First World War movie, a challenge for Jenny Spelling, who was heading up hair and makeup). With our young performers assembled, we needed a "voice of authority" in the cameo role as the theater director. Although David Sterne had been busy the previous several months in *Vanity Fair* with Reese Witherspoon and Gabriel Byrne, as well as in his regular TV spot as Professor Dust in *The Mysti Show*, he had worked with Maureen Murray on a number of occasions and agreed to join us for the one day the part required. Finally, we needed a black taxi; Tim Pierce supplied his cab and, though unseen, drove with the conviction we have come to expect from a London cabbie.

CREWING

Jean-Philippe provided a mixture of passion and professionalism at the casting sessions and brought his regular camera crew with him to film *Greta May*. After casting, we toured the locations making a video storyboard. Jean-Philippe and I were in agreement about how the film should look, but my shot list turned out to be inadequate, with elements missing from most scenes when it came to the shoot. In future, I will draw traditional storyboards with matchstick men to illustrate each shot. The video version is better than nothing, but pencil on paper has yet to be supplanted and I learned from experience that it is vital to draw a detailed study of each shot, the angle, camera movement, lighting, point of view, background, choice of lens, what the audience can see in the frame, and the way you want the audience to interpret the scene. The more the director and director of photography (DOP) map out the shoot, the less time you lose in discussion on set.

For Jean-Philippe, the director and his DOP are like lovers. "You are a couple. The director supports his actors and the narrative. The cinematographer is loyal to the aesthetic. Sometimes they clash. If the narrative is weak, the DOP will cover the weakness by making the film flashy or glossy. He will leave space for the narrative. The DOP must learn to adapt to the director, but this is not a one-way street. It is a shared experience. Each half of the partnership must have great respect for the other but, in the end, the director has the final word."[2]

The DOP and director must also work closely with the production designer, the look and feel and texture of the film relying on all the departments running in harmony. The cinematographer invites the director into his world of lenses and filtration. He is the eyes of the director. "They must connect. Ideally, they will be people who share the same tastes and envisage the same aesthetic."

Jean-Philippe had worked with Maja Meschede on another film and she was duly engaged to bring her flair and visual talents to the wardrobe department; her last job had been with the Royal Opera House, so I knew we were in safe hands. Likewise, Maja recommended Julian Nagel as production designer and together they gave the costumes and sets a coherence that enhances the film. Jean-Philippe's camera team consisted of grip Pete Nash, camera operator Renee Willis, and gaffer Pete Carrier, all skilled craftsmen who enjoy the sense of adventure in making a short.

The rest of the crew came to us through notices on Shooting People, the essential indie and short film Internet exchange operating in both London and New York. Through it we found sound man Daniel Rosen and boom operator Daniel Owen; Jenny Spelling, who makes a living with stills photographers but prefers to work in the makeup department on a film; continuity supervisor Susan Hodgetts, who had given up a career as an economist to retrain for the film industry; stills photographer Alexander Atwater; and runners Max Thurlow, Nick Burgess, Adam Greves, Charlie Lass, Igor Degtiarev, Adam Partridge, and Luc Tremoulet. Sydney Florence came to assist Maja, and Julian Nagel's usual assistant John Pearce not only put in many long hours as our art director, but created some great graphics for the theater flyer, the magazine cover used in the film, and the DVD artwork. Assistants in the various departments—camera, set design, wardrobe, sound, makeup—will often get more responsibility on a short and the experience will help them rise up the ladder to become a head of department; the head honcho on a successful short is more likely to get the same role on a feature.

67 Sound man Daniel Rosen wires up Emma Rand

P.239

STILLS PHOTOGRAPHER

When films were silent, a stills photographer on set could click and flash to his heart's content. When sound came, the snap of a shutter would ruin a take and the stills man was reduced to restaging scenes, much to the annoyance of the actors. Directors flexing their muscles would, after banning the writer from the set, then often pick on the stills photographer.

In 1959, the Los Angeles photographer and inventor Irving Jacobson had come up with the cordless battery pack, a design—sold later to Nikon—that saved many a photographer from choking himself on his own cables at the worst possible moment. In the mid-1960s Jacobson designed and built the first sound blimp, which effectively silenced the camera's shutter and finally allowed the set photographer to shoot while the actors were performing.

Life for the stills man may have become easier with digital cameras, but they still operate via a shutter and make a noise loud enough to ruin a take. On *Greta May*, Alexander Atwater used two Nikon film SLRs, one camera with black-and-white film, the other with color. He carried a 20-mm lens, a 50-mm lens, and a 28–105-mm lens. Since the shoot he has switched to Leicas, which are quieter and more discreet.

Atwater views set photography as being similar to reportage: "Readiness is probably the most important thing, because the actors and the rest of the crew won't wait around for you to take pictures. Like reportage, you never know what's going to happen—or when. There is a lot of waiting around but you still have to be constantly alert. The best time to photograph a scene is before and after a take; never during."

Does the stills photographer try and disappear into the background?

Alexander explains: "I try and be unobtrusive, move slowly, and take my time. The best shots come when the actors aren't really aware of your presence and are therefore not too posed. It helps to be *in the background* and to stay out of people's way."

Does the stills photographer ever make suggestions?

He explains: "If I want a specific shot I might ask the actors to play the scene again for my camera. Regarding the shooting of the film, I don't think it is the photographer's place to make suggestions, except in an extreme situation."

What kind of shots is the photographer trying to get?

Alexander elaborates: "Shots that relate to the narrative of the film. Portraits of actors in (and out) of character. Scene shots. Behind the scenes, for example makeup, filming, various technical aspects of the set. Shots that capture the essence and the atmosphere of the film. One of the easy things about set photography is that you don't have to worry too much about lighting: everybody is already beautifully lit. For set photography it is important to be able to work with available light. Flash ruins photographs. Also it is very important to be able to build good relationships with the director, actors, and crew so they feel comfortable and have trust in you. This is when you get honest and occasionally intimate pictures."

www.alexanderatwater.com

BUDGET

When Sacha and I first sat down with our coffees, we were planning to make the film for about £4,000. Many short films are made with everyone taking part working for nothing but a credit. Once we had employed professional cast, the budget had to be rewritten. There is a special arrangement with Equity, the actors' union in the UK, that allows members to work for a minimum fee of £100 a day on low-budget projects, and we set that as the benchmark for everyone working on *Greta May*.

The cost of cast and crew, coupled with the added expense of shooting on Super 16 mm, resulted in a final budget of £10,000, and it would have been about 50 percent more had Sacha and Maureen not cut some amazing deals for the hire of camera equipment and the panoply of lighting the DOP needed to give the sets the desired high production values we had envisaged.

THE SHOOT

68 Clapperboard
 ▶▶ P.239

We had started planning *Greta May* in the spring of 2004 and finally did the shoot in four days in November, when the weather was particularly kind, and the team gathered for Day 1 at the Battersea Arts Centre. On a big-budget movie, the production team would be expected to get an average of about 3½ minutes of finished film a day: about 3½ pages of script, 5–6 weeks to shoot a feature. In that time, the crew becomes a team and learns to work quickly and efficiently. On *Greta May*, we only managed to get 2½ minutes of film in the can on the first day and overran by about five hours. Was everyone a perfectionist, or just too slow? Time would tell.

The film was developed overnight at Soho Images[3] and when we looked at the rushes the next day, we were satisfied with what we had. No one seemed to mind when the pattern of working late into the night, set on Day 1, continued on the next three days of the shoot. At least at Battersea Arts Centre there is a good café and the army was well fed.

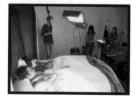

69 Bedroom scene
▶▶ P.240

Day 1 had been demanding for Jess Murphy, who spent about eight hours in her underwear being slapped around by Thomas as Oliver Morrell and growled at by the theater director David Sterne, who brought such authority to the role, even I as the director had to think twice when he roared: "No, no, no. For heaven's sake. Do it again."

The mood remained buoyant and at midnight we were still unloading the lighting into the house where we would be for the next two full days, shooting interiors. I have tried to bring to mind any dramas, beyond the drama of *Greta May*, and really can't remember any. I recall, nostalgically, Maureen Murray screaming at Jean-Philippe that if he tweaked the lights one more time she would close down the set. But he kept tweaking, she kept on urging him on, and the film got made at the same slow rate of 2½ minutes a day.

70 Philip Desmeules gets slapped

▶▶ P.240

When twenty or so people work in a small house for forty-eight hours, it tends to become cramped, and it was a pleasure to do the exteriors on the last day. It is the final reel of Greta May's drama, where she goes to the apartment of Richard Bates, as if there she will resolve her dilemma. The scene requires a long corridor (the tunnel from one state of being to another) and Niccoló Gioia, who had been following our progress, not only volunteered his home for the night, but we used his kitchen to prepare the last feast for the cast and crew.

Jess, as Greta May, arrives in a taxi in a breathtaking black dress made by couturiere Breege Collins especially for the production; Breege gave Jess the dress after the shoot and Jess duly modeled for Breege when she prepared her spring collection, a marvelous example of the indie aesthetic. Greta steps out of the cab and paces assertively along the pavement. At the blue-painted door, she hesitates, changes her mind and dawdles back along the street to the newsagent's. It was an unseasonably warm evening. Jean-Philippe, Pete Carrier, and the runners labored for hours to give the street a *film noir* feeling that justified Jean-Philippe's extravagance with the lights (we'd rented enough for a feature!) and when I got the rushes back next day, I knew that even if we had made a lousy picture, we did have some super night shots of London. Jean-Philippe brings a French sensibility to his camera work. With sets by Julian Nagel and costumes by Maja, both from Germany, *Greta May* has the European flavor faithful to the original short story.

We finished at around 4.00 a.m. I was home at 6.00 a.m., and back at the rental houses at 9.00 a.m. to return the gear in order to avoid having to pay for an extra day. It was sad to see the team break up, although now the production was over, the long journey through post-production was about to begin.

When you make a film, you should draw up a budget and stick to it. Sacha had been reminding me of that every day and it was through my excesses that the river had run dry, regardless of all the people who had donated their time, flats, and expertise to the production. Along with the rest of the crew, we had three associate producers helping along the way: Gerardo Silano, Cedric Behrel, and Keith Eyles.

71 Greta May dressing for a stranger

 ▶▶ P.**240**

72 Greta's ex hits the headlines

▶▶ P.**240**

POST-PRODUCTION

We were fortunate that Trevor Georges agreed to compose an original score, a moody jazz piece that brings out the tone I'd been aiming for, and as final proof that filmmakers are the most generous people in the world, Ron Lloyd at True Media let us loose in his facilities in Soho's Golden Square during his editor's downtime on *The Constant Gardener*, directed by Fernando Meirelles, with Ralph Fiennes and Rachel Weisz. I worked odd hours, late afternoons, and late nights for a month with editor Tony Appleton, who covered the inevitable gaps left by me as the director and teased out the emotional heart of *Greta May* with his adroit grasp of rhythm and timing. After adding sound effects and music, I came to appreciate Coppola's oft-quoted remark: "A film is created three times: first you write it, second you shoot it, third you edit."

Greta May premiered at the Curzon in Soho at the launch of the first edition of *Making Short Films* in 2005. It was shown at various screenings in the UK and at CinéGuernsey; it was audience-selected at the Savannah Film Festival, Georgia, and was runner-up for best short film at the Marbella Film Festival, Spain, in September 2006. *Greta May* got its first broadcast credit on Sky on March 31, 2007 in the First Film series produced by Propeller TV, and can now be seen on YouTube. Jess Murphy went from *Greta May* to appear

on stage with the Mexican actor Gael García Bernal in *Blood Wedding* at the Almeida Theatre, London; Emma Rand was cast with substantial roles in two TV shows, *Casualty* and *Judge John Deed*; Philip Desmeules has appeared in the movies *Trafalgar Battle Surgeon* and *Twice Upon A Time*.
www.YouTube.com

I had set out, with *Greta May*, with the lofty goal of writing and directing a short film that would win major prizes. It makes sense to aim high and, while the mega-success was not realized, I learned so much through the hands-on experience that I am optimistic that my next effort will put some silverware on the shelf. Taking the advice of Daniel Mulloy (see Chapter 15: *Daniel Mulloy*), I am in pre-production with the tricky second short (new bands have the same problem with their second album); and, with Maureen Murray, have recently completed *The Dalí Triangle*, a documentary about the commercial benefits the Dalí name and past presence bring to the Catalan villages where he once lived and worked.

You learn by doing. A mistake made by many first-time filmmakers is that they compare their first efforts with *Star Wars* when they should be looking at George Lucas's film school shorts. In making a film, you run the risk of being criticized or appearing foolish. All creative work runs the same risk and only when you take the risk, and keep taking risks, do you cut through the cliché and the formula to create something truly original. Like good wine, filmmakers mature with time. The secret is to keep going.

THE SHORT STORY

It will be a useful exercise for filmmakers to study the short story below and make notes before reading the script. Decide how you would adapt the story, and compare it with my own adaptation. There is no right or wrong way, but it will be interesting to see how I've done it, and how similar or dissimilar your own take on the story is.

GRETA MAY

She was glancing at the night's TV listings in the *Standard* when she became aware of the man staring at her. Studying her. It's something that just isn't done. Not on the tube. It's so intimate. While your body's rubbing against other bodies the last thing you want to do is make eye contact. She looked away. There was a movie with Jack Black, Channel 4, nine o'clock. Shame about the commercials. She'd microwave something during the breaks. Drink a glass of wine. Or two.

She glanced up. He was looking still. He smiled. Good teeth. She frowned. If she'd been in a pub she would have liked his brown eyes and broad shoulders. She looked down, then back up again, instinctively, as if against her will. He was writing something in a notebook.

He tore out the page and gave it to her as the train slowed at Gloucester Road.

"My stop," he said, and squeezed through the sliding doors before they closed.

His name was Richard. His number was 05557 757 777. She wondered how he managed to get so many sevens. Was it lucky? For him? For her?

She screwed up the piece of paper and let it drop to the floor among the fast-food bags and abandoned newspapers. She'd grown to despise the tube in the two years she'd worked in the shop. A shop assistant. How did it happen? Why? Two years at drama school. Two on the boards. Two in a shop. And another birthday in June. She didn't even bother to read the trades anymore. Twenty-five. That's almost thirty. She'd be looking at comfy slippers next.

She picked up the piece of paper again. Richard. 05557 757 777. Black jacket. Blue shirt. Dark jeans. Media: television, advertising, web design.

The train pulled in at Hammersmith. As she stumbled along behind two girls in gray veils she thought about the crowd at Gloucester Road. Well-heeled. Closer to the action. London was a chessboard. Blacks and voids.

As soon as she got home, she spread the slip of paper flat on the kitchen counter. She called the number. She let it ring twice. Then hung up. It was ridiculous to call a total stranger. Then, it was ridiculous not to. What did she have to lose? She lit a cigarette and poured a glass of wine. The first drag and the first sip are the best. Life's like that. An unfulfilled promise. She'd played at the Royal Court in Sloane Square when she was nineteen. She was Polly in *The Raw Edge*, a pilot for a soap that had never got made. There had been hundreds of girls up for it. But she'd got the part. At twenty she could play fifteen. They liked that. She looked like the girl next door who gets raped and murdered.

She lifted the receiver and phoned again. Her sister.

"Alison. It's me."

They talked: Alison's child. Alison's partner. Alison's stiff joints; she was learning to be a yoga teacher. Alison was about to hang up. Then remembered.

"How's things with you?"

"A man gave me his telephone number on the tube."

"How exciting."

"I know." Greta paused.

"Well?"

"Nothing. He was a stranger."

"What was he like?"

"Mmm. Tall, dark, nice accent."

"Lucky devil."

They talked some more. Said goodbye.

Greta finished her wine and started to pour a second glass, stopping herself and adding just a touch. She had decided to make the call while Alison was going on about her aches and pains and was bracing herself to actually do it. What would she say? What if she got an answerphone? No problem. She'd hang up.

There was no answerphone. He answered.

"It's me."

"I knew you'd call."

"How?"

"Nothing ventured …" He trailed off. "Come over."

"What for?"

"I could say a plate of spaghetti."

"Why don't you, then?"

"Okay. A plate of spaghetti." She knew he was smiling. He gave her the address.

"Do you need to write it down?"

"I have a trained memory," she told him.

"I'll put the water on."

She replaced the receiver. A chill ran through her. This was insanity. He was an axe murderer. A madman. *American Psycho*!

It wasn't her that went through to the bathroom and took a shower. Shaved her legs. Perfumed her parts. It wasn't Greta May. It was someone like Greta May, a mirror image that stared from the mirror as she slid into black underwear. She cleaned her teeth. Lit a cigarette. Smiled at the absurdity of it. Of everything. She put on a black dress, looked down at her breasts, and took it off again. She tried blue jeans and a shirt. Good hips, she thought; she took off the jeans and put on a skirt instead. Clothes help you find the character. Then, when you're up there, out there, you're no longer you, but then you are, even more so. Yes, they really were someone else's eyes peering back as she did her mascara. Someone who didn't work in the shoe department in a big store. She removed the skirt, slid back into the black dress, then swivelled round just quickly enough to catch a glimpse of Polly in *The Raw Edge*.

A taxi stopped as she was about to enter the tube and she stepped in the back. She despised London taxi drivers. But she loved their cabs. It was like returning to the womb. You were coddled. Luxuriated. You learned how to love yourself, your reflection opaque and vaguely surreal in the dark glass, amber streaks of light crossing the sky. She imagined dying and being carried to her funeral in the back of a taxi. Nirvana on the radio.

He lived in a red brick building divided into five flats. His bell was the bottom one. She stood there on the threshold, her finger hovering before the shiny brass button. This really was madness. The taxi had gone. The street was silent. She marched off back the way she had come and only slowed her pace when she reached the newsagent's on the corner. She studied the magazines. She flicked through the pages of *The Stage* and put it back in the rack. If she hurried, she'd get home in time to see the movie on Channel 4.

She lit a cigarette and blew a long stream of smoke into the sky. The night was clear. Full of stars. She had every intention of going home and watching the film, but found herself crushing the cigarette below her heel, cleaning her teeth with her tongue, and setting out again for the red brick building. She took a deep breath and hit the bell. The door buzzed open almost immediately. She heard his voice.

"Come in."

It was hollow. Like an echo. She heard the sound of her shoes tapping over the black-and-white tiles in the hall. There was a table piled with letters, a gilt mirror reflecting an image of herself she didn't recognize. Richard stood in the doorway to his flat. He was wearing jogging pants, a polo shirt. Bare feet. It's very familiar. Bare feet.

As she stepped into the hall he pushed the door just hard enough for it to catch. They stood motionless in the half-light. He leaned toward her, placing his two palms flat on the wall, her head trapped in the space between them. He wasn't smiling. He just stared. And she stared back. He had dark eyes. Jet-black hair. She wondered if he would ever be cast as a leading man.

The slap came as a complete surprise. It stung her cheek. It really stung; and so loud in the silence. It was hard. Not so hard as to bruise, but hard enough for her teeth to cut the inside of her mouth. She tasted blood. She slapped him back, just as hard. Her breath caught in her throat. She would have screamed, but his lips were on her mouth, sucking at her and she responded to his kiss. His hands slid down the wall, across her back, over her bottom. He pulled up her dress and ripped the side of her knickers. They fell to her feet. She remembered reading in *Cosmo* that women got wet when they were excited. It had never happened to her. Never. But it did now.

She could feel a dampness inside her stomach. She felt that dampness grow liquid and leak from her, wetting her thighs. The feeling was … *luxurious*. The sound of the word ran through her mind as he turned her round and pulled her down on the floor. He entered her in one swift movement. The cheek where he'd hit her was pressed against the coarse floor covering. Her breath came in short gasps. She could feel his breath, hot against her ear. He rammed deep inside her, harder and harder, and when he came the warm feeling in her stomach filled her whole body and that feeling was … luxurious.

Now that he'd finished she imagined he was going to open the door and toss her back out again. But he didn't. He turned her over and did something she had not been expecting. He kissed her cheek. He lifted her awkwardly into his arms and carried her through to the bathroom. He didn't say anything. He turned on the taps, filled the big bath and added blue crystals to the flow. She was reaching for the zip on her black dress automatically, her fingers doing the thinking for her. He turned off the taps and she stepped out of her dress into the foaming blue water.

He was about to go, but leaned back through the door: "What kind of pizza do you like?" he asked.

"What about the spaghetti?"

"Takes too long."

"Spinach with an egg."

"Anything else?" he asked her.

"Yes, you can get this week's *Stage* at the newsagent's."

"You're an actress?" he asked, and she nodded. "I thought so. What's your name?"

"Greta May."

"Nice one."

He closed the door and she held her breath as she sank for a moment beneath the dark blue water. Luxurious.

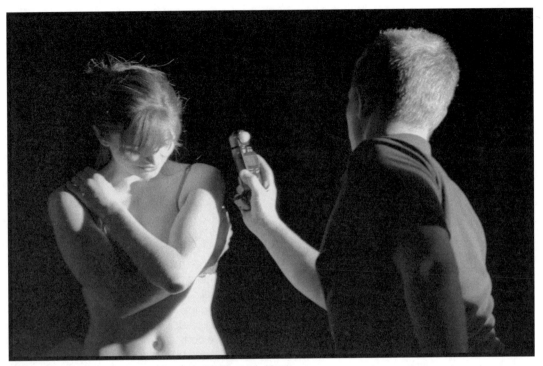

62 Lighting check. DOP Jean-Philippe Gossart with actress Jess Murphy.
Photo by Alexander Atwater

63 Jess Murphy doing her Audrey Hepburn impression.
Photo by Alexander Atwater

64 Emma Rand as Rachel, advises Greta that the only
way to get over someone is to get under someone else!
Photo by Alexander Atwater

65 Jean-Philippe Gossart lighting Philip Desmeules.
Photo by Alexander Atwater

66 Makeup artist Jenny Spelling steps in to work the
clapper—making short films is a multitasking pursuit.
Photo by Alexander Atwater

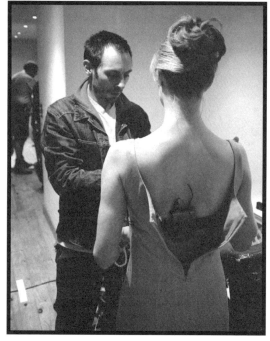

67 Sound man Daniel Rosen wires up Emma Rand for
action. Photo by Alexander Atwater

68 Clapperboard. Photo by Alexander Atwater

69 Bedroom scene: a big crowd in a small room.
Photo by Alexander Atwater

70 Philip Desmeules gets a good slapping.
Photo by Alexander Atwater

71 Pensive Greta May dressing for a stranger.
Photo by Alexander Atwater

72 There's that man again—Greta's ex hits the headlines.
Photo by Alexander Atwater

START ▶	TITLE

GRETA MAY

Script / direction by Clifford Thurlow
Produced by Sacha Van Spall and Maureen Murray

Note: Numbers in bold denote the timing of each sequence

1 INT. THEATER FOYER - EARLY EVENING

GRETA MAY descends the stairs and peruses the flyers in a theater foyer. She is twenty-five, attractive, down in the dumps. **5**

She removes a flyer with a picture of a powerful, handsome guy below the play title: *You're Not Alone.* **4**

RICHARD BATES, twenty-five, confident but not pushy, carries a newspaper. He recognizes GRETA and approaches.

> **RICHARD**
> Hi, it's Greta May.

She tries to place him ...

> **RICHARD (CONT'D)**
> Richard. Richard Bates.

She acts like she's kind of remembering him. He doesn't press.

> **RICHARD (CONT'D)**
> I saw you in your last play, *Hope Express* ...
> (Notices the flyer)
> ... with Oliver Morrell. Of course. You were terrific.

> **GRETA**
> But I'm not in this one, though.

> **RICHARD**
> It's not that good. What are you doing now?

> **GRETA**
> I'm sorry?

>   RICHARD
> What are you in?

>   GRETA
> I'm reading scripts; considering things.

>   RICHARD
> Listen, do you want to have a coffee or
> something?

>   GRETA
> Another time. I've got to ...

GRETA moves past RICHARD. **50**

RICHARD scribbles his name and number on his newspaper: *Richard* 05557 757 777. He
tears off the corner and hurries after Greta.

>   RICHARD (CONT'D)
> Next time you're in something, you know
> ...

GRETA reluctantly takes the scrap of paper, and glances at it. **20**

Richard watches her wander toward the exit, shoulders slumped, and sees her shove
the piece of paper in her pocket. **5**
(1.24)

2 INT. GRETA'S KITCHEN - NIGHT

On the kitchen counter there is a half-eaten chocolate cake, an ashtray with
a smoking cigarette, a glass of wine, a bottle of wine, a mobile phone and the
theater flier from *You're Not Alone*.

GRETA sips wine. Wine drops in red tears down her front.

She studies Oliver's face on the flyer, wipes away the wine with her fingers and
real tears well up into her eyes ... **8**

FLASHBACK

There is a fleeting image of GRETA dressed in an ultra-sexy outfit consisting of a red
bra and pants, teetering heels, and sheer nylons. She looks terrified... **3**

GRETA'S name, called off-screen, shakes her from her reverie.

>   RACHEL (VO)
> Greta. Greta.

GRETA cuts and takes a big slice of cake. **4**

RACHEL GOLD, GRETA'S flatmate, enters: same age as GRETA, sophisticated in a slinky
dress and ready for an evening out. She carries a pearl necklace, which she twirls
around her finger. GRETA remains silent and looks shaken.

RACHEL ignores her, arranges the flowers. GRETA breaks off a piece of cake and shoves it in her mouth. RACHEL approaches, picks up the flyer and puts it back down again.

> **RACHEL**
> You know something, I've been dumped more times than you've had hot ...

> **GRETA**
> (Cutting in)
> ... sex?

> **RACHEL**
> ... Tell me about it.

> **GRETA**
> I was chatted up today. Some bloke saying he knew me. What a jerk. **9**

> **RACHEL**
> Handsome jerk or an ugly jerk?

> **GRETA**
> You're so shallow, Rachel. "Shallow Rachel!" Sounds like a bad play.

> **RACHEL**
> Yeah, you should be in it. You're not doing anything else. Can you?

RACHEL releases the necklace, like a conjuring trick, from her palm. GRETA stands to help.

> **GRETA**
> I'm resting.

GRETA hooks the necklace in place. RACHEL turns and looks at the cake.

> **RACHEL**
> Is that what you call it?

GRETA straightens Rachel's sleeve. She looks great. GRETA looks sad. **1.02**

RACHEL grabs the flyer and screws it up.

> **GRETA**
> Rachel ...

RACHEL crosses the kitchen ...

> **RACHEL (CONT'D)**
> Oliver would step over his own grandmother to get a part. He's just a bastard.

> GRETA
> Don't ...

... and drops the flyer in the pedal bin.

> RACHEL (CONT'D)
> The way to get over one man is to get
> under another.

RACHEL kisses GRETA'S forehead and makes her way to the door. GRETA sits and cuts into the cake. RACHEL turns and holds her own slender waist as she nods toward the cake.

> RACHEL
> Cake is not the answer. 35

RACHEL exits. GRETA speaks to the cake.

> GRETA
> Depends on the question. 4

A door slams from above. **(2.18)**

3 INT. GRETA'S KITCHEN (LATER) - NIGHT

GRETA spins her mobile. She stares thoughtfully at the keyboard, then stabs in a number. It rings and she hangs up. She takes a sip of wine. Then presses RECALL.

INTERCUT TELEPHONE CONVERSATION: **(15 jumps)**

4 INT. RICHARD'S LIVING ROOM - NIGHT

Nice pad. Richard reads the *Evening Standard* (corner is torn).

> RICHARD
> Yeah ... Richard.

> GRETA
> So what about that coffee?

> RICHARD
> What ... Greta ... You kept my number.

> GRETA
> Nooo. I've got a trained memory.

> RICHARD
> You didn't remember me.

> GRETA
> I'm sorry. Where do I know you from?

> RICHARD
> I work in the theater. I've seen you in
> the spotlight.

>   **GRETA**
> Agh, that's right, in *Hope Express.*
> Why don't you ask me over and you
> can tell me why Oliver Morrell was so
> *amazing*!

>   **RICHARD**
> Yeah! ... I'll give you the address. Are
> you ready? **40**

GRETA listens. Hangs up. She stands, takes the whole cake and slides it into the bin on top of the flyer. **5 (45)**

5 INT. GRETA'S BEDROOM - NIGHT

GRETA stands in front of the mirror in modest underwear — moving to her own music. **2**

The same fleeting image of GRETA, dressed in the sexy red underwear, crosses the mirror and for a moment she sees OLIVER standing behind her. **2**

She shakes away the image. Quick Cut to: **2**

GRETA dressed in blue jeans, T-shirt and a leather **3** jacket, hair carefully scruffy. She faces CAMERA and spins round to catch her reflection in the mirror - very James Dean with the fag in the corner of her mouth.

>   **GRETA (VO)**
> Biker girl ...

She wriggles out of her clothes and tosses them on the bed. She gazes at her image and combs her hair.

Quick cut to GRETA dressed in a formal black dress — a demure Audrey Hepburn. She poses for the mirror. **9**

>   **GRETA (VO)**
> Socialite ...

GRETA undresses and stands staring into the dark wardrobe. Car lights flicker over the ceiling. **5 (21)**

>   **GRETA (VO)**
> Femme fatale ...

6 EXT. BLACK CAB - NIGHT

A black cab going around Hyde Park Corner, lights streaming by; GRETA'S reflection in the black glass flickers into a momentary flashback:

7 INT. THEATER STAGE - NIGHT

GRETA wears the sexy red outfit from Sc. 4 flashback. She looks panicky as OLIVER MORRELL crosses a darkened room, empty but for a sofa.

OLIVER slaps her across the face. He enjoys abusing her. OLIVER kisses GRETA violently, and as she struggles to get away he pushes her roughly down on the sofa.

> **GRETA**
> You bastard, what are you doing? What
> the hell ...   **10**

The voice of the dissatisfied **DIRECTOR** intervenes from the darkened auditorium. We see now that the action is not "live" but is taking place on stage.

> **DIRECTOR (VO)**
> No, no, no, Greta, for heaven's sake.
> Let's try again.   **8**

OLIVER bends and touches GRETA'S shoulder in a sweet way. He raises his eyebrows as if to say he can't understand what's wrong with the DIRECTOR and takes GRETA's hand to pull her up from the sofa.

GRETA smiles ...   **5**

Close-up on GRETA becomes her reflection in the cab window as the cab plunges into the tunnel at Hyde Park Corner and disappears.   **7 (30)**

8 EXT. RICHARD'S HOUSE - NIGHT

GRETA crosses the pavement, climbs three steps and her finger hovers over the doorbell. The sound of the taxi disappears into a silence that is deep, oppressive.   **3**

GRETA reads the nameplate: Richard Bates. Her hand trembles, and she backs away. The cab has vanished. GRETA's shoulders drop. She dawdles along the street in her heels, turns the corner ...   **10 (13)**

9 EXT. NEWSAGENT'S - NIGHT

... and stops at the rack of magazines outside the late-night newsagent's. It's gloomy inside, the dim yellow light casting an insipid glow over the sidewalk. She slips a cigarette into her mouth.

GRETA notices *The Stage*.

She pulls *The Stage* out of the rack and OLIVER MORRELL is staring from the front page below the heading: "*You're Not Alone—Oliver Morrell Strikes Again.*"

She shakes herself and takes a deep breath.

She pushes the magazine back in place, removes her unlit cigarette and stamps it out anyway.   **(20)**

10 EXT/INT. RICHARD'S HOUSE - NIGHT

GRETA marches back to Richard's building and gives the bell a decisive press.

> **GRETA (VO)**
> Femme fatale.

The door buzzes open. **4**

GRETA enters the darkness. As she opens the interior doors, the door to Richard's flat opens. **5**

RICHARD is in an open doorway at the end of the hall; in sharp silhouette, the light behind him. **2**

GRETA walks the long corridor toward him.

(11)

11 INT. RICHARD'S LIVING ROOM - NIGHT

GRETA is composed, ostensibly in control. Richard, unsure of himself, while trying to conceal his pleasure that she's there. **4**

She studies RICHARD: his polo shirt, jogging pants, bare feet. She looks from his feet to his dark eyes and down to his feet again. **4**

It's difficult to know who is going to look away first — but it is RICHARD.

> **RICHARD**
> Coffee? Drink ...

Greta glances around the room, taking everything in. Looks back over her shoulder, seems bored as she answers.

> **GRETA**
> Red wine.

He produces a bottle, glasses, corkscrew. **4**

> **RICHARD**
> I didn't really think you were going to
> come. I mean, I'm glad you did ...

> **GRETA**
> Don't they all come? The girls you give
> your number to. **10**

GRETA glances at the photos on the shelf: they show RICHARD as a little boy, in school uniform, getting into a car, with mummy: family snaps, all very normal. **5**

> **RICHARD**
> I don't make a habit of it.

As RICHARD points out something in one of the photos, he places his hand gently on her bare shoulder (the same action as OLIVER when he was being sympathetic on stage).

>   RICHARD (CONT'D)
>   Look, that was ...

GRETA flinches, as if she has woken from a dream, and with the jerk of the movement wine spills down her front. **5**

RICHARD puts his glass down. So does GRETA. GRETA'S hand is covered in wine. **3**

RICHARD goes to take her hand, and GRETA slaps him across the face in exactly the same way that OLIVER hit her on stage.

>   RICHARD (CONT'D)
>   What the... (52)

As GRETA goes to hit him again ... Quick Cut:

12 INT. THEATER STAGE - NIGHT

... Oliver hits Greta across the face.

He kisses her violently, and as she struggles to get away he pushes her roughly down on the sofa.

>   GRETA
>   You bastard, what are you doing? What
>   the hell ... No.

OLIVER slides his belt out of his trousers and roughly ties Greta's hands. He hits her again.

>   OLIVER
>   You're going to enjoy this, you little
>   bitch.

>   GRETA
>   What? Why are you doing this ...

INTERCUT   (20)

13 INT. RICHARD'S LIVING ROOM - NIGHT

GRETA moves toward RICHARD, grips the side of his head, and kisses him violently, the action mirroring OLIVER kissing her.

As RICHARD moves back, he stumbles over a chair and lands on the floor. GRETA falls on top of RICHARD, straddling him.
She kisses his neck. She pulls off his shirt, her actions frantic, violent. She slides out of her dress, revealing the red underwear from the theater costume.
(20)
As RICHARD goes to embrace her, she pushes his hands away.

CUT BACK TO SCENE 12

>   DIRECTOR (VO)
>   He's not going to do anything.

The DIRECTOR'S voice brings the action to an end.

The DIRECTOR comes into view, a ghostly figure in the dark auditorium. He sits in an end seat beside the aisle.

He is a middle-aged man in black trousers, a turtleneck, and distinctive polished black leather shoes.

> **DIRECTOR (CONT'D)**
> Oliver, a word please.

OLIVER makes his way off stage. The DIRECTOR stands as OLIVER approaches. His voice is like an echo inside GRETA's head. **5**

> **DIRECTOR (CONT'D)**
> I know you've worked together before,
> but this isn't doing it for me. I'm going
> to use the French girl ... **12**

The DIRECTOR turns and his footsteps recede up the aisle. OLIVER looks back at GRETA for a moment, then follows the DIRECTOR. **6**

Close-up on GRETA lit by a single spotlight. **2**

Close-up on RICHARD: the lighting operator working in the control booth. **3 (28)**

14 RICHARD'S LIVING ROOM - NIGHT

GRETA has tears in her eyes.

> **RICHARD**
> It's okay ... I understand ...

RICHARD caresses GRETA.

At first she is unsure. Then she returns his caress, truly focusing on him for the first time.

The caresses become more passionate. RICHARD gently rolls GRETA over and kisses her eyes, kissing away her tears. Their lips meet. They kiss, discovering each other. **(17)**

INT. RICHARD'S BEDROOM - MORNING

Sunlight streams into the room. GRETA is in bed wearing RICHARD'S polo shirt. Her eyes adjust to the light. **3**

She snuggles up to RICHARD and the movement wakes him. He opens his eyes and they look at each other for a long moment.

> **GRETA**
> Where's that coffee you promised?

RICHARD still can't quite believe she's there. He smiles ...

> **GRETA (CONT'D)**
> What did you really think of me in *Hope Express*?

> **RICHARD**
> You were adorable ...

She pulls him toward her, pulling his ears, and kisses him tenderly.

RICHARD is about to get up, but she pulls him back.

> **GRETA (CONT'D)**
> There's no hurry.

They kiss.   **30**
 (33)

FADE OUT

30 seconds end credit
Total 10 minutes

STOP

PART

VI

TITLE
Useful information

CHAPTER 22

Press Kit

Once a film is complete it is essential, in order to enter it for festivals, to have a press kit containing supplementary publicity material. It should include:

- A synopsis.
- Production stills.
- Director's and/or producer's statement.
- News, reviews, production notes, and anecdotes.
- Résumés for key cast and crew, including biographies, filmographies, and photos.

Press kits are not even looked at until a film is selected, but it is best to assemble the information early and send it off at the same time as the film and entry form. On the other hand, some festival organizers request that you *don't* send a press kit with your film, but will ask you to do so if it is selected. Just follow the rules.It is crucial to have at least one great production still, which is likely to be used over and over again. A poster, too, is useful. If the film is selected, you get a real rush of adrenaline when you arrive at the event and see your poster up in the foyer. Some filmmakers try to bamboozle festival selectors with a flashy folder of photos and PR material. It doesn't work. The film has to stand on its own and, in general, it is better to keep the press kit brief and honest.

The time for producers to think about publicity is before the first day of principal photography. Producers normally have some down time while the director is rehearsing cast and making the shot list with the director of photography. This is the time to contact the local newspaper and invite the press along to the shoot; actors (and likewise directors) like being interviewed, it's good for their CV and, if you have a star on board, you'll get more column inches for your film. This won't necessarily bring more people in, unless the film is being shown to a local audience, but either way, the clippings make a positive addition in the press kit and show that the filmmakers are approaching the enterprise in a serious and professional manner.

A website for a short can also be useful tool, not only for festival selectors and filmgoers, but also to keep the cast and crew up to date with the film's progress. The film will probably not be shown for several months after the wrap party (you can invite the press along to that, too), but those who have played a role in making the short will be keen to know how it's doing. If the shoot went well, these are the people you're going to work with on the next short.

At Withoutabox, the major registration service for film festivals, there is an option to create an online press kit, where registered members can upload photographs, press coverage, and website details.
www.withoutabox.com

Opposite is the press kit for *Greta May:*

Metro 7 Presents
Greta May

Written & Directed By **Clifford Thurlow**

BACKGROUND

Produced by Metro Seven Films, *Greta May* is a contemporary, character-driven drama that tells a fully realized story in a 10-minute short. Written and directed by Clifford Thurlow, it was shot on Super 16mm on location in London.

Producer Sacha Van Spall endows the project with high production values. Maureen Murray, as the executive producer, brings a keen eye for detail, and French director of photography Jean-Philippe Gossart washes the screen in radiant light. Composer Trevor Georges provides a moving jazz score, and Jess Murphy in the title role as Greta May puts in a captivating performance.

The film stands alone as a short, indie movie and there is the additional interest of it being one of five short films studied in Clifford Thurlow's book *Making Short Films: The Complete Guide From Script To Screen.* The screenplay for *Greta May* was adapted from a short story first published in *The Dream Zone*. Then follows the Eight-Point Guide to Making Short Films devised for the book. Combined with the film, it provides an insight into the adaptation process.

GRETA MAY SYNOPSIS

Actress Greta May has lost her confidence. She has lost her boyfriend, rising star Oliver Morrell. And she has lost her big break in a major new play that Oliver has made a roaring success.

When a stranger gives Greta his telephone number it only adds to her sense of desolation until her worldly-wise flatmate Rachel tells her: "The only way to get over one man is to get under another."

Greta is uncertain about Rachel's shallow advice but, left alone, she makes the telephone call in the vain hope that an encounter with the stranger will change her life and put her back in the spotlight.

METRO SEVEN MISSION STATEMENT

Metro Seven is committed to making profitable movies that are innovative, distinctive, compelling and engaging; movies that create an intercultural dialogue; movies that make us contemplate our life's journey and touch our brightest moments and our darkest secrets.

We will endeavor to develop projects that have universal themes that embrace a wide variety of moviegoers and maintain high production values to ensure their commercial viability. This will enable us to compete with any major film studio and protect our investors while never losing sight of our main responsibility—to entertain.

Writer/Director

Clifford Thurlow received a European Media Development Award (EMDA) for his feature adaptation of the Freya North novel *Sally*. He is the author of a number of books, including *Making Short Films*.

Producer

With a keen understanding of a good story and a sense of obligation to the audience, Sacha Van Spall is ideally suited to the role of producer. His dedication and attention to detail enable the highest standard of filmmaking.

Executive Producer

Maureen Murray cut her producing teeth working with controversial film director Ken Russell. She is a member of the Production Guild of Great Britain, a former board member of Women In Film and Television, and a graduate of Media 2000's European Audio-Visual Entrepreneurs.

Director of Photography

Jean-Philippe Gossart graduated in film and journalism before moving from France to the UK in 2002. He has spent the last three years as a lighting cameraman working on features, short films, and documentaries. His passion for camera and lighting is endless and he works to translate words into visual images.

Composer

Trevor Georges began his career as a performer at Glyndebourne Opera. He moved through the music genres from Latin, playing bass for King Salsa, to being a rock trombonist, assistant musical director for *The Buddy Holly Story*, the composer for *Tapping Harlem*, and Sam in the West End production of *Casablanca*.

Editor

Tony Appleton has spent almost twenty years editing commercials, documentaries, and movies for TV and the cinema. He sees short films as the ideal training ground for new filmmakers and enjoys the challenge of working with first-time directors on projects with tight budgets, and all the constraints of creating viable drama within the limitations of the genre.

Jess Murphy

Jess Murphy brings total passion and commitment to the title role as Greta May. Before drama school, Jess graduated from the Royal Academy of Music with a B.Mus. (violin performance). She played the lead in ITV's *How Not To Find A Husband*. *Greta May* is her first film.

Produced by Metro Seven

A

Above-the-line costs
The creative elements as detailed at the top of the budget sheet. Includes story rights and screenplay, producer and executive producer, director, principal cast, and all associated costs.

ADR (automated dialog replacement); looping
Rerecorded dialogue to replace unfit recordings. Normally done back at a studio with the actors lip-synching.

AMPAS (Academy of Motion Picture Arts and Sciences)
American professional honorary organization composed of more than 6,000 motion picture craftsmen and women.

Ambient sound
Background sound in addition to dialogue picked up by the mike.

Anamorphic lens
A projection lens used to produce widescreen images at the cinema.

Ancillary rights
Rights to the commercial potential of a project aside from direct exploitation of the film. Includes computer games rights, television spin-off, prequel, sequel and remake, book publishing rights, merchandising rights, soundtrack album rights, and the music publishing rights to the score.

Answer print
The composition print that emerges from the laboratory after the combining of the graded picture with sound, soundtrack, and optical effects.

Aperture
Camera opening controlling the amount of light that touches the film; its size can be varied to vary the amount of light.

Aspect ratio
The width-to-height ratio of a movie frame and screen. Standard aspect ratio is 1.33 to 1; CinemaScope uses 2.35 to 1.

Audience positioning
The relationship between the audience and the media product. The way the media tries to determine the response of an audience to its products.

Auteur
A filmmaker, usually a writer/director, with a recognizable strong personal style.

B

Backlighting
Lighting placed behind a subject to create a silhouette.

BAFTA (British Academy of Film and Television Arts)
British professional honorary organization.

BBFC (British Board of Film Classification)
The organization that issues certificates to films and videos, stating whether they are suitable for children or young people to watch.

Below-the-line costs
Section of budget that includes technical, insurance, production, general expenses, editing, and post-production costs.

Best boy
The chief assistant to the gaffer on a set.

Bollywood
Nickname of the Indian film industry (a fusion of "Bombay" and "Hollywood").

Boom
A movable arm that holds a microphone over actors' heads during filming.

Buzz track, presence, atmos
Recorded atmospheric sound. The sound of silence. Also used as a backdrop for ADR.

C

Call sheet
Schedule of each day's filming normally created by the line producer.

CGI (computer-generated imagery)
Used for creating everything from full-on *Lord of the Rings* battle scenes to cleaning up minor details such as an errant watch on Napoleon's wrist.

Chain of title
The route by which the producer's right to use copyright material may be traced from the author to the producer through a "chain" of assignments and transfers.

Chromakey
A device that allows an image to be filmed in front of a background that has been produced elsewhere.

Cineaste
A film or movie enthusiast.

CinemaScope
The trademark used for an anamorphic widescreen process.

Cinéma-vérité
A style of filmmaking that stresses unbiased realism and often contains unedited sequences.

Cinerama
A widescreen process using three projectors to produce an image on a curved screen.

Clapperboard
A board on which details of each take are written in chalk, and which is "clapped" in order to synchronize sound and vision.

Cliffhanger
Device used principally in early film serials, and latterly on television, whereby the action ends at the highest point of the drama ensuring that the audience tunes in for the next episode.

Collection agent
A mutually agreed company appointed to collect the proceeds from a film and distribute to the financiers and other contractually agreed benefactors.

Completion guarantee
An agreement under which a guaranteeing company guarantees to financiers that a film will be completed and delivered by a given date.

Contingency
An amount added to the budget of a film to cover unforeseen circumstances; usually 10 percent of the budgeted costs.

Continuity
Ensuring that each shot in a film or TV program has details that match.

Contra-zoom
Technique of adjusting the zoom to keep subject the same size in the frame as the camera moves toward or away from the subject.

Co-production treaty
An arrangement between two or more countries allowing filmmakers to access tax incentives in each country.

Coverage
The shots, including close-ups and reverse angles, which a director takes in addition to the master shot.

Crane shot
A shot from above, using a device of the same name.

Crash-zoom
A rapid zoom in on a subject; *see also* **Zoom in/Zoom out.**

Cross-collateralization
Used by distributors and sales agents to apply costs from one territory or exploitation right to all other income revenues from all other territories and exploitations.

CU
Close-up.

Cut
1. The instruction to stop the camera and the action in front of the camera. 2. The process of editing a film or shortening a scene.

Cutaway
A brief shot that interrupts the continuity of the main action of a film, often used to depict related matter or indicate concurrent action.

D

DAT (digital audio tape)
Tape used to store digital recordings of a high quality.

Day for night
A shot filmed during the day, which appears on the screen as a night scene. (Title of a 1973 movie by François Truffaut.)

Deep focus
A cinematic technique whereby objects are kept in focus in both foreground and background.

Deferment
Payment from revenues derived from the exploitation of a film, after the deduction of distribution fees and expenses and, usually, after financiers have recovered all of the sums. Most short films are made with deferments.

Degeneration or Drop out
The lowering of quality as images and sound are transferred from tape to tape.

Diegetic sound
Sound that naturally belongs with what can be seen in the picture.

Diffusion
The reduction of the harshness or intensity of light achieved by using a screen, glass filter, or smoke.

Director of photography (DOP)
The movie photographer responsible for camera technique and lighting during production. Also called cinematographer.

Director's cut
Director's version of a film, which usually includes scenes cut from the original.

Dissolve
The gradual transformation of one scene to the next by overlapping a fade-out with a fade-in.

Distributor
Company responsible for the distribution and placement of a film in cinemas and other agreed media.

Dolby
A technique in sound recording that helps cut out background noise and distortion.

Dolly shot
A moving shot that uses a wheeled camera platform known as a dolly.

Domestic rights
The rights to distribute a film in North America or other originating country where specified.

DOP, *see* **Director of photography**

Down time
The late hours and off-peak times at an editing suite, where you may be able to cut your film on a budget.

E

E&O (errors and omissions insurance)
Insurance against claims arising out of infringements of copyright, defamation, and unauthorized use of names, trade names, trademarks, or characters.

Establishing shot
The first shot of a scene, showing a wide shot of the location in which the action takes place.

Edit controller
Machine linking a player, or video camera, to a recorder in order to assemble and edit shots; it comes in various sizes with a range of extras.

Editor
The person usually responsible for the final structure of a film.

Equity
Union of British actors. Equivalent of the Screen Actors' Guild in the US.

External microphone
Mic that plugs into the camera.

F

Fade-in
A gradual transition from complete black to full exposure.

Fade-out
A gradual transition from full exposure to complete black.

Field of vision
The area a camera *sees* and will record.

Film gauge
The size or width of film, e.g. 35mm or 16mm.

Final cut
The last version of an edited film prior to release.

Flickers
Early nickname for the movies, stemming from the flickering effect they had.

Foreign rights
Opposite of domestic rights: the rights to distribute a film outside America or the originating country.

Four-walling
The renting of a cinema by a producer for a period allowing for the retention of all box office returns.

Frame-accurate editing
Editing system that allows editors to stop and start cuts exactly where they want.

Frame/frames per second
An individual unit of movie film. The American standard film speed is 24 frames per second (FPS); there are 16 frames per foot of 35-mm film.

Freeze-frame
A still picture during a movie, made by running a series of identical frames.

FX
Short for "effects"; used to refer to special effects; *see also* **SFX**.

G

Gaffer
The main electrician and supervisor of lighting on set.

Gaffer tape
A strong and versatile multipurpose cloth tape used for everything from marking floor positions to fixing equipment.

Gag
A furry object for reducing the amount of wind sound a mic picks up.

Gap financing
Lending arrangement whereby a bank will lend the difference between production finance raised and the minimum expected from sales by a reputable sales agent.

Gate
The part of a camera or projector that is in front of the lens, through which the film passes.

Gel
Colored transparent sheets that are placed in front of lights to change the color and ambience, or over windows to maintain a white balance in the picture.

General release
The exhibition of a film that is shown in cinemas across a country.

Grip
Crew member who adjusts scenery, flags lights, and often operates the camera cranes and dollies.

Gross participation
An arrangement whereby a participant in a film, usually a major artist, takes a share in the gross, rather than net receipts.

H

Holdback
A period during which a particular form of exploitation is not allowed. An example would be a six-month holdback on video rentals to allow sufficient time for a theatrical release.

Hook
The special "selling" point that gets the buyers interested in your script and keeps the audience in their seats when the film is made. Every tale must have one.

I

In-camera editing
A technique used when shooting on video. Requires shooting in sequence and rerecording over unwanted scenes.

J

Jump cut
A cut made in the middle of a continuous shot rather than between shots, creating discontinuity in time and drawing attention to the film itself instead of its content.

K

Key grip
The head grip, who supervises the grip crew and receives orders from the gaffer.

Key light
The primary light in a scene.

Klieg light
A powerful carbon-arc lamp producing an intense light that is commonly used in filmmaking.

L

Laveliers
Small omni-directional microphones usually attached to an actor's chest.

Loan-out agreement
An agreement where the services of an individual are made available through a production company, usually owned or controlled by that individual.

Low-angle shot
Shot with the camera placed low (which makes people look bigger and stronger) as opposed to a high-angle shot (which makes you look small and insignificant). An aerial shot is a bird's-eye view of a scene.

M

M&E track
A mixed music and effects track, which contains no dialog. Used for foreign language versions.

Master shot
A continuous take that covers the entire set or all of the action in a scene.

Matching
It's all about the money. This is a funding process where funds are granted to equal those that are already in the pot.

Matte shot
A partially opaque shot in the frame area. The shot can be printed with another frame, hiding unwanted content and permitting the addition of another scene on a reverse matte.

Minimum guarantee
The minimum sum a distributor guarantees will be payable to a producer as a result of the distributor's distribution of the film.

Mise-en-scène
From the French, meaning "arranging the scene." The physical setting of the action and environment. It defines the mood, color, style and feeling of the world. It includes the style of art, camera movement and lighting; architecture, terrain atmosphere and color palettes.

Mix
To put together sound or images programs, or the sounds on a record.

Montage
The putting-together of visual images to form a sequence.

N

Negative
An image that has been shot on to film, from which a print or positive is taken.

Negative pick-up
A distribution agreement where the advance is payable only on delivery of the finished film to the distributor.

Net profits
The revenues from the exploitation of the film after distribution fees and expenses, deferments, and repayment of any loans and investments raised to finance production.

Non-diegetic sound
Sound that does not come from anything that can be seen in the picture—i.e. the musical score or a voiceover (VO).

Non-linear editing
Editing style where shots can be edited in a way that does not conform to, or affect, the scheduled story order.

NTSC (National Television Standards Committee)
A broadcast and video format using a fixed vertical resolution of 525 horizontal lines. NTSC countries are: USA, Antigua, Bahamas, Barbados, Belize, Bermuda, Bolivia, Burma, Canada, Chile, Colombia, Costa Rica, Cuba, Dominican Republic, Ecuador, El Salvador, Greenland, Guam, Guatemala, Guyana, Honduras, Jamaica, Japan, South Korea, Mexico, Netherlands Antilles, Nicaragua, Panama, Peru, Philippines, Puerto Rico, St Vincent and the Grenadines, St Kitts, Saipan, Samoa, Surinam, Taiwan, Tobago, Trinidad, Venezuela, Virgin Islands.

O

Optical
A visual device such as a fade, dissolve or wipe; also includes superimposing and other special effects.

Option agreement
The right to exploit, during a specific period of time, for a specific sum, a book, screenplay, short story or contributors services for the making of a film.

Out-take
A shot or scene that is shot but not used in the final print of the film.

Overages
Distribution revenues payable to the producer after the advance or minimum guarantee has been recouped.

Overexposure
When too much light gets through the aperture during filming, often caused by the sun's sudden appearance through clouds. This makes faces and shiny surfaces glossy. It is more commonly called flare or bleach. You may wish to overexpose film for dream sequences and flashbacks; *see also* **Underexposure**.

P

P&A commitments/spend
A contractual obligation imposed on a distributor to spend specified minimum sums on prints and advertising to support the initial theatrical release of a film.

Pact (Producers' Alliance for Cinema and Television)
Pact is the UK trade association for film and television producers.

PAL (phase alternating line)
Broadcast and video standard which is used mainly in Western Europe, Australia, and some areas of Africa and the Middle East. It provides a clearer image than NTSC. This standard is based on 625 horizontal scan lines and 50 frames per second.

Pan
A horizontal movement of the camera from a fixed point; *see also* **PU**.

Paper edit
Written guide to the planned chronology of the film footage, soundtrack, and other effects; also called the edit script.

Pay or play
A commitment to pay a director or performer made before production commences, regardless of whether the production actually goes ahead.

Pitch
Verbal summary of a film delivered to busy executives; the *elevator pitch* gives the filmmaker two minutes to tell his story and get backing.

Points
Shares of the net profits of a film, measured in percentage points.

POV (point of view)
A shot that depicts the outlook or position of a character.

Post-production
The final stage in the production of a film or a television program, typically involving editing and the addition of soundtracks. Also called "post."

Pre-production
The planning stage of a film or television program, involving budgeting, scheduling, casting, design, and location selection.

Pre-screen
To see a movie before it is released for the public.

Press kit
Essential marketing document containing filmmakers' contact details, film synopsis, behind the scenes production details, key profiles and photos, credits of key players, and press clippings. Other handy tools: flyers, posters, stickers and business cards.

Producer
The person responsible for initiating, organizing, and financing a venture.

Product placement
A form of sponsorship in which advertisers pay the producers of films to have characters use their products.

PU
Pan up from exterior below; *see also* **Pan**.

R

Reaction shot
Just what it says. It's usually a cutaway shot to show someone's reaction; the bigger the close-up, the greater the reaction.

Recce
Short for "reconnaissance"; this is an essential part of pre-production, where the director and key personnel go and look at locations prior to filming.

Recoupment order
The order in which investors and financiers are repaid their loans and investments.

Redhead
Standard type of lighting equipment.

Reverse shot
Filming from opposite angles. In this way, a moving object can appear to change directions.

Rush
The print of the camera footage from one day's shooting. Also called the *daily*.

S

SAG (Screen Actors' Guild)
American equivalent of British actors' union, Equity.

Sales agent
An agent appointed by the producer to act as agent for the sale of a film.

SCART
A 21-pin plug connector for audio and video between VCRs, camcorders, and televisions.

Scene
A succession of shots that conveys a unified element of a movie's story.

Screenplay
The script for a film.

Set
This is the place where it all happens: where the actors act, the technicians set up their gear, the DOP rolls that camera and the director yells (through a megaphone if need be) "Action." This is an interior space decorated by the set designer, as opposed to an exterior location.

Sequence
A succession of scenes that comprises a dramatic unit of the film.

SFX
Special effects or devices used to create particular visual illusions; *see also* **FX**.

Shooting script
The final version of a script, with the scenes arranged in the sequence in which the film is to be shot.

Short subject
Before the term "short film" was coined, films of this nature were termed "short subject." Studios in the United States sold their short subject as part of a block booking package that included the feature, a cartoon, news clips, a comedy and occasionally a travelog.

Shot
The basic building block of film narrative—the single unedited piece of film.

Slate
The digital board that is held in front of the camera and identifies shot number, director, cameraperson, studio and title. The data was originally written with chalk on a piece of slate. This footage is used in the laboratory and editing room to identify the shot.

Soft focus
The device of shooting the subject a little out of focus to create a specific effect, usually to do with nostalgia, an attractive female star, or dreams.

Sotto
Short for *sotto voce*: speaking in an undertone.

Sound stage
A soundproof room or studio used in movie production.

Source material
The original work on which the screenplay for a film is based.

Steadicam
A hydraulically balanced apparatus that harnesses a camera to an operator's body, providing smooth tracking shots without using a track.

Stop date
The last date on which a performer or director can be obliged to work. Allows an agent to schedule projects for a client.

Storyboard
The sketches depicting plot, action, and characters in the sequential scenes of a film, television show, or advertisement.

Streaming
The transfer of data (as audio or video material) in a continuous stream for immediate processing or playback.

Strobing
A system of digital editing employed to make video look more like film.

Sub-genre
A genre within a genre.

Sync
When sound and images are linked properly together in time.

T

Take

The filming of a shot in a particular camera set-up. The director usually films several takes before approving the shot.

Takeover

Completion guarantors and some financiers require the right to take over the production of a film if the producer becomes insolvent, commits a material breach of his obligations to the completion guarantor, or if the financier encounters serious production problems.

Television rights

The collective expression for different forms of television, i.e. free and pay television, terrestrial, cable, and satellite television.

Third-party material

Such things as music, film clips or text used but not owned by the filmmaker.

Tilt

A vertical camera movement from a fixed position.

Timecode

The numerical sequence shown in a camera viewfinder or tape player to help locate shots.

Time lapse

A technique of filming single frames of action at delayed intervals and replaying them at normal speed, to dramatically speed up an action or event.

Tracking shot

A shot that moves in one plane by moving the camera dolly along fixed tracks.

Trailer

A short filmed preview or advertisement for a movie.

Treatment

A detailed synopsis of a movie's story, with action and character rendered in prose form. An essential weapon.

Turnaround

Occurs when an agreed period in which to put a project into production expires. The producer is entitled to buy the project back from the financier, usually for all or a proportion of the sums advanced by the financier.

Two shot

Just as it sounds: a shot with two people dominating the frame.

U

Underexposure

The opposite of overexposure, underexposure occurs when the sun suddenly vanishes into clouds, or from not having the aperture open enough. Underexposure is useful to create the effect of night and twilight.

V

Video assist

Video assist (or video tap) takes some of the image and sends it to a video monitor that allows the crew/director to check footage immediately.

Voiceover

The voice of an unseen narrator, or of an onscreen character not seen speaking in a movie.

W

Whip-pan

Favorite of MTV directors. Like a pan, only quicker, in fact so quick the shot comes out streaked or blurred.

Wildtrack

A recording of background or atmospheric noise that can be used at the editing stage; *see also* **Buzz track**

Z

Zoom in/Zoom out

Zooming in is to move a camera closer to a subject, making the object in the frame steadily larger. Zooming out is to move further away, making the object steadily smaller.

▶

CHAPTER 24

Film Festivals

There are now more than 2,000 film festivals worldwide, and the number grows each year. Festivals used to be free. Most now charge for entry—anything from $10 to $50; the sky's the limit. Those that encourage mass applications may merely have found a lucrative way to finance their festival. Be warned, and be aware that research is the key to finding the right festival for a short film.

Withoutabox is a good place—actually the best place—to start. This US-based site facilitates registered members to apply to festivals online. Members can make as many applications to festivals as they wish (they still have to pay the entry fee, but Withoutabox acquires discounts at many festivals).

At Withoutabox, filmmakers can track their submission status, find fests that fit the film, even get e-mail reminders for upcoming festivals. There is a message board for filmmakers to network, and an online guide for creating a press kit.

www.withoutabox.com

There are innumerable festivals, but only prizes from the majors are going to help filmmakers in their career. I have chosen a dozen of the best: eight in North America, four in Europe. (Short film and online festivals follow.)

Note: Festival addressed and details change frequently. A search on the internet will find them.

PICK OF THE FESTIVALS

North America

Chicago Film Festival (October)
32 West Randolf St, Suite 600
Chicago, IL 60601-9803
Tel: 312 425-9400
info@chicagofilmfestival.org
www.chicagofilmfestival.org

Cinequest: The San José Film Festival (Feb–March)
476 Park Avenue, Room 204
San José, CA 95110
Tel: 408 995-5033
sjfilmfest@aol.org
www.cinequest.org

Florida Film Festival (June)
1300 South Orlando Ave
Maitland, FL 32751
Tel: 407 644-6579
filmfest@gate.net
www.floridafilmfest.com

Slamdance Film Festival (January)
5634 Melrose Ave
Los Angeles, CA 90038
Tel: 323 466-1786
mail@slamdance.com
www.slamdance.com

Sundance (January)
Park City, UT 84068
Tel: 435 658 3456
programming@sundance.org
www.sundance.org

SXSW Film Festival (March)
Box 4999
Austin, TX 78765
Tel: 512 467-7979
sxsw@sxsw.com
www.sxsw.com

Telluride Film Festival (July)
800 Jones St
Berkeley
CA 94710
Fax: 510 665 9589
tellufilm@aol.com
www.telluridefilmfestival.org

Toronto Intl Film Festival
(September)
2 Carlton Street, Suite 1600
Toronto, Ontario MFB 1J3
Tel: 416 967-7371
tiffg@torfilmfest.ca
www.tiff07.ca

Europe

Berlin Film Festival (February)
Potsdamer Strasse 5
Berlin D-10785
Tel: 30-259-200
program@berlinale.de
www.berlinale.de

Cannes Film Festival (May)
3, rue Amelie
75007 Paris
Tel: 1 53 596100
festival@festival-cannes.fr
www.festival-cannes.fr

London Film Festival (November)
National Film Theatre
South Bank, Waterloo
London SE1 8XT
Tel: 020 7928 3535
info@bfi.org.uk
www.ibmpcug.co.uk

Venice Film Festival (Aug–Sept)
Palazzo Giustinian Lolin
San Vidal
San Marco 2893
Tel: 041 521 8711
cinema@labiennale.org
www.labiennale.org

Australia

Brisbane International Film Festival (August)
Level 3, 167 Queen Street
Brisbane, Qld 4000
Tel: 61 7 3007 3003
www.biff.com.au

Flickerfest Short Film Festival (January)
Bondi Beach
www.flickerfest.com.au
(Australia's biggest short film fest)

Melbourne International Film Festival (July–Aug)
See new address and
details at the website
www.melbournefilmfestival.com.au

Melbourne Queer Film Festival (March)
6 Claremont Street
Sth Yarra, Victoria 3142
Tel: 61 03 9827 2022
www.melbournequeerfilm.com.au

Sydney Film Festival (June)
PO Box 96
Strawberry Hills, NSW 2012
Tel: 61 2 9318 0999
www.sydneyfilmfestival.org

FILM FESTIVALS FOR SHORT FILMS
(There are some repetitions
with main twelve above; only
websites are listed.)

North America

AFI Fest
www.afifest.com

Anchorage Film Festival
www.anchoragefilmfestival.com

The Angelus Awards
www.angelus.org

Ann Arbor Film Festival
http://aafilmfest.org

Aspen Shortsfest
www.aspenfilm.org

Atlantic (Canada's
premier film festival)
www.atlanticfilm.com

Atlantic City Film and Music Festival
www.atlanticcityfilmfestival.com

Austin Film Festival
www.austinfilmfestival.com

Boston Film Festival
www.bostonfilmfestival.org

Chicago International
Children's Film Festival
www.cicff.org

Chicago International Film Festival
www.chicagofilmfestival.org

Chicago Underground Film Festival
www.cuff.org

Cinema of the Spirit
(Saratoga, New York)
www.parabola.org

Cinequest Film Festival
www.cinequest.org

Cinematexas Film Festival
www.cinematexas.org

Crested Butte Reel Fest
www.crestedbuttereelfest.com

Dances With Films Festival
www.danceswithfilms.com

Denver Film Festival
www.denverfilm.org

Film Fest New Haven
www.filmfest.org

Florida Film Festival
www.floridafilmfestival.com

Fort Lauderdale International Film
Festival
www.fliff.com

Gen Art Film Festival
www.genart.org

Hamptons International Film
Festival
www.hamptonsfest.org

Hawaii International Film Festival
www.hiff.org

Heartland Film Festival
www.heartlandfilmfestival.org

Hollywood Film Festival
www.hollywoodawards.com

IFP Market
www.ifp.org

Johns Hopkins Film Festival
www.hopkinsfilmfest.com

Los Angeles Film Festival
www.lafilmfest.com

Los Angeles International Short
Film Festival
www.lashortsfest.com

Lost Film Fest
www.lostfilmfest.com

Marco Island Film Festival
www.marcoislandfilmfest.com

Maryland Film Festival
www.md-filmfest.com

Method Fest Film Festival
www.methodfest.com

Miami Film Festival
www.miamifilmfestival.com

Mill Valley Film Festival
www.mvff.com

Montreal World Film Festival
www.ffm-montreal.org

Montreal Just For Laughs—Eat My
Shorts
www.hahaha.com

Nashville Independent Film Festival
www.nashvillefilmfestival.org

New Orleans Film Festival
www.neworleansfilmfest.com

New York Underground Film
Festival
www.nyuff.com

New York Film Festival
www.filmlinc.com/nyff/nyff.htm

NewFest: The New York Lesbian
and Gay Film Festival
www.newfestival.org

Newport Beach Film Festival
www.newportbeachfilmfest.com

NoDance Film Festival
www.nodance.com

Palm Springs International Festival
of Short Films
www.psfilmfest.org

Parabola Film and Video Festival
www.parabola.org

RESFEST Digital Film Festival
www.resfest.com

San Francisco International Film
Festival
www.sffs.org/festival

Santa Barbara International Film
Festival
www.sbfilmfestival.org

Savannah Film Festival
www.scad.edu/filmfest

Seattle International Film Festival
www.seattlefilm.com

Short Shorts Film Festival
www.shortshorts.org

Slamdance Film Festival
www.slamdance.com

Slamdunk Film Festival
www.slamdunk.cc

St Louis International Film Festival
www.cinemastlouis.org

Sundance Film Festival
www.sundance.org/festival

SXSW Film Conference and
Festival
www.sxsw.com

Tallgrass Film Festival
www.tallgrassfilmfest.com

Taos Talking Picture Festival
www.ttpix.org

Telluride Film Festival
www.telluridefilmfestival.com

Toronto International Film Festival
www.tiff07.ca

Toronto Worldwide Short Film Festival
www.worldwideshortfilmfest.com

Tribeca Film Festival
www.tribecafilmfestival.org

Vancouver International Film Festival
www.viff.org

WorldFest-Houston International FilmFestival
www.worldfest.org

Europe and Worldwide

Berlin Film Festival
www.berlinale.de

Bermuda International Film Festival
www.bermudafilmfest.com

Brest Festival
www.film-festival.brest.com

Brief Encounters: Bristol International Short Film Festival
www.brief-encounters.org.uk

Cannes International Film Festival
www.festival-cannes.org

CineFestival
http://guadalupeculturalarts.org

Clermont-Ferrand Short Film Festival
www.clermont-filmfest.com
(Biggest shorts festival in the world; full details listed under "Useful Addresses")

Fresh Films Cologne
www.short-cuts-cologne.de

Copenhagen International Film Festival
www.copenhagenfilmfestival.com

Edinburgh International Film Festival
www.edfilmfest.org.uk

Flanders International Film Festival—Ghent
www.filmfestival.be

Flickerfest International Short Film Festival
www.flickerfest.com.au

Greek and International Short Film Festival
www.dramafilmfestival.gr

Hamburg International Short Film Festival
www.shortfilm.com

London Film Festival
www.lff.org.uk

Marbella Film Festival
www.marbellafilmfestival.com

Oberhausen International Short Film Festival
www.kurzfilmtage.de

Raindance Film Festival
www.raindance.co.uk
(Largest shorts festival in the UK)

Rotterdam International Film Festival
www.filmfestivalrotterdam.com

Rushes Soho Shorts Festival
www.sohoshorts.com

Venice Film Festival
www.labiennale.org

Vila do Conde International Short Film Festival
www.curtasmetragens.pt

Young People's Film and Video Festival
www.nwfilm.org

Online Film Festivals

Alwaysi
www.alwaysi.com

American Short Shorts
www.shortshorts.org

Big Film Shorts
www.bigfilmshorts.com

Bijou Café
www.bijoucafe.com

The BiT Screen
www.thebitscreen.com

DDPTV Weekly Film Festival
www.ddptv.com

DfiLM
www.dfilm.com

DiGiDance DiGital Cinema Festival
www.digidanceonline.com

Hayden Films
www.haydenfilms.com

ifilm
www.ifilm.com

New Venue
www.newvenue.com

ShortTV
www.shorttv.com

Sputnik7
www.sputnik7.com

Undergroundfilm.com
www.undergroundfilm.com

Urbanchillers.com
www.urbanchillers.com

Yahoo Film Fest
www.onlinefilmfestival.com

Zoie Films Internet
www.zoiefilms.com

Useful Addresses

Academy of Motion Picture Arts and Sciences (AMPAS)
Academy Foundation
8949 Wilshire Boulevard
Beverly Hills
CA 90211, USA
Tel: 310 247-3000
ampas@oscars.org
www.oscars.org

American Film Institute (AFI)
2021 N. Western Ave
Los Angeles
CA 90027, USA
Tel: 323 856-7628
www.afi.com

Arista Development
11 Wells Mews
London W1T 3HD, UK
Tel: 020 7323 1775
arista@aristotle.co.uk
www.aristadevelopment.co.uk

Arts Council
Visual Arts Department
14 Great Peter Street
London W1P 3NQ, UK
Tel: 020 7973 6410
www.artscouncil.org.uk

Association of Film Commissioners International
109 E 17th St.
Suite 18
Cheyenne
WY 82001, USA
info@afci.org
www.afci.org

BECTU (Broadcasting Entertainment Cinematograph and Theatre Union)
373–377 Clapham Road
London SW9 9BT, UK
Tel: 020 7346 0901
www.bectu.org.uk

British Board of Film Classification
3 Soho Square
London W1V 6HD, UK
Tel: 020 7440 1570.
www.bbfc.co.uk

British Federation of Film Societies
Unit 315
The Workstation
15 Paternoster Road
Sheffield S1 2BX, UK
Tel: 0114 221 0314
www.bffs.org.uk

British Film Institute (BFI)
21 Stephen Street
London W1P 2LN, UK
Tel: 020 7255 1444
www.bfi.org.uk

British Universities Film and Video Council
77 Wells Street
London W1T 3QJ, UK
Tel: 020 7393 1500
www.bufvc.ac.uk

BritShorts
(See below, under Distributors.)

Cineuropa (Italia Cinema Srl)
Via Aureliana 63
00187 Roma, Italy
Tel: 06 4200 3530
www.cineuropa.org

Clermont-Ferrand FilmFestival
Festival du Court Métrage à
Clermont-Ferrand La Jette
6 place Michel-de-L'Hospital
63058 Clermont-Ferrand
Cedex 1, France
Tel: 473 01 65 73
info@clermont-filmfest.com
www.clermont-filmfest.com

Dazzle Films
(See below, under Distributors.)

Directors Guild of Great Britain
4 Windmill Street
London, W1T 2HZ, UK
Tel: 020 7580 9131
www.dggb.co.uk

European Coordination of Film Festivals
64 rue Philippe le Bon
B-1000 Brussels, Belgium
Tel: 2 280 1376
yblairon@eurofilmfest.org
www.eurofilmfest.org
(Essential site for latest festival information.)

Europscript
64 Hemmingford Rd
London N1 1DB, UK
Tel: 07958 244656
www.euroscript.co.uk

Fb Films
(Movie-budgeting software.)
www.fbfilms.co.uk

Film Council
10 Little Portland Street
London W1W 7JG, UK
Tel: 020 7861 7861
www.ukfilmcouncil.org.uk
(Filmmakers should apply directly to
the partner organizations for funding.
They can contact the Film Council by
e-mailing shorts@filmcouncil.org.uk
with general enquiries about any
of the short film schemes)

London

Film London
Tel: 020 7613 7676
info@filmlondon.org.uk
www.filmlondon.org.uk

Scotland

Glasgow Media Access Centre Ltd
Tel: 0141 553 2620
admin@g-mac.co.uk
www.g-mac.co.uk

East of England

Screen East
Tel: 01603 776920
production@screeneast.co.uk

East Midlands

**EMMI/ Intermedia Film and Video
Ltd.**
Tel: 0115 955 6909
info@intermedianotts.co.uk

South of England

Lighthouse
Tel: 01273 647197
film@lighthouse.org.uk

West Midlands

Screen West Midlands
Tel: 0121 265 7120
info@screenwm.co.uk
www.@screenwm.co.uk

North West of England

**Moving Image Development
Agency**
Tel: 0151 708 9858
enquiries@mida.demon.co.uk

Northern Ireland

Northern Ireland Film Commission
Tel: 028 9023 2444
info@nifc.co.uk
www.nifc.co.uk

North of England

Northern Film and Media
Tel: 0191 269 9200
info@northernmedia.org.uk

South West of England

South West Screen
Tel: 0117 0952 9977
info@swscreen.co.uk
www.swscreen.co.uk

Yorkshire and Humberside

**Yorkshire Media Production
Agency**
Tel: 0114 249 2204
admin.ympa@workstation.org.uk

Film Distributors' Association
(formerly the Society of
Film Distributors)
22 Golden Square
London W1R 3PA, UK
Tel: 020 7437 4383
www.launchingfilms.com

The Film Foundation
110 W 57th St.
New York, NY 10019, USA
www.film-foundation.org

First Film Foundation
9 Bourlet Close
London W1P 7PJ, UK
Tel: 020 7580 2111
info@firstfilm.co.uk
www.firstfilm.co.uk
(Supports short filmmakers preparing
to make their first feature.)

The Global Film School
(Professional Internet training)
www.globalfilmschool.com

Inside Pictures
Kuhn & Co.
42–44 Beak Street
London W1F 9RH, UK
Tel 020 7440 5924
snuttall@kuhnco.co.uk
www.inside-pictures.com

Internet Movie Database
(The IMDb is an invaluable source of
information containing credits from
virtually every film ever released)
www.imdb.com

Kodak
(Always willing to cut a deal)
www.kodak.co.uk

London Arts Development Fund
2 Pear Tree Court
London EC1R ODS, UK
Tel: 020 7608 6100
info@lonab.co.uk
www.arts.org.uk/londonarts

New Producers Alliance
7.03 Tea Building
56 Shoreditch High Street
London E1 6JJ, UK
Tel: 020 7613 0440
queries@npa.org.uk
www.newproducer.co.uk

The Oscar Moore Foundation
c/o Screen International
33–39 Bowling Green Lane
London EC1R ODA, UK
Tel 020 7508 8080
www.screendaily.com

Panavision
(Equipment hire)
www.panavision.co.uk

**Producers Alliance for Cinema &
Television (Pact)**
Procter House
1 Procter Street
London WC1V 6DW, UK
Tel: 020 7067 4367
www.pact.co.uk

Propeller TV
46 The Calls
Leeds
LS2 7EY, UK
www.propeller.tv.co.uk

Raindance
81 Berwick Street
London W1F 8TW, UK
Tel: 020 7287 3833
www.raindance.co.uk
(Incorporates the British Independent
Film Awards; the annual festival is
the largest showcase of short films in
the UK; also makes shorts available
on limited edition DVDs)

Rocliffe
www.rocliffe.com
("Connecting established
industry to emerging writing and
filmmaking talent." Show cases
short filmmakers at BAFTA)

Screen International
(UK trade paper "Updated around
the clock from around the world.")
33–39 Bowling Green Lane
London EC1R ODA, UK
Tel: 020 7505 8102
screeninternational@compuserve.com
www.screendaily.com

**The Screenwriter's Store
Screenwriters' Workshop**
802 Capital Tower
91 Waterloo Road
London SE1 8RT, UK
Tel: 0845 094 6061
info@thesws.com
www.screenwritersstore.net

Script Factory
Linton House
24 Wells Street
London W1T 3PH, UK
Tel: 020 7323 1414
general@scriptfactory.freeserve.co.uk
www.scriptfactory.co.uk

Shooting People
34 Keeling House
Claredale Street
London E2 6PG, UK
www.shootingpeople.org
(Internet community of filmmakers)

Short Circuit
(See below, under Distributors)

**Skillset (The Sector Skills Council
for the Audio Visual Industries)**
Prospect House
80–110 New Oxford Street
London WC1A 1HB, UK
Tel: 020 7520 5757
info@skillset.org
www.skillset.org

TriggerStreet
www.triggerstreet.com
(Kevin Spacey's TriggerStreet
provides a showcase for short films
and uploaded scripts—open to
industry and public feedback. Three
short film festivals are screened
annually over the net with judges
including Tim Burton, Cameron
Crowe, Danny de Vito, Mike Myers,
Ed Norton, and Sean Penn.)

Writers' Guild of Great Britain
15 Britannia Street
London WC1 9JN, UK
Tel: 020 7833 0777
www.writersguild.org.uk

Zoetrope Virtual Studio
www.zoetrope.com
(Founded by Francis Ford Coppola in
1998 to launch the literary magazine
Zoetrope: All-Story, it has grown
into a virtual studio with facilities
to upload scripts and a forum for
producers willing to help new writers
get projects seen by the industry)

Zoo Cinemas
20 Rushcroft Road
London SW2 1LA, UK
Tel: 020 7733 8989

SHORT FILM DISTRIBUTORS

United States

**Apollo Cinema
Short Film Distribution**
1160 Alvira Street
Los Angeles, CA 90035
Tel: 323 939-1122
www.ApolloCinema.com

AtomFilms
Attn: Submissions
225 Bush Street
Suite 1200
San Francisco, CA 94104
www.atomfilms.shockwave.com

Big Film Shorts
100 S. Sunrise Way, #289
Palm Springs, CA 92262
Tel: 760 219 6269
www.bigfilmshorts.com/home.htm

IFILM
1024 N. Orange Drive
Hollywood, CA 90038
www.ifilm.com

Image Union
WTTW/Channel 11
5400 North St. Louis Ave
Chicago, IL 60625
www.wttw.com/imageunion

The Independent Film Channel
200 Jericho Quadrangle
Jericho, NY 11753
www.ifctv.com

Omni Short Films
PO Box 64397
Los Angeles, CA 90064
Tel: 310 478-4700
www.omnifilmdistribution.com

Seventh Art Releasing
7551 Sunset Blvd., Suite 104
Los Angeles, CA 90046
Tel: 323 845-1455
www.7thArt.com

Short Movies
1223 Wilshire Boulevard, # 421
Santa Monica, CA 90403-5400
Tel: 310 586-9678
www.shortmovies.com

United Kingdom

Britshorts Limited
25 Beak Street
Soho
London W1F 9RT
Tel: 020 7734 2277
www.britshorts.com

Dazzle Films
Unit 102
Penn Street Studio
23-28 Penn Street
London N1 5DL
Tel: 020 7739 7716
www.dazzlefilms.co.uk

Short Circuit
15 Paternoster Row
Sheffield S1 2BX
Tel: 0114 221 0569
shortcircuit@workstation.org.uk
www.shortcircuitfilms.com

France

Talantis Films
36 Rue Milton
75009 Paris.
Tel: 1 45 26 13 02
www.talantisfilms.com

AUSTRALIAN FILM DISTRIBUTORS

Beyond International
(Australia's largest
independent distributor)
109 Reserve Road
Artarmon, NSW 2064
Tel: 61 2 9437 2000
www.beyond.com.au

Hopscotch Films
Suite 102, 4–14 Buckingham Street
Surry Hills, NSW 2010
Tel: 61 2 9319 0233
www.hopscotchfilms.com.au

NewVision Film Distributors
Level 2, 252 Bay Street
Port Melbourne, Victoria 3207
Tel: 613 9646-5555
www.newvision.com.au

Potential Films
PO Box 569
North Melbourne, Victoria 3051
Tel: 61 3 9328 5000
www.potentialfilms.com

Ronin Films
PO Box 1005, Civic Square
Canberra, ACT 2608
Tel: 02 6248 0851
www.roninfilms.com.au

STOP

START

Acknowledgements

The aim of this book has been to place the short film in its historic context and trace the journey through the process from writing to screening shorts.

In this revised and expanded edition, we have added new chapters on the history of short films, crewing, locations, casting, sound design, unions, music and post-production, and finding a career in film. There is an analysis of *Broken*, a low-budget, high-concept short made by two filmmakers based in Florida, some insider tips from documentary-maker Jack Pizzey, and the multi-award-winning short filmmaker Daniel Mulloy.

The joys and struggles of filmmaking are universal. If you are sweating for months writing a script, or spending months raising funds to shoot a film, the struggle is the same if you are based in New Jersey or the Isle of Jersey, in Melbourne or in Middlesborough. I am based in London, and many references in this book come from my experiences of filming in London. For example, I ran over budget on my short film *Greta May* and had to seek an editor willing to cut my film without a fee; the same experience is likely to occur wherever you are. Yet an editor appeared and spent many weeks editing my film out of the goodness of his heart—I believe this experience is also universal, that filmmakers everywhere have a sense of camaraderie, an innate feeling that what we do is worthwhile and worthy of support. Film is the language of our times and I hope that with *Making Short Films* as your guide and inspiration, many more new and young filmmakers will go out and shoot film—wherever they are in the world.

I am particularly indebted to Sacha Van Spall for compiling the glossary of film terms and the list of film festivals, as well as reading and making valuable comments on the manuscript. Likewise, many thanks to Iris Gioia for checking my facts, as well as my prose.

There is no film without the script and this book would be incomplete without the screenplays of Alex Ferrari and Jorge F. Rodriguez, Terence Doyle, Eoin O'Callaghan, and Martin Pickles, who have kindly allowed me to reproduce their work. For the insightful comments on directing shorts, and the pleasure it has given me from being able to study their films, I am grateful to Cedric Behrel, Alexis Bicât, Clive Brill, Alex Ferrari, and Dušan.

I am forever indebted to my film editor Tony Appleton for the long hours he spent patiently working with me at True Media to make the best of my footage on *Greta May*.

Many thanks for all the valuable help, advice, and suggestions I received from Crawford Anderson-Dillon at Hub Media, Colin Brown, Juan Luis Buñuel, Andrea Calderwood, Mac Chakaveh at the Marbella Film Festival, Peter Chipping, Spencer Cobrin, Breege Collins, Andrew Ellis, Dirk Fieldhouse, Trevor Georges, Niccolò Gioia, Jean-Philippe Gossart, Elliot Grove at Raindance, Jennifer Fate-Velaise, Nancy Harrison at *Vertigo*, Bina Harding at the BFI, Trish Healy at Empower Training, Petter Hegre and Luba Shumeyko, Sally Hibbin, Simon Hinkley, Phil Hunt, Himesh Kar of the Film Council, Ashvin Kumar, Ron Lloyd, Elizabeth MacLeod Matthews, Maedhbh McMahon, Andy Martin, Daniel Mulloy, John Offord at Propeller TV, Tristan Palmer at Berg Publishers, Phil Parker, Kevin Phelan, Jack Pizzey, Mick Ratman and the Guild of Location Managers, Danny Richman at Castnet, Philip Robertson, Christina Routhier at the Savannah Film Festival, Daniel San, Dawn Sharpless at Dazzle Films, Boyd Skinner at the Film Centre, Sam Small, Elisabeth Tsychrkow, Catriona Stares at CinéGuernsey, my sons David and Max Thurlow, and sister Ruth Thurlow, Roger Tooley, Tom Treadwell, Alexis Varouxakis, Mike Von Joel at *State of Art*, Ben Watson, Tiffany Whittome of Piper Films for her valuable insights on product placement, Michael Zeffertt for his constant support, and the staff at the Curzon Cinema, Soho.

A *warm* thank you to Maureen Murray, who has taught me how to write (that is rewrite) screenplays, and who took me out in the sub-zero January weather to work as an extra on the short film *Room Eleven*. I am indebted to Mark Duffield for clarifying the technical aspects described in the book, and stills photographers Alexander Atwater, Cleo Bicât, Chika Kobari, Emma Critchley, and Kalpesh Lathigra for allowing me to reproduce their work. Thanks yet again to Urve Landers for her intuitive comments, and in memory to my mentor Tudor Gates, for the gift of his time and experience.

The Making Short Films website was built by Jonny White, who is also webmaster and keeps the site constantly updated with new information.

www.making-short-films.com

Clifford Thurlow
London
info@making-short-films.com

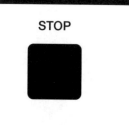

STOP

START

Illustrations

Figure 27 Carol White and Ray Brooks in a scene from Ken Loach's moving account of homelessness, *Cathy Come Home*. © BFI.

Figure 28 Crowds line up for the opening of *Citizen Kane*.

Figure 29 The Director's Chair—as only Orson Welles would have it. On set during the shooting of *Citizen Kane*. © BFI.

Figure 30 Sergei Eisenstein making the final cut.

Figure 31 Propeller Studios.

Figure 32 Propeller Studios.

Figure 33 Propeller Studios.

Figure 34 *Perfume* film poster. © BFI.

Figure 35 *"I love the smell of napalm in the morning."* Robert Duvall as Colonel Kilgore in *Apocalypse Now*. © BFI.

Figure 36 Spencer Cobrin at East River, New York. Photo by Chika Kobari.

Figure 37 Daniel Mulloy on set. Photo by Emma Critchley.

Figure 38 Daniel Mulloy takes a risk to work with children! Photo by Emma Critchley.

Figure 39 Jack Pizzey.

Figure 40 DVD cover.

Figure 41 Concept art.

Figure 42 Concept art.

Figure 43 Costume design.

Figure 44 Costume design.

Figure 45 Poster designs from film stills no. 1.

Figure 46 Poster designs from film stills no. 2.

Figure 47 Poster designs from film stills no. 3.

Figure 48 Screen capture.

Figure 49 Nick Moran. Photo by Cleo Bicât.

Figure 50 The cast and crew of *Noise Control* fake Wales in a Gloucestershire garden. Photo by Cleo Bicât.

Figure 51 Director of photography Simon Dinsel frames the shot with director Alexis Bicât. Photo by Cleo Bicât.

Figure 52 Alexis Bicât and Nick Moran. Photo by Cleo Bicât.

Figure 53 Bicât readies his stars for the next take. Photo by Cleo Bicât.

Figure 54 The cast and crew look on as Bicât directs the action on the set of *Noise Control*. Photo by Cleo Bicât.

Figure 55 Leading man Nigel Hastings readies himself for his final cinematic moment. Photo by Cleo Bicât.

Figure 56 *G.M.* director Martin Pickles. Photo by Kalpesh Lathigra.

Figure 57 Neil Edmond takes to the streets. Photo by Kalpesh Lathigra.

Figure 58 Isabel Rocamora in *G.M.* Photo by Kalpesh Lathigra.

Figure 59 *G.M.* set. Photo by Kalpesh Lathigra.

Figure 60 Tracking shot. Photo by Kalpesh Lathigra.

Figure 61 The storyboards for *G.M.* Artwork by Martin Pickles.

Figure 62 Lighting check DOP Jean-Philippe Gossart with actress Jess Murphy. Photo by Alexander Atwater.

Figure 63 Jess Murphy doing her Audrey Hepburn impression. Photo by Alexander Atwater.

Figure 64 Emma Rand, as Rachel, advises Greta that *the only way to get over someone is to get under someone else!* Photo by Alexander Atwater.

STOP

START

Notes

CHAPTER 1 INTRODUCTION TO MAKING SHORT FILMS

1. Paul Hammond's excellent study L'Âge d'Or is published by the BFI. All books and articles quoted in the text are listed in the Bibliography.

CHAPTER 2 A BRIEF HISTORY OF SHORT FILMS

1. Steve Parker, *The Lumière Brothers and Cinema* (Belitha Press, 1995).
2. Tim Dirks, www.filmsite.org.
3. The Bill Douglas Centre for the History of Cinema and Popular Culture www.centres.ex.ac.uk.
4. Gordon Hendricks, *Edweard Muybridge* (Dover Publications, 2001).
5. Marta Braun and Etienne-Jules Marey, *Picturing Time: Work of Etienne-Jules Marey* (University of Chicago Press, 1994).
6. Neal Baldwin, *Edison: Inventing the Century* (Hyperion, 1995).
7. Charles Tepperman, www.canadianfilm.com.
8. See www.biographycompany.com.
9. Alec Worley, *Empires of the Imagination: A Critical Survey of Fantasy Cinema from Georges Méliès to the Lord of the Rings* (McFarland, 2005).
10. Luke McKernan, www.victorian-cinema.net.
11. Sandra Brennan, *All Movie Guide* at www.allmovie.com, accessed 2006.
12. Aaron Delwiche, www.firstworldwar.com.
13. Chris Wiegand, *French New Wave* (Pocket Essentials, 2005).
14. Dan Glaister, *Guardian*, December 15, 2006.

CHAPTER 3 CAREERS

1. Withoutabox is the world's largest film festival guide and submissions coordinator.

CHAPTER 4 THE SCRIPT

1. Throughout the text, I use masculine nouns and pronouns to refer to both sexes; while this avoids clumsy tags such as cameraman/woman or soundperson, it should also be made clear that there are now just as many female producers in the industry as males, as indeed there are many female directors, editors, etc.
2. Joseph Campbell, *The Hero With A Thousand Faces* (Fontana Press, 1993).

3. Callie Khouri, *Thelma and Louise.*
4. Truman Capote.
5. Jean Cocteau.

CHAPTER 5 THE PRODUCER

1. John Walker.
2. Franz Kafka.
3. Samuel Beckett.
4. Michael Wakelin, *J. Arthur Rank* (Lion Hudson, 1997).
5. The quotations in this chapter from Dawn Sharpless and Elliot Grove are from interviews with the author, 2004.
6. *Minghella on Minghella*, edited by Timothy Bricknell (Faber and Faber, 2005).

CHAPTER 6 THE DIRECTOR

1. John Gibbs, *Mise-en-Scène, Film Style and Interpretation* (Wallflower Press, 2002).
2. Gary Oldman.
3. Burt Lancaster, in a live interview at the National Film Theatre, 1988.
4. Steve Biddulph.
5. Paul Wells, *The Horror Genre* (Wallflower Press, 2001).
6. John Berger, *Ways of Seeing* (Penguin, 1972).
7. Federico Fellini.
8. Andrew Sarris.
9. Hollis Alpert, *Fellini, A Life* (Atheneum Publishing, 1986).
10. The quotations in this chapter from Cedric Behrel, Alexis Bicât, and Terence Doyle are from interviews with the author, 2004.
11. *Minghella on Minghella*, edited by Timothy Bricknell (Faber and Faber, 2005).

CHAPTER 7 THE EDITOR

1. Simon Callow, *Orson Welles, The Road to Xanadu* (Jonathan Cape, 1995).
2. Ibid.
3. Ibid.
4. Paul Hammond, *L'Âge d'Or* (BFI Publishing, 1997).
5. Cecil B. DeMille.
6. Frank Capra.
7. Hedda Hopper.
8. The quotations from Martin Scorsese and Harvey Weinstein are from an interview by Alex Williams, *The Guardian*, January 3, 2003.
9. The quotations in this chapter from Sam Small are from an interview with the author, 2004.
10. Roger Crittenden, *Film Editing* (Thames and Hudson, 1981).

CHAPTER 8 FINANCE AND DISTRIBUTION

1. Rachel Cooke, *The Observer*, January 7, 2007.
2. The quotations in this chapter from Tiffany Whittome, Amanda Nevill, Dawn Sharpless, and Dušan Tolmac are from interviews with the author, 2004 and 2007.
3. Sir Alan Parker, *Building a Sustainable UK Film Industry*, notes from a UK Film Council speech, 2002.
4. Mark Duffield wrote and directed *Ghost of Mae Nak*, 2005; trailer at www.video.google.com.

CHAPTER 10 LOCATIONS

1. The quotations in this chapter from Mick Ratman are from interviews with the author, 2007.

CHAPTER 11 CASTING

1. Judith Weston, *Directing Actors: Creating Memorable Performances for Film and Television* (Michael Wise, 1999). There is a chapter devoted to the casting process.
2. Quotations and tips from Danny Richman are from an interview with the author, 2007.

CHAPTER 12 SOUND DESIGN

1. Neal Baldwin, *Edison: Inventing the Century* (Hyperion, 1995).
2. David Cook, *A History of Narrative Film* (W. W. Norton, 2004).
3. Michael Chion (foreword Walter Murch), *Audio-Vision: Sound on Screen* (Columbia University Press, 1994).
4. See www.en.wikipedia.org.

CHAPTER 13 MUSIC AND POST-PRODUCTION

1. The quotations in this chapter from Spencer Cobrin are from an interview with the author, 2007.

CHAPTER 14 TRADE UNIONS

1. Benjamin Craig, www.filmmaking.net.

CHAPTER 15 INTERVIEW WITH DANIEL MULLOY

1. Interviewed in 2007.

CHAPTER 16 INTERVIEW WITH JACK PIZZEY, DOCUMENTARY FILMMAKER

1. Interviewed in 2007.

CHAPTER 17 *BROKEN*

1. Roger Ebert, *Chicago Sun-Times*, December 21, 2005.

CHAPTER 18 *NOISE CONTROL*

1. The quotations in this chapter from Terence Doyle and Danielle Anneman are from interviews with the author, 2004.

CHAPTER 19 *G.M.*

1. Martin Pickles, script notes.
2. The quotations in this chapter from Martin Pickles are from an interview with the author, 2004.

CHAPTER 20 *ROOM ELEVEN*

1. The quotations in this chapter from Maureen Murray, Philip Robertson, Roger Tooley, Clive Brill, and Maedhbh McMahon are from interviews with the author, 2004 and 2007.
2. Garrett Brown, in John Baxter, *Stanley Kubrick, A Biography* (HarperCollins, 1997).
3. Ibid.

CHAPTER 21 *GRETA MAY*—THE ADAPTATION

1. *Zoetrope: All-Story* runs online workshops and short story competitions. See www.all-story.com.
2. The quotations in this chapter from Jean-Philippe Gossart and Alexander Atwater are from an interview with the author, 2004.
3. Soho Images is a full-service film laboratory and digital post-production facility, all located under one roof in the heart of Soho's post-production community.

GLOSSARY

1. Research for glossary by Sacha Van Spall.

FILM FESTIVALS

1. Research for film festivals by Sacha Van Spall

USEFUL ADDRESSES

1. Research for useful addresses by Sacha Van Spall

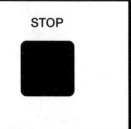

STOP

Bibliography

Alpert, Hollis (1986), *Fellini, A Life*, New York: Atheneum Publishing.

Ashcroft, James (2006), *Making A Killing*, London: Virgin Books.

Baldwin, Neal (1995), *Edison: Inventing the Century*, New York: Hyperion.

Baxter, John (1997), *Stanley Kubrick, A Biography*, London: HarperCollins.

Berger, John (1972), *Ways of Seeing*, London: Penguin.

Biskind, Peter (1983), *Seeing is Believing*, London: Bloomsbury Publishing.

Braun, Marta and Etienne-Jules Marey (1994), *Picturing Time: The Work of Etienne-Jules Marey*, Chicago, IL: University of Chicago Press.

Brown, Garrett (1997), in John Baxter, *Stanley Kubrick, A Biography*, London: HarperCollins.

Callow, Simon (1995), *Orson Welles The Road to Xanadu*, London: Jonathan Cape.

Cameron, Julia (1995), *The Artist's Way*, London: Pan Books.

Campbell, Joseph (1993), *The Hero with a Thousand Faces*, London: Fontana Press.

Chion, Michael (1994), *Audio-Vision: Sound on Screen*, foreword Walter Murch, New York: Columbia University Press.

Cook, David (2004), *A History of Narrative Film*, New York: W.W. Norton.

Cook, Pam (1999), The Cinema Book, London: BFI (British Film Institute) Publishing.

Crittenden, Roger (1981), *Film Editing*, London: Thames and Hudson.

Crofts, Andrew (2002), *The Freelance Writer's Handbook*, London: Piatkus Publishing.

Eisenstein, Serge (1970), *The Film Sense*, London: Faber and Faber.

Field, Syd (1984), *The Screenwriter's Workbook*, New York: Dell Publishing.

Field, Syd (1998), *The Screenwriter's Problem Solver*, New York: Dell Publishing.

Fonda, Afdera (1987), *Never Before Noon*, London: Weidenfeld & Nicolson.

Freeman, D. J. (1995), *The Language of Film Finance*, London: Pact.

Frensham, Raymond G. (1996), *Teach Yourself Screenwriting*, London: Teach Yourself Books.

Gates, Tudor (1995), *How to Get into the Film and TV Business*, London: Alma House.

Gates, Tudor (2002), *Scenario, The Craft of Screenwriting*, London: Wallflower Press.

Gibbs, John (2002), *Mise-en-Scène, Film Style and Interpretation*, London: Wallflower Press.

Giles, Jane (2001), *A Filmmaker's Guide to Distribution and Exhibition*, London: Film Council.

Goldman, William (1997), *Adventures in the Screen Trade*, London: Abacus.

Goldman, William (2000), *Which Lie Did I Tell? More Adventures in the Screen Trade*, London: Bloomsbury.

Gore, Chris (2001), *The Ultimate Film Festival Survival Guide*, Los Angeles, CA: Lone Eagle Publishing.

Hammond, Paul (1997), *L'Âge d'Or*, London: BFI Publishing.

Hancock, Caroline and Nic Wistreich (2003), *Get Your Film Funded*, *UK Film Finance Guide*, London: Shooting People Press.

Hendricks, Gordon (2001), *Edweard Muybridge*, New York: Dover Publications.

Hill, John and Pamela Church Gibson (1997), *The Oxford Guide to Film Studies*, Oxford: Oxford University Press.

Houghton, Buck (1991), *What a Producer Does, The Art of Moviemaking*, Los Angeles, CA: Silman-James Press.

Jones, Chris and Genevieve Jolliffe (2000), *The Guerrilla Film Maker's Handbook*, London: Continuum.

Minghella, Anthony (2005), *Minghella on Minghella*, ed. Timothy Bricknell, London: Faber and Faber.

Parker, Philip (1998), *The Art and Science of Screenwriting*, Bristol: Intellect Books.

Parker, Steve (1995), *The Lumière Brothers and Cinema*, London: Belitha Press.

Thompson, Kristin and David Bordwell (2002), *Film History: An Introduction*, Columbus, OH: McGraw-Hill.

Thurlow, Clifford (2000), *Sex, Surrealism, Dalí and Me,* Penryn: Razor Books.

Tobias, Ronald B. (1993), *Twenty Master Plots and How To Build Them*, London: Piatkus Publishing.

Vogler, Christopher (1998), *The Writer's Journey*, Studio City, CA: Michael Wiese Productions.

Wakelin, Michael (1997), *J. Arthur Rank*, Oxford: Lion Hudson.

Wells, Paul (2001), *The Horror Genre*, London: Wallflower Press.

Weston, Judith (1999), *Directing Actors: Creating Memorable Performances for Film and Television*, London: Michael Wise.

Wexman Wright, Virginia (2005), *A History of Film, Sixth Edition*, Boston, MA: Allyn & Bacon.

White, Carol (1982), *Carol Comes Home, An Autobiography*, London: New English Library.

Wiegand, Chris (2005), *French New Wave*, Harpenden: Pocket Essentials.

Worley Alec, (2005), *Empires of the Imagination: A Critical Survey of Fantasy Cinema from Georges Méliès to the* Lord of the Rings, Jefferson, NC: McFarland.

STOP

START

▶

Index

STOP